HEARTS
AND
MINDS

www.**penguin**.co.uk

HEARTS
AND
MINDS

*The Untold Story of the Great Pilgrimage
and How Women Won the Vote*

Jane Robinson

Doubleday

LONDON · TORONTO · SYDNEY · AUCKLAND · JOHANNESBURG

TRANSWORLD PUBLISHERS
61–63 Uxbridge Road, London W5 5SA
www.penguin.co.uk

Transworld is part of the Penguin Random House group of companies
whose addresses can be found at global.penguinrandomhouse.com

Penguin
Random House
UK

First published in Great Britain in 2018 by Doubleday
an imprint of Transworld Publishers

A CIP catalogue record for this book
is available from the British Library.

ISBN 9780857523914

Typeset in 13¾/15¼pt by Falcon Oast Graphic Art Ltd.
Printed and bound by Clays Ltd, Bungay, Suffolk.

Penguin Random House is committed to a sustainable
future for our business, our readers and our planet. This book
is made from Forest Stewardship Council® certified paper.

For Bruce,
Heart and Mind

LONDON SOCIETY FOR WOMEN'S SUFFRAGE.

(Nat. Union of Women's Suffrage Societies.)

A
MEETING
Will be held

LAW-ABIDING.   NO PARTY.

A blank poster issued for NUWSS meetings.

Contents

Acknowledgements

MANY OF THE people who feature in this book were not thought important enough to record in official chronicles of the fight for the vote, or were too modest to imagine anyone being interested in who they were. It has not always been possible to acknowledge those individuals by name. There is nothing I can do about that except wait for serendipitous discoveries from readers. What I *can* do is acknowledge the support I have had in bringing their stories to light. Information, time, family histories, expertise, research tips, encouragement and inspiration have all been offered to me with generosity and enthusiasm, and I am enormously grateful.

Particular thanks must go to archivists and staff at the following cities, counties, museums and places of learning: Angus; Ashburne Hall at the University of Manchester; Birmingham; the Bodleian Library, Oxford; the British Library at Boston Spa and in London; Cambridge University Library; Cambridgeshire; Cheshire; Columbia University, New York (Rare Book and Manuscript Library); Cornwall; Cumbria; Duke University, North Carolina (David M. Rubenstein Rare Book and Manuscript Library); East Sussex; Elizabeth Roberts' Working Class Oral History Archive, Regional Heritage Centre, Lancaster University; Essex; Girton College, Cambridge; Guernsey; Houses of Parliament; Huddersfield (Kirklees); Ipswich; Lancashire; University of Leeds; Museum of London; The National Archives; Newnham College, Cambridge; Nottinghamshire; Oldham; Orkney; Portsmouth; Royal Albert

Hall; Royal College of Physicians; Scotland at Edinburgh; Somerville College, Oxford; Southampton; Teesside; Walsall; Wolverhampton; and LSE library staff for access to The Women's Library collection.

Extracts detailed in my notes and references are reprinted courtesy of Birmingham Archives and Heritage; the Bodleian Library; Cambridgeshire Archives; Cornwall Record Office; Elizabeth Crawford with Francis Boutle Publishers and Routledge; Cumbria Archive Centre, Carlisle; Essex Record Office; Island Archives, Guernsey (Tooley Collection); Lancashire Archives; Museum of London Suffragette Collections; The National Archives; Newnham College, Cambridge; Nottinghamshire Archives; Oldham Local Studies and Archives; Parliamentary Archives; Portsmouth Library and Archive Service, Portsmouth City Council; David M. Rubenstein Rare Book and Manuscript Library (Baskin Collection), Duke University, North Carolina; by kind permission of the Principal and Fellows of Somerville College, Oxford; Suffolk Record Office; West Yorkshire Archive Service, Kirklees; and Wolverhampton City Archives. While every effort has been made to contact copyright holders, the publishers would be pleased to hear from any not here acknowledged.

So many people have contributed to the book, one way or another, including Barbara Andrew, Kath Ashcroft, Neil Ashcroft, Peter Barratt, Lisa Baskin, Michael Blackamore, Anne Blunt, Kathleen Boet, Liz Carter, Rev. Colin Cartwright, Simon Colbeck, Beverley Cook, Elizabeth Crawford, Joe Davies, Minty and Binks Day, Dr Anne Dingsdale, Anne Blessley Evans, Roddy Greig, Sheila Griffiths, Catherine Harkin, Helen Howell, Anne Hughes, Victoria Iglikowski, Jess Jenkins, Jenny Kendall-Tobias, Dr Simon Murray, C. Oates, David Patrick, Lucy Pollard, Neil Preston, Alastair and Duncan Rabagliati, Josette Reeves, Stephen Robertson, Ruth Rowling, Caroline Rutter, Caroline Schimmel, Deborah Scriven, Diana Spence, Pat Stevens, Margaret Stewart, Dr Mari Takayanagi, Melanie Unwin, Brenda Updegraff, Valerie Warrior, Marie-France

Weiner, Richard White, Catherine Wood and Neil Worthington. I should have got absolutely nowhere without them.

There is always a danger of getting carried away with acknowledgements: I feel like a best-supported actress flailing her arms in the spotlight and anxious not to leave anyone out. If I have neglected to name those I should have named, I apologize. And if I have made factual mistakes, it is my fault and no one else's. Before I am tempted to put on a sparkly dress, look for the kindest camera-angle and start sobbing with gratitude, I must just thank Dr Anne Manuel, Kate O'Donnell, Sue Purver and Matthew Roper, my colleagues at Somerville College, Oxford, who have been forced to listen to the book's progress week by week over morning coffee and biscuits; my peerless agent Veronique Baxter at David Higham Associates and editor Susanna Wadeson at Transworld; and finally Richard, Ed and Bruce, who are my heroes.

Introduction

Status incompatible with gender

THIS IS A book about ordinary people doing extraordinary things for the sake of democracy. At its heart is one of the most inspiring and neglected episodes in British history: a six-week protest march undertaken just before the First World War by thousands of suffragists, or non-militant supporters of votes for women, which changed their world and ours. They called it the Great Pilgrimage.

Mention 'votes for women' to most people and a succession of stock images inevitably leaps to mind. In a haze of green, white and violet, a group of determined-looking Edwardian women strides towards us wearing sashes and top-heavy hats or the aprons and clogs of the factory floor. They carry placards – 'Who Would be Free Must Strike the Blow' – or bricks; a few of them are being manhandled by policemen while the others raise their fists in protest. Ethel Smyth's 'March of the Women' is playing in the background. Alternatively, we see a young prisoner with wild eyes and loose hair, strapped down in her cell and being forcibly fed through a tube, or Emily Wilding Davison lying on the Epsom turf with her broken head wrapped in newspaper.

Ah yes, we say. Votes for women? It's all about the suffragettes.

It is more complicated than that. Firstly, not all suffragettes – militant campaigners, in other words – were the glorious or tragic heroines we imagine them today. At the beginning of the twentieth century, the press and cartoonists caricatured them as lunatic harridans. One of them wryly described her own species in a suffragette journal: 'a gaunt, unprepossessing female of uncertain age, with a raucous voice and a truculent demeanour, who invariably seems to wear elastic-sided boots and to carry a big "gampy" umbrella which she uses as occasion demands either to brandish ferociously by way of emphasising her arguments, or to belabour any unfortunate member of the opposite sex who happens to displease her.'[1] The 'gampy' reference is to Charles Dickens's grotesque and laughable anti-heroine in *Martin Chuzzlewit*, Nurse Sarah Gamp, who was rarely seen without her battered brolly.

Being a suffragette did not necessarily mean that you were an extremist, or even a rebel. Victoria Liddiard was a proud follower of suffragette leader Emmeline Pankhurst and a member of the militant Women's Social and Political Union, but she would never have dreamed of going on hunger strike, because her mother said she mustn't. Her colleague Grace Roe was appalled at the bra-burning antics of women's libbers in the 1960s. She considered first-wave feminism – the fight for the vote – to be a spiritual campaign. This did not preclude violence, but did at least lend it the gloss of evangelism. According to her, it was simply bad taste to show off.[2]

Secondly, and much more importantly, this movement was *not* all about the suffragettes. They played a vital part and, as we shall discover, some lost their health, families, even their lives in defence of their beliefs. But they were a minority, the ones who caught the headlines. Their confrontational approach distracted public attention from the imaginative and quietly courageous work done by tens of thousands of others across Britain, dressed not in amethyst and emerald but in their own uniform of berry-red and leaf-green; not singing Ethel's anthem about battle and strife but Parry's 'Jerusalem' instead. They were the suffragists, who were just as determined about emancipation as their suffragette sisters, but more persuasive.

Some say victory might have been won much sooner had it not been for the militants, and if someone in your family fought for the vote, they are far more likely to have been a ''gist' than a ''gette'. Many men campaigned for women's suffrage too, and plenty of women opposed it. So as well as being a people's history, based on contemporary first-hand and largely unpublished accounts, this – like all my books – is also an exercise in shattering stereotypes.

Recently I met a retired academic who told me a story. In the early 1990s she moved house, which meant registering with a new doctor. She went along to the surgery and provided her details to the receptionist, who entered them straight into the practice's shiny new computer. When my friend gave her title – Professor So-and-so – the computer stopped in its tracks. Up flashed a message on the screen: 'status incompatible with gender'.

My friend sighed in exasperation. She had hoped the 'but only men do that!' response to her job was history. There were very few no-go areas for women, in theory at least, when her GP's computer said 'no' at the end of the twentieth century, and there are even fewer now. But in her mother's day the story was different. During the latter half of the nineteenth century and the first two or three decades of the twentieth, women were defined by low expectation and limited opportunity. Traditionally they acquiesced while the powerful debated; looked down while the educated scanned the horizon; did what they were told. Without a vote, they had neither the influence nor the authority to challenge the domestic stereotype. They were voiceless; locked out of the system, like my friend.

The campaign to change all that began in earnest in 1866, when Parliament received a massed women's petition demanding political enfranchisement. It continued after the first (few) women voted in a General Election in 1918, until universal suffrage was achieved at last in 1928. During the turbulent years between, it was not the cartoon characters of popular history who turned the world upside down, but our own families: our grandmothers, great-grandmothers, great-aunts and their male friends. Some shouted and were angry, but most of them spoke with grace, infectious good humour, and utter conviction.

Theirs are the voices you are about to hear.

An anti-suffrage 'sandwich man' joins a deputation in 1910.

Suffrage Organizations

Main organizations

MOST SUFFRAGE CAMPAIGNERS belonged to one, or sometimes both, of these two organizations:

NUWSS – National Union of Women's Suffrage Societies (1896–1918)
◆ The non-militant or 'constitutionalist' NUWSS was set up after a conference in 1896 to consider amalgamating a growing number of separate women's suffrage societies around the country. Its leader was Millicent Fawcett. Members of the NUWSS were suffragists, not suffragettes; that is, they believed in the power of peaceful demonstration and persuasion rather than in forcing the issue by violence. The majority of campaigners for votes for women were members of the NUWSS; by 1914 there were six hundred branches with tens of thousands of members and an annual expenditure exceeding £45,000. Constituent societies were arranged into nineteen geographical federations with a central office in London. Members took part in some of the most spectacular processions of the age, and were responsible for the Great Pilgrimage of 1913 – a protest march in favour of votes for women and against militancy – which was arguably the single most influential event in the fight for the vote.

WSPU – Women's Social and Political Union (1903–17) ◆ Emmeline Pankhurst was a disaffected suffragist when she set up the WSPU in

Manchester, angered by the campaign's forty-year history of what she considered to be fruitless agitation for the vote. It was originally designed to be a ginger-group within the Independent Labour Party, but soon developed into a society in its own right. The organization's headquarters moved to London in 1906, where its members were christened 'suffragettes' by a journalist on the *Daily Mail*. Inspired by the violence of past campaigns for men's suffrage, the suffragettes turned to militancy to counter the perceived complacency of the **NUWSS** and to force the government's hand. Over one thousand were jailed, not as political prisoners but as common criminals; many went on hunger strike and were forcibly fed. Despite this, and various high-profile personality clashes, few lost their commitment to the Cause. Although the WSPU was a smaller organization than the NUWSS in terms of membership, branches and revenue, its members remain icons of the campaign for the vote and their slogan, 'Deeds, not Words', is one of the most enduring in British politics.

Other major pro- and anti-suffrage organizations

Langham Place Group (1857–66) ◆ Founded by dissenters Barbara Leigh Smith Bodichon and her friend Bessie Rayner Parkes, this largely middle-class organization campaigned on several fronts for an improvement in the lot of women. Members lobbied for political enfranchisement together with access to higher education and better employment opportunities, legal rights and working conditions. They helped make Victorian feminism respectable. Running the group's activities gave invaluable experience to those members who later became officers of women's suffrage societies.

MLWS – Men's League for Women's Suffrage (1907–18) ◆ Though largely opposed to direct action, members of this organization supported the militant suffragettes of the **WSPU** as well as the **NUWSS**

and the **WFL.** Its members – who belonged to all political parties and none – concentrated on propaganda, public protest and lobbying.

MPU – Men's Political Union for Women's Enfranchisement (1910–c.1918) ◆ Victor Duval, whose wife was a suffragette, founded the militant MPU as a counterpart to the **WSPU,** which was exclusively for women. Several of the first members, dubbed male suffragettes, belonged formerly to the non-militant **MLWS.** Branches soon spread from London throughout the country. Activist and hunger striker Hugh Franklin was an organizer and Henry Nevinson a committee chairman.

NLOWS – National League for Opposing Woman Suffrage (1910–18) ◆ This was the flagship organization of the anti-suffrage campaign. It developed from two earlier groups, the Women's National Anti-Suffrage League and the Men's League for Opposing Woman Suffrage, both of which were founded in 1908. The NLOWS had a high-profile executive, including the best-selling novelist Mrs Humphry Ward, Lords Curzon and Cromer, and fashionable medical man Sir Almroth Wright. They based their opposition to female enfranchisement on the grounds that it would degrade Britain's imperial power, its constitution and political system, its national safety, family harmony, and the feminine charms of its womenfolk. Ladies were not considered fit to vote because of their innately sentimental nature and because menstruation was deemed to render them physically and mentally incapable for at least a week a month.

NUSEC – National Union of Societies for Equal Citizenship (1919–28) ◆ After partial enfranchisement was won in 1918, the **NUWSS** changed its name to this under the leadership of Eleanor Rathbone and campaigned for universal suffrage, eventually achieved in 1928.

SWH – Scottish Women's Hospitals (1914–19) ◆ This medical unit was founded by suffragist Dr Elsie Inglis on the outbreak of the Great War, and supported by **NUWSS** fundraising. Medical staff at Scottish Women's Hospitals in France, Serbia, Greece, Romania, Corsica and Russia were all women (though not all Scottish). Most of them were also NUWSS members, although some were suffragettes. Conditions were terrible – several SWH workers lost their lives – and the women's experience of field medicine was negligible, yet these units were among the most progressive, efficient and successful of all field hospitals during the war.

WFL – Women's Freedom League (1907–61) ◆ This group was created by three dissident **WSPU** members, Charlotte Despard, Teresa Billington-Greig and Edith How Martyn, who felt unable to support the Pankhurst regime after 1907. They – and those who defected with them – disagreed with Emmeline Pankhurst's growing opposition to the Labour Party, her autocratic mien and the increasing violence of WSPU protests. The WFL still termed itself a militant organization, but for its members militancy meant disruption and civil disobedience, demonstrated by the Census boycott of 1911. Like the **Langham Place Group,** the WFL declared an intention to campaign beyond political enfranchisement. It was the longest-running of all women's suffrage organizations.

Women's Franchise League (1889–97) ◆ Richard Pankhurst and his wife Emmeline were both members of this short-lived group, formed 'to establish for all women equal civil and political rights with men' in opposition to those suffrage campaigners who thought that married women should be excluded from the franchise. It was dissolved on the creation of the **NUWSS** in 1897.

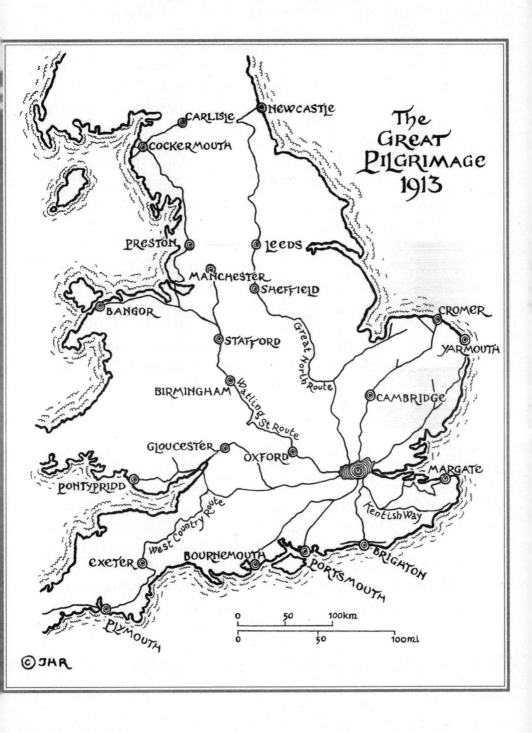

The
GREAT
PILGRIMAGE
1913

CARLISLE
COCKERMOUTH
NEWCASTLE
PRESTON
LEEDS
MANCHESTER
SHEFFIELD
BANGOR
STAFFORD
CROMER
YARMOUTH
Great North Route
BIRMINGHAM
Watling St Route
CAMBRIDGE
GLOUCESTER
OXFORD
MARGATE
PONTYPRIDD
Kentish Way
West Country Route
EXETER
BOURNEMOUTH
PORTSMOUTH
BRIGHTON
PLYMOUTH

0   50   100km
0   50   100mi

© JHR

1

BREAD AND ROSES

1913

It is more important that a woman should possess a voter than a vote.[1]

MARJORY LEES WAS off duty. Some of the others had cut along an alleyway leading from the recreation ground to the market place to hold another open-air meeting, but Marjory, Milly Field, Eda Sharples and Mary Siddall had done more than their bit yesterday and were stood down. It was a peaceful Monday evening in July 1913. The view of the Chiltern Hills was much gentler than the Lancashire fell Marjory and her friends were used to; the air was soft, dusk was drawing in, and after two weeks on the road the women felt ready for a rest.

They had left Oxford at 9.30 that morning in a strange procession of around seventy women, many of whom were unfashionably tanned, some carrying slightly grubby banners, several on bicycles and one even riding astride a horse and shockingly dressed in khaki trousers. A few men marched with them, including an elderly fellow who had walked all the way from Carlisle and a handful of Oxford undergraduates so entranced by this curious company of women that they had decided, there and then, to go with them to London. One of the lads was six foot seven inches tall: a useful attribute when scanning the crowds for trouble in the Badlands of the Home Counties.

Everyone paused at Headington, a suburb of Oxford, for a group photograph to be taken with an elderly lady who – it was said – had signed that famous suffrage petition to Parliament way back in 1866. They arrived at the village of Wheatley, five miles down the road, at noon. The scheduled luncheon at the Merry Bells did not go entirely to plan: when the innkeeper saw how many of them there were he blanched. He had only seven cutlets and a few hardboiled eggs available. It was a little like the parable of the loaves and fishes but without the happy ending. He refused to cook them anything else, so many went hungry. But they were used to that by now, and at least they weren't chased off the premises or pelted with stinking, rotten potatoes.

The vicar's wife at the next village tried her best, but the open-air tea she had prepared didn't quite stretch far enough either. Still, she was apparently a doctor as well as a clergy wife and drove her own motor car. That was inspirational enough, without tackling mass catering too.

Now they had arrived at Thame, Marjory could feel herself relaxing. This was a lovely spot. She and her friends sat mending their increasingly tattered linen and giggling about a picnic near Banbury a couple of days ago when Mrs Fletcher ate so much toasted cheese that her deckchair collapsed; then someone dropped a plate of cakes on people's heads while trying to negotiate the steps of the *Ark* – their nickname for the caravan that had been their home since leaving Oldham – and Annie Davies sat on her hat, after warning everyone else not to, and flattened it.

The weather was so fine at Thame that the groom, Scholes, pitched a tent on the recreation ground for Miss Field and Miss Sharples before leaving for a local inn with the horses, so they had no need to cram themselves into the *Ark* tonight with Marjory and Mrs Siddall. It was eight o'clock. They could hear the faint sounds of people singing (not very well) and high-voiced rhetoric floating across from the town centre: all was well.

Marjory Lees (far right) with the Ark and other caravans in Thame.

There were three wooden caravans parked in Thame that night. Two belonged to the Oldham contingent – the *Ark*, drawn by a horse called Noah, and the *Sandwich*, drawn by Ham – and the third to a group from Birkenhead, pulled along by Polly. The *Ark*'s comforts were limited: the bunks were surrounded by tins of food, boxes of pamphlets, a change of clothes for everyone, spare hats (luckily), countless jars of marmalade, crockery, washing basins, books and fold-up furniture. Given the space available, it was a relief that two of the friends would be sleeping outside. The women bade one another goodnight and were just beginning to get undressed when the tone of the music and speeches they had been half aware of in the background began to change. They heard jeering and shouting, women screaming and someone blaring a hunting horn, over and over. The noise grew louder. By now it was dark. Two voices approached the tent: a couple of breathless policemen had hurried from the market place to warn the women that trouble was on its way. The meeting had broken up in chaos and a gang of hooligans was making for the recreation ground.

Milly and Eda immediately crept out of the tent and into the *Ark*. Marjory snuffed out the candles, barred the door of the caravan and barricaded the windows with cushions. The clamour of the crowd hooting and shouting obscenities swelled terrifyingly as the four women pushed themselves as far to the back of the vehicle as they could and tried to sit perfectly still. It was difficult to know how many men were outside; certainly over a hundred. The noise went on for about twenty minutes (though to Marjory it seemed much longer) and then began to die away. But the women became aware of different sounds now: the muttered oaths of men tripping over guy-ropes and a weird, repeated rasping which they realized with horror was the sound of matches being struck. The policemen had retreated, overwhelmed; the Oxford undergraduates were nowhere to be seen; and Scholes was probably nursing a well-earned pint in the Spread Eagle.

Once alight, the *Ark* would burn like tinder.

How did these four respectable women find themselves in an Oxfordshire field, in the last long summer before the war, in fear of their lives? They were far from home at a time when few people strayed from their own corner of the country and ladies rarely travelled without a gentleman, rather than a mere man like the groom Scholes, to part the waves for them. Even though they were out on the streets accosting people every day, just as common prostitutes did, they were hardly women of ill repute. They had abandoned their families and factories, professional commitments and domestic duties deliberately to put themselves in danger, but they were neither mad nor reckless. Yet here they were at an unknown town, cowering from a mob of ordinary British citizens threatening to kill them.

It was all for the sake of the vote. Marjory and her companions were suffragists; not suffra*gettes* but suffra*gists*. They were on a mission, taking part in one of the most successful and largest-scale public demonstrations this country has ever known, the 'Great Pilgrimage' of 1913. At a time when the unpopular militant campaign was at its height, this was an orderly and dignified crusade. It was a march that would change lives.

The Pilgrimage involved crowds of women and a number of men setting off from all across the country: from Newcastle and Carlisle in the north, Cromer and Yarmouth in the east, Bangor in Wales and Land's End, Portsmouth, Brighton and Margate in the south. There were six major routes, with further routes feeding into these main ones like tributaries, all flowing to the capital city. Following carefully planned timetables, people joined in or dropped out along the way, everyone sparing as much time as possible from the ordinary round of daily life. Many stayed the whole course, travelling as much as three hundred miles between the middle of June and the end of July.

Most of the pilgrims walked. They were expected to cover up to twenty miles each day, day after day, in rain as well as full sun. One bemused journalist noted how strong and confident they looked: not like ladies at all. Others rode in caravans like the *Ark*, on horseback, in the occasional motor car or charabanc, and on bicycles. The cyclists were particularly useful in pedalling ahead to arrange meals or extra beds at the next destination.

They were a motley lot. Pilgrim Lady Rochdale commented afterwards that she had been privileged to meet all sorts of women on the road, from duchesses to fishwives. By the end of the march she considered herself indistinguishable from a fishwife herself: 'hot and smelly' and proud to be so. Some marched for themselves, to demonstrate their personal support for the enfranchisement of women; others represented sympathetic friends too busy or frail to take part, or commemorated strong-minded mothers and grandmothers. A young woman from Kent took her children with her, while a suffragist daughter accompanied her eighty-year-old father, and an elderly married couple lifted everyone's spirits as they strode along together. 'Are we fools or heroes?' one of them asked a friend. 'A little bit of both,' he replied.

They were often cheered by onlookers. In Bangor two hundred quarrymen just off shift turned out to line the road, and pupils filed out of schools to wave flags and sing them bracing songs. One woman in Nottinghamshire, though she had neither the money nor the time to join them herself, saved up scraps of her family's food to offer the pilgrims a tiny packed lunch as they passed by: that was her precious contribution to the fight for the vote. In Durham, when a crowd of snooty theological students who should have known better started making trouble, local coalminers hefted the young men away and dunked them in the River Wear.

But sometimes they went hungry, as at Wheatley when the local innkeeper refused to serve them or when no farmer would sell them food. Danger was never far away. Pilgrim Harriet Blessley from Portsmouth overheard a Guildford publican wishing that someone would 'dig a big 'ole' and bury these feckless women alive, what with their racing all over the country . . . Why were they not at home like good little wives, mending stockings or their husband's shirts? When a banner carried from Keswick to London was rediscovered in a local archive recently, pellets of lead shot rolled out from its folds, presumably fired at the pilgrims by a furious onlooker mistaking them for militants or just looking for some easy entertainment.

The purpose of the Great Pilgrimage was peaceful. It was organized by the National Union of Women's Suffrage Societies (NUWSS) to demonstrate to Parliament and the people how many 'quiet, home-loving' women of Great Britain wanted the vote. It was important that the pilgrims should be non-threatening and disciplined, so that people wouldn't confuse them with the violent suffragettes; in this it was as much a march against militancy as it was for women's rights. They wore a neat and serviceable skirt and coat in black, grey or navy blue (violet was strictly banned) with a white blouse, a simple hat in a matching colour with a traditional cockleshell badge, a sash and a threepenny rosette in the NUWSS colours of red, green and white. Optional extras were knapsacks in red oilskin edged in green and white, a printed band advertising the name of the route being taken – the Watling Street route, perhaps, or the Pilgrims' Way in Kent – and, of course, a large umbrella.

The Pilgrimage was no mere show of solidarity. As though wearing out multiple pairs of boots in a month or rarely being able to wash properly were not enough, those taking part were expected to hold several meetings a day at which a resolution to persuade Parliament to enfranchise women was democratically put to the vote, with attendant speeches. It was not always possible to gauge what the level of public support was likely to be. On one occasion Marjory Lees's contingent turned up at the appointed place and time with an audience no more numerous than a gaggle of rude little boys and a dog. 'Mrs Fletcher spoke to the children about citizenship' (they weren't impressed), 'and a kind lady gave everyone tea in her garden,'[2] whether out of sympathy with the children or the suffragists is unclear.

Accidents were common, from traffic, recalcitrant horses fed up of towing caravans, stumbles into potholes or heavy mud. Some women's health broke down, and worried relatives were occasionally dispatched to collect wayward wives or daughters and bring them home, having had their fun. The pilgrims' most serious problem, however, stemmed from their supposed association with the unruly suffragettes. Anywhere they went they were likely to be kicked and trampled by crowds who assumed them to be arsonists and stone-throwers. To counter this, pilgrims' banners, while still attempting to rouse support, were gracefully conciliatory, with elaborately embroidered slogans like 'By Faith Not Force', and 'Better is Wisdom than Weapons of War'. Gertrude Jekyll's design for Godalming's banner was swathed in bountiful swags of silken garden flowers. The one from Keswick, targeted by a rifle, could hardly have been less provocative, saying simply 'Keswick Urban District Council Prays for Women's Suffrage'.

All pilgrims were encouraged to be unfailingly polite and tactful. When a woman in a Potteries village outside Stoke-on-Trent told Marjory she was a disgrace to her sex and ought to be 'drownded', Marjory cheerfully explained that this lady sounded suspiciously like a militant herself, 'at which she had to laugh.' Before they left the Potteries, the pilgrims were presented with new crockery to replace anything broken in attacks on their caravans, and with much good will. It was crucial to be ladylike at all times, both to belie the stock images of anyone campaigning for the vote (a hook-nosed harridan, a withered spinster or a battleaxe) and in the canny acknowledgement that men were as likely to support them out of chivalry as political conviction. This was possibly politically incorrect in feminist circles even then, but it worked. Harriet Blessley was presented with a fulsome bunch of sweet peas by an admirer in Kingston upon Thames, which would have been lovely had they not all been purple and white. She had to hide them away for fear of being taken (yet again) for a suffragette.

As well as the odd bouquet, pilgrims were regularly gifted addled eggs specially saved up by hostile shopkeepers and sold to protestors as ammunition, mouldy vegetables, dead rats, elderly herring, pebbles, rocks, cow pats, even bottles of hydrogen sulphide, a poisonous gas. Most of these were hurled at them as they tried to hold open-air meetings: the Pilgrimage was no picnic.

A vociferous anti-suffrage campaign ran parallel to the fight for women's votes. Its supporters, nicknamed 'antis', were comparatively few in number and some of their tactics somewhat crass – employing men in top hats to wander about sporting sandwich-boards with 'Women Do Not Want the Vote' printed on them, for example – but at its head were some highly respected names, and no history of the suffrage movement would be complete without them. Queen Victoria's splenetic attitude to enfranchising women is well known.

As early as 1870 she declared herself 'anxious to enlist everyone who can speak or write to join in checking this mad, wicked folly of "Women's Rights," with all its attendant horrors, on which her poor, feeble sex is bent, forgetting every sense of womanly feeling and propriety.'[3] For good measure, she added that Lady Amberley, a flamboyant and unconventional member of the suffrage campaign, 'ought to get a good whipping.'

Gertrude Bell is celebrated as one of the bravest and most influential explorers of the Edwardian age, travelling alone through the empty quarters of the Middle East and eventually settling in Iraq as a political advisor to King Faisal. Yet she staunchly upheld her right not to be allowed to vote. Parliament, she said, was no place for ladies. Even more unlikely is the position of novelist Mrs Humphry Ward as president of the National League for Opposing Woman Suffrage (NLOWS). She was a founder of Somerville College for women in Oxford, surely one of the most important institutions in the history of British feminism.

Her friend Lord Curzon was Viceroy of India between 1899 and 1905, Vice-Chancellor of Oxford University, and perhaps the most ardent of the antis. In 1909 he published *Fifteen Good Reasons Against the Grant of Female Suffrage*, summing up the opposition's arguments. Firstly, he said, political activity would take women away from their 'proper sphere and highest duty', which is motherhood. If we give women the vote their political opinions might differ from those of their husbands, which will 'break up the harmony of the home.' Women as a sex or class are not blessed with the 'calmness of temperament or the balance of mind' necessary to exercise a vote, nor have they any training in political judgement. Besides, there is no evidence that the large majority of women *want* the vote. Even if they did get it, their innate volatility would render it useless. 'If the vote were granted,' he pontificated, 'it is probable that a very large number of women would not use it at all. But in emergencies or on occasions of national excitement, a large, and in the last resort,

owing to the numerical majority of women, a preponderant force
might suddenly be mobilised, the political effect of which would be
wholly uncertain.[4] As a distinguished ornament of Empire, Curzon
was gravely concerned that admitting women to the electorate
would weaken Great Britain in the estimation of foreign powers and
diminish its hold over India. And where would it end, this enfranchisement business? 'The vote once given, it would be impossible to
stop . . . Women would then demand the right of becoming M.P.s,
Cabinet Ministers, Judges, &c. Nor could the demand be logically
refused.'[5] It was his opinion that no one should be allowed to make
a law who is incapable of enforcing it, and as women cannot possibly become soldiers, sailors or policemen – the very thought! – they
should not become law-makers either: 'They are incapacitated from
discharging the ultimate obligations of citizenship.'

With this last point he was getting to the nub of the matter.
According to anti-suffragists, women were not only intellectually
incapable of meaningful political activity; they were physiologically
and emotionally a mess and this could be calamitous. Just as the eminent Dr Henry Maudsley claimed in 1874 that if women used their
brains too much their wombs would wither,[6] so Sir Almroth Wright
wrote some forty years later that 'no doctor can ever lose sight of the
fact that the mind of woman is always threatened with danger from
the reverberations of her physiological emergencies . . . there is
mixed up in the women's movement much mental disorder.'[7]
According to Sir Almroth, peace would not ensue when a woman
got the vote; on the contrary, it would be achieved only when she
gave up, calmed down, accepted her 'natural disabilities' and stopped
picking on men; when she ceased to resent the fact 'that man cannot
and does not wish to work side by side with her.'

In a diatribe that even at the time seemed extreme, Sir Almroth
(another medical doctor, incidentally) went on to state that only
'unfledged girls and the sexually embittered'[8] were likely to be
moved by arguments in favour of women's suffrage; that women

didn't deserve the vote because they didn't earn enough money; and that they only wanted it in the first place because they were (naturally) jealous of men. Then he pulled out his trump card: the world was fashioned by men and therefore men should have sole dominion over it. It wouldn't be *fair* if women muscled in, now the job was done.

It is a mistake to think that everyone opposed to giving women a vote thought in the same terms as Sir Almroth Wright. The popular argument was that women had their proper sphere, the home, and that their strengths were more spiritual than political. They could and should exercise influence solely through bringing up the family in piety and economy, and supporting their menfolk in all things. Everyone knows that behind every successful man there stands a woman, after all, and it is better to possess a voter than a vote. Be satisfied, ladies, with that.

Nevertheless, there were plenty who agreed that women were somehow the common enemy of the electorate. A gentleman in Guernsey, Harold Augustus Tooley, wrote an unpublished essay in 1909 with the title *The Militant Suffragette*. His was not an unusual point of view. He called her 'the man-woman or the woman-man', a particular class of person who expressed a stubborn resistance to the laws of nature and the will of God. 'It may be taken fairly for granted that the suffragette is a disappointed woman . . . She is a mistake that sooner or later will, by the laws of nature, be rectified.'[9]

Disappointed they certainly were. Not necessarily sexually disappointed, which was Tooley's implication, but deeply frustrated by the calibre of arguments against suffrage. 'Ought Women to be Abolished?' asked a sardonic pamphlet published in response to Sir Almroth Wright's invective:

Is she fit to live? Obviously on her merits (if she can be said to have any merits) she is not. I find that she is subject to periodically recurring phases of hypersensitiveness, unreasonableness, and loss of a sense of proportion. In fact she is mentally unbalanced for the greater part of her adult life, till she arrives at the period when she ought to be shut up. What can you do with a sex that is first unsound and then insane?[10]

Sir Almroth's book, *The Unexpurgated Case Against Woman Suffrage*, was dismissively reviewed by suffragist Ethel Williams in the *Common Cause*, the organ of the NUWSS. She cheerfully confessed that reading it made her feel as though the cause of anti-suffrage was 'such a very dead donkey' it was 'unseemly, if not an unsavoury task to kick it.'[11] What both suffragettes and suffragists preferred to do was explain why women should have the vote, one group famously with deeds, not words, and the other with both. They declined to waste too much energy countering the likes of Lord Curzon and Sir Almroth Wright, taking their justifications to the heart of government instead.

A popular pro-suffrage argument centred on the improving moral influence of women: the very same argument used by the antis to dismiss the idea of enfranchisement. It went something like this. Parliament runs the country as though it were some hidebound bachelor establishment; without the input of women, men lack the checks and balances to create a just legislature. Much of that legislature should concern the treatment of women and children by men in law and in person. Think of the Custody of Infants Act, so fiercely argued by Caroline Norton in the 1830s; centuries of legislation denying women rights in divorce cases; the double standard of the Contagious Diseases Acts, subjecting any woman suspected of prostitution to medical examination and incarceration but ignoring the men who infected them. Shouldn't women have a hand in shaping the moral and material reform of laws in which they have such a vested interest? Besides, women are habitually more temperate, more conscientious than men. They are by nature loving, gentle, sociable, modest and intuitive. Give them a chance to share those complementary qualities with men at the highest possible level, and to enshrine them in law.

These points were all valid, but rather abstract and a little wishy-washy. They are reminiscent of a letter written by a lady advising young emigrants how to conduct themselves with propriety in the immoral society of 1850s New Zealand. Always keep a mannequin of a lady 'carefully draped' in your sitting room, she suggested, 'and behave before it as if it were your mother, or some other dignified lady'.[12] It's as though some women wanted the vote only in order to remind men of their mothers and embarrass them into playing nicely together.

A little more robust were the arguments based on logic. By 1913, women already had the vote in New Zealand, Australia, Finland, Norway and in a dozen states of America. Chaos had not ensued, so why not try it in Britain? It was nonsensical that a farm labourer might have the franchise but not the female farmer who employed him. The best way to educate a woman about politics was to involve her; the best way to teach responsibility was to confer it. Historically, women had wielded political power with wisdom and acuity – medieval businesswomen, aristocratic matriarchs, queens – so the precedent was there. Even though Queen Victoria did not like the idea of ladies sullying themselves in the polling booth, in practice she was a consummate stateswoman. And if the hand that rocks the cradle rules the world anyway, why not dignify the nation's mothers, sisters and daughters with a vote? Especially now that they were admitted to universities and medical schools.

In January 1913 a deputation of working women organized by the suffragettes of the Women's Social and Political Union (WSPU) appeared before the Chancellor of the Exchequer, David Lloyd George, and other members of Parliament to present the strongest case for women's suffrage they could think of. Women had been at the heart of the manufacturing powerhouse driving the Empire forward since the Industrial Revolution. They frequently outnumbered men in factories, in the coalfields, in workshops, schools and now in hospitals, yet because they lacked political influence, in most cases their hours were longer and their pay lower. This was fundamentally unjust.

Miss Bonwick, the headmistress of a large school in London, was the first to appear before Lloyd George and his august, moustachioed panel. She explained that she earned two thirds of the salary commanded by the male teachers under her authority. Next came Sister Townsend, a night nurse who worked a seven-day, eighty-eight-hour week. She owned her own home and paid taxes, but had no vote. Nor a lunchbreak, she added. Not only would she improve her own working conditions if she could, she would introduce a nursing register so that the entire profession was regulated and reformed.

Mrs Wood worked in a sweatshop in the East End of London for 1s 3d a day, machining pinafores for which she had to provide her own cotton thread and source of light. The average wage for men at the time was £3 a week; hers was 9s. Mrs Bigwood was another East End worker whose sister, she said, was contemplating going on the streets to earn a living wage. 'I am not here as a cat's paw for the middle class,' she assured Lloyd George, 'I am here for the working classes. I think if you give us our votes we should get on much better. So do it at once. Be gentlemen.'[13]

Even though Alice Hawkins from Leicester was a member of a trade union for boot- and shoemakers, her wages were still lower than those of men doing the equivalent – or less – work. She had brought two sons into the world who were likely to get the vote before her; it was as though she couldn't be trusted, she said, and that hurt. She took the lack of a vote personally. Mrs Ward Brown was a laundress. Ironers where she worked got tuppence for every dozen collars they pressed, or sixpence for 144 collars washed: 'Gentlemen, think of that.'

Mrs King had travelled four hundred miles from Newhaven

near Edinburgh to join the deputation (subsidized, like the others, by the WSPU – and with no guarantee of keeping her job once she returned). She was a fishwife. 'Grant us the vote and let me take it home to Scotland,' she pleaded. And so it went on, with contributions from a weaver, a pit-brow girl, a tailoress, a cotton-mill operative and a shop assistant. 'We are absolutely helpless,' said one of them. Suffragist Beatrice Chapman put it well when she wrote to her local paper in Kent:

> Some people may be asking why the women of England are taking so much trouble to get the vote. Well, they do not ask for it as they would ask for a new hat, a Sunday dress or a piano to put in their front parlour. They do not want it as a trophy. They want it as an instrument of reform, and in nine cases out of ten they want it to make the home life of the working people better and easier and more decent. 'Bread for all, and roses too.'[14]

2

SILENCE IS REQUESTED

Campaigning before 1903

Most of us who were married found that Votes for Women were of less interest to our husbands than their own dinners.[1]

ONE OF THE most potent arguments for women's suffrage was also the most consistent: people had been seeking it for centuries, asking politely, angrily, demanding or wheedling, singly and in crowds of solidarity. Historians like to date the orchestrated campaign for female enfranchisement back to the publication of feminist Mary Wollstonecraft's *A Vindication of the Rights of Women* in 1792, but women were involved in activism long before that. Over the centuries, almost 16,500 petitions had been presented to Parliament before partial victory in 1918.[2] There had been countless deputations like the working women's one, starting in 1427 when a group of women in London complained to the House of Commons about a husband's inhumane treatment of his wife. The Levellers were early campaigners for universal suffrage for men; some of their female members wanted to extend that concept by lobbying Parliament for a vote themselves and in 1649 ten thousand of them signed a petition for the right to represent their grievances to the government. It got nowhere, of course.

Even then, in the seventeenth and eighteenth centuries when expectations were low, campaigners grew frustrated. Like Mrs Ward

Brown, who spoke to Lloyd George, Mary Collier was a London washerwoman. Though formally uneducated, she wrote and self-published a poem in 1739 inspired by her exasperation at constantly being told by peevish men how tirelessly they worked for poor reward. You don't know the meaning of hard labour, she insists:

> For my own Part, I many a Summer's Day
> Have spent in throwing, turning, making Hay;
> But ne'er could see, what you have lately found,
> Our Wages paid for sitting on the Ground . . .
>
> When Ev'ning does approach, we homeward hie,
> And our domestic Toils Incessant ply:
> Against your coming Home prepare to get
> Our Work all done, our House in order set;
> Bacon and Dumpling in the Pot we boil,
> Our Beds we make; our Swine we see the while;
> Then wait at Door to see you coming Home,
> And set the Table out against you come;
> Early next Morning we on you attend;
> Our Children dress and feed, their Cloaths we mend;
> And in the Field our daily Task renew,
> Soon as the rising Sun has dry'd the dew . . .

She continues relentlessly for some 250 lines, making quite clear how women maintain at least two full-time jobs (ruinous to health and dignity) and are properly rewarded for neither. And she finishes with a flourish:

> So the industrious Bees do hourly strive
> To bring their loads of Honey to the Hive;
> Their sordid Owners always reap the Gains,
> And poorly recompense their Toil and Pains.[3]

That same year someone rather higher up the social scale –
'Sophia, a Person of Quality' – produced a pamphlet foreshadowing
Wollstonecraft's book, called *Woman not inferior to man: or, a short and
modest vindication of the natural right of the Fair Sex to a perfect equality of
Power, Dignity and Esteem with the Men*. She was more succinct than
Mrs Collier: 'Why is learning so useless to us? Because we have
no share in Public Offices. And why have we no share in Public
Offices? Because we have no learning.'[4]

Had Mary Collier and Sophia been born in later times, they
would surely have made fine suffragettes. So would the women who
campaigned with working men for electoral and other reforms in
1819. Before the Peterloo Massacre on 16 August that year, women
in Manchester, Blackburn, Oldham and other local towns formed
Female Reform Societies and held meetings – calling themselves
'Sisters of the Earth' – to demand political rights not for their own
sex so much as for their labouring husbands and sons. Women were
there on the front lines during the massacre itself, when troops on
horseback broke up a peaceful demonstration of about a hundred
thousand campaigners in Manchester's St Peter's Fields, killing at
least eighteen and injuring many more. One of them, 'with her face
all bloody, her hair streaming about her, her bonnet hanging by
the string, and her apron weighted with stones',[5] fought an assailant,
unhorsing him by hurling a brick, and managed to survive; another
– Margaret Downes – was killed by a sabre, while Mary Heys was
trampled to death by the cavalry.

That night in Oldham, where the cavalry provocatively displayed
a flag captured on the field from the Manchester Female Reformers,
women protesters started a riot, throwing stones at shop windows
and allegedly shouting things it would not be proper to repeat. This
was the political heritage to which local girl Emmeline Goulden was
born a generation later; she was to become Emmeline Pankhurst,
the leader of the suffragettes. And Oldham, of course, was where
Marjory Lees and the *Ark* were from.

In 1832, the Great Reform Act was passed by a Whig government led by Lord Grey, wiping out 'rotten' boroughs by creating new constituencies to even out the number of electors around the country, and widening the franchise to include small landowners, tenant farmers and shopkeepers. All householders who lived in boroughs and paid an annual rent of £10 or more were eligible to vote unless disqualified on other grounds, being lunatics or criminals – or women. For the first time in British legislation, the Act used the term 'male person' when describing those eligible to vote, rather than the more ambiguous 'person' which, if challenged by a madwoman, might just hint at a loophole and give her a vote.

These limited changes increased the electorate from about 500,000 to 813,000: at 7 per cent of the population, this was not deemed enough for radical reformers. There were riots, during which Nottingham Castle was burned down, while calmer protesters went on to form the Chartist movement demanding an end to all property qualifications for the vote; secret ballots (until 1872 one voted in public by shouting one's allegiance in front of others in the polling booth); a new Parliament to be elected every year; and a salary for MPs to help neutralize corruption. Just as there had been women Levellers, there were women Chartists too, many of whom became members of the first women's suffrage societies.

One of the first individual women's petitions to Parliament was presented in the wake of the Great Reform Act on 3 August 1832. Hansard records its progress. The MP bringing it to the House of Commons, a Mr Hunt, suggested to members that they might enjoy listening to this: he had been asked by a Mary Smith of Stanmore in Yorkshire – 'a lady of rank' – to explain why she did not have a share in the election of a representative since she paid taxes. And since she was liable to all the punishments of the law, decided by a male judge and jury, why did she have no part in making the legislation?

Someone in the House made the point that it would be rather awkward if juries were half male and half female: what would happen if they had to be locked up for the night together? This might lead to some . . . embarrassment. Hunt replied, no doubt to guffaws from the floor, that he knew that the Honourable Member was frequently in the company of ladies for whole nights, but wasn't aware of any ensuing mischief . . .

The petition was then 'laid on the Table'; in other words, like all the others, it was thrown out. But now, once the Act had set the precedent of broadening the franchise just a little, a more concerted campaign for women's suffrage began to emerge with real hope of success. Not immediate success, perhaps, but a steady progression through the next few decades towards votes for women on the same terms as they were granted to men. Supporters were heartened by news of the Declaration of Sentiments at the Seneca Falls Convention in New York State in 1848, when Lucretia Mott, Martha Wright, Elizabeth Cady Stanton and Mary Ann McClintock kickstarted the feminist movement in the United States. Their statement, based on the Declaration of Independence, averred their rights as 'one-half the people of this country' not to be oppressed by men, nor to remain entirely disenfranchised, but to be allowed to use their voices for the good of their country and of their souls.

A few years later, in 1851, there appeared in the *Westminster Review* an essay responding to the burgeoning women's movement in America inspired by Seneca Falls. The writer did not reveal a name and therefore her gender; in fact it was Harriet Taylor Mill, newly married to the philosopher and political economist John Stuart Mill, to whom she had been scandalously close (while married to someone else) for some twenty years.

'The Enfranchisement of Women' is a remarkable piece of writing. With all the authority of cold, reasoned logic, she upholds Mary Smith's points about taxation without representation and the right to be tried by one's peers. She goes on to claim that, as a civilized country proud to have outlawed slavery, Britain should be ashamed to uphold a political system which makes one half of the population dependent on, and subject to, the other. To those who say women should confine themselves to their 'proper sphere' she retorts that everyone's proper sphere should be the 'largest and highest which they are able to attain to.'

Taylor Mill denies that she lives in an age when women require protection from men, largely because men in general behave rather better nowadays than they used to, so are not so dangerous. And if women can be educated to be men's companions, why not the other way round? 'The most eminent men cease to improve if they associate only with disciples.'[6] She refers to a petition sent to the House of Lords earlier in the year by the Sheffield Association for Female Franchise, asking for 'the entire enfranchisement of our sex' and presented by Lord Carlisle, an eminent male supporter of women's suffrage (of which there was an increasing number). She welcomes the signal it gives, endorsing the American activists', that women are no longer content to be servile, merely ancillary, or little more than appendages to a male society.

This, for all its pragmatism, was strong stuff. John Stuart Mill himself was deeply impressed. It inspired his seminal work *The Subjection of Women* which, though not published until 1869, was probably written jointly with his wife much earlier. It also gave confidence to a new movement of pioneering women emerging in the fields of journalism, education, medicine and the creative professions who dared to acknowledge the intoxicating possibility of there being strength in numbers, even if those numbers were women. As somebody said (rather poetically) at a suffrage meeting in Suffolk a little later: up until now, women's voices had only been allowed to join in the chorus of life; perhaps now they could begin to sing a song of their own.[7]

Before 1950, the scrolls on which petitions were presented to Parliament were routinely consigned to the furnace. A few have survived, but the most significant petition of all in the history of women's suffrage in Britain is, sadly, not among them. It was drawn up in haste in 1866 and included 1,521 signatures, ranging from the female celebrities of the day (there weren't many), like the scientist Mary Somerville and writer Harriet Martineau, to Ellen Nichols, a governess from Hampshire, the divinely named Bathsheba Pilbeam, a former grocer, and charwoman Emma Tingle.[8]

Many of the signatories shared a background of temperance or anti-slavery campaigning and a Quaker or Unitarian heritage. They were all, de facto, involved in politics. Some knew one another well. Two of them were particularly close friends and used to reminisce about an absurdly ambitious conversation they had had back in 1860. 'Well, Elizabeth,' Emily had said at the end of the evening, 'it is clear what has to be done. I must devote myself to securing higher education while you open the medical profession for women.' Emily (Davies) went on to found Girton College, Cambridge, while Elizabeth (Garrett, later Garrett Anderson) was the first woman to qualify as a medical doctor in England. Emily concluded: 'After these things are done, we must see about getting the vote.'[9]

Emily and Elizabeth were both members of the Langham Place Ladies, a network of progressive women who set up a club in London. We would call them feminists now, though the term wasn't used in England till the 1890s. The club had a reading room, a committee room, an employment bureau for governesses and domestic staff, and from 1858 it produced the *English Woman's Journal*, the first national publication to discuss women's issues, including, of course, the prospects for parliamentary suffrage. *Any* suffrage: women were not even allowed to vote on parish, municipal or borough councils at this stage.

The editor of the *English Woman's Journal* was political campaigner Barbara Bodichon, heroine of England's divorced and would-be divorced women for her efforts in support of the Matrimonial Causes Act of 1857, which gave women the legal right to divorce adulterous

Emily Davies (left) and Dr Elizabeth Garrett Anderson.

husbands for the first time. She was also a founder member of the Kensington Society. This was more of a discussion group than the Langham Place outfit; it was an intellectual sorority formed in 1865 by about a dozen women who had never been told, or certainly never believed, that for a woman to think, and act on her thoughts, 'flew in the face of nature.'[10] Emily and Elizabeth joined Barbara in the Kensington Society; so did Jessie Boucherett, a founder of the Society for Promoting the Employment of Women; the legendary headmistresses Dorothea Beale and Frances Buss; another teacher from Lancashire called Elizabeth Wolstenholme, who campaigned with Josephine Butler against the Contagious Diseases Acts; and Helen Taylor, daughter of Harriet Taylor Mill (who had died in 1858) and, like her mother and stepfather, a committed suffragist.

It is hardly surprising that one of the Kensington Society's first subjects of debate was the vote. On 21 November 1865 it met as usual at 44 Phillimore Gardens, Kensington (the home of member

Charlotte Manning) and addressed the question, 'Is the extension of
the Parliamentary suffrage to women desirable, and if so, under what
conditions?' You can guess the outcome.

Meanwhile, John Stuart Mill was garnering his reputation as
a champion of what soon came to be known simply as 'the Cause'.
He subscribed to Jessie Boucherett's Society for the Employment of
Women; he joined the committee of Elizabeth Garrett's Dispensary
for Women and Children in London; and started to discuss with
politicians the possibility of complete equality for men and women
in the professions and in Parliament. In March 1865 he was asked
to stand as Liberal candidate for the Westminster constituency and,
though he had mixed feelings, he agreed.

Mill was something of an eccentric. His patent devotion to
Harriet, both before and after their marriage, made him appear
somewhat soppy to his more robust peers, and his judgement was
questioned even more when he formally renounced any of the traditional legal privileges of a husband over his wife. He refused to
allow any money to be spent on his election campaign and would
not even canvass, believing both practices to be distasteful and corrupt. So to all intents and purposes he was an absentee candidate,
only attending the odd meeting before the General Election in July
(saying very little) and writing a letter to *The Times* stating his belief
in enfranchising 'all grown persons, both men and women, who can
read, write, and perform a sum in the rule of three, and who have
not, within some small number of years, received parish relief.'[11]

He was well known already as a writer on philosophy and economics – in fact, the one aspect of his election campaign he enjoyed
was the gratifying effect it had on book sales – and perhaps it was this
reputation that carried him into the House of Commons. He won the
seat, much to the delight of his stepdaughter Helen and her friends
in the Kensington Society, who had supported him wholeheartedly.

The following year a new Reform Bill came under debate. Mill
was well aware of the possibilities for widening the franchise to

women, or at least *some* women, and, after rising Tory star Benjamin Disraeli expressed his qualified support for women's suffrage, Mill suggested to Helen that a petition to Parliament might help – but only if it contained more than one hundred signatures. It was the end of April 1866. Members of the Kensington Society had already discussed 'a subdued kind of agitation for the franchise'[12] (not wanting, for all their radical tendencies, to be thought vulgar) and immediately formed a committee to work on a petition which Mill said he would sponsor in the House at the beginning of June.

Time was short. Helen drafted the wording; a covering letter was composed, lithographed two thousand times, and posted to friends and acquaintances around the country with another two thousand printed petition forms to be filled in and sent back to London. The letter was admirably unemotional:

> An impression is widely prevalent that the extension of the Parliamentary suffrage to women, whether it would be in itself desirable or not, is at any rate not desired by women. In the hope of in some way removing this impression, it is proposed to present to the House of Commons, at an early date, a Petition briefly expressing the opinion of women on this point . . . The Petitioners do not attempt to enumerate the reasons which might be urged in support of their claim, and by which they are severally influenced. They simply adopt what appears to be the most direct method of expressing their wishes on a matter which they hold to be of great importance.[13]

Members of the Kensington Society appear to have walked the streets canvassing for names. They sent sheaves of petition forms to relatives, hence a little glut of contributors from Aldeburgh in Suffolk, where Elizabeth Garrett's family lived, and Elizabeth Wolstenholme collected some three hundred signatures in and around her native Manchester. On the printed version of the completed petition – which is all we have left – there are 1,499 names, but it is known that a handful of signatories was added to the original at the very last moment, making the final total 1,521.[14]

As the inclusion of Bathsheba Pilbeam and Emma Tingle suggests, there must have been a good deal of propaganda work done in a very limited time by the compilers of the petition. Luminaries and activists like Josephine Butler, Bessie Rayner Parkes or Frances Power Cobbe would have heard about it on the intellectual grapevine, or been personally invited by a member of the organizing committee, but what about Maria Mondy, a teacher who lived in Cold Bath Street, Greenwich? Matilda Hays, who was an actress? All the milliners, seamstresses, shopkeepers? Frances Lumley, a laundress from Leeds, or pattern-setter Mary Shepherd from Nottingham? How were they not only contacted but persuaded, if not personally by campaigners?

It is apparent that as well as being gentlewomen, career women, professionals or working women (so interested in bread *and* roses), the majority of the signatories were heads of household and would therefore be immediately eligible to use any vote granted them on property qualification.[15] Others were divorced, so had already benefited from the efforts of activists like Barbara Bodichon. In other words, within little more than a month the Petition Committee managed to target their canvassing and present to Parliament an array of valid names across geographical and social divides. The implication was that these were not only supporters of the Cause their own right, but representatives of all sorts of different classes of women suffragists, just as concerned with the material things of life as with the concept of respect, esteem and natural justice. The 1866 petition showed merely a cross-section of potential voters. This was surely a powerful message.

Once the responses had been collected and collated on a committee member's dining table, on Thursday, 7 June the resulting scroll – presumably rather heavy and cumbersome – was carried by Emily Davies and Elizabeth Garrett to the Palace of Westminster. There the two women enquired for Mill, and while they were waiting rather bizarrely asked an apple-seller outside to hide the scroll under her stall. Whether they were embarrassed or fearful of somehow losing it is not clear, but like the Nottinghamshire lady who made the pilgrims a packed lunch in 1913, this anonymous apple-seller thus played her own little cameo role in the fight for the vote.

Mill eventually appeared, the scroll was retrieved, and off he marched into the House, delighted that he now had something substantial to brandish at the opposition. Emily and Elizabeth returned home with optimism and not a little pride. 'It is indeed a wonderful success,' wrote Helen Taylor to Barbara Bodichon (who was supposed to have joined Emily and Elizabeth on the day but, frustratingly, fell ill). 'It does honour to the energy of those who have worked on it and promises well . . .'[16]

It almost sounds as though she imagined the battle was over.

The incident of the apple-seller and the hidden petition has been immortalized in a 1910 painting by suffragist Bertha Newcombe. It would be difficult to imagine a less appropriate depiction. Emily Davies (who was in reality a sober woman in her late thirties) is bedecked in creamy frills and furbelows, while Elizabeth Garrett (rather severe and, according to one contemporary, 'hard and Godless') simpers in the background in lettuce green with a lacy shawl and satin ribbons. The apple-seller sits passively next to a heap of decorative fruit, like a paid extra, and John Stuart Mill looks like an elongated Mr Pickwick, twinkly, benign, and ultimately ineffectual.

In truth, though the image does the petitioners no favours, unfortunately Mill *was* ineffectual in Parliament, certainly on the issue of women's enfranchisement. A total of over fifteen hundred names, when he had asked for only one hundred, was a remarkable achievement, particularly in such a short time; he was right to be optimistic as he turned on his heels with the scroll under his arm and strode back into the House. And it's not surprising that the petition's organizers felt galvanized: they had run an efficient campaign, which they were convinced was just and timely. 'I think there must be truth in your theory as to the peculiar fitness of women for fighting,' wrote an invigorated Emily Davies to Mill's stepdaughter, Helen Taylor. 'I cannot help enjoying it.'[17]

But few outside their own circle took the campaigners or their champion seriously. Once the newspaper reports were published it became clear that the press was far more interested in the comedic value of Mr Mill's mission than in his politics. He was a man who usually spoke sense, they admitted; a great writer and thinker. On this occasion, however, his judgement had obviously been clouded by infatuation with his late wife, who was a paragon among women (in her beauty and her mind if not her morals). Women's suffrage was patently a false and unworkable concept. 'Mr Mill's crochet of a female franchise [is] the most fanciful of all the "fancy" franchises.'[18] 'We are quite sure that those strong-minded ladies by whom Mr Mill is instructed – who are eager to plunge into the area of party politics, and to drag with them, sooner or later, the entire female population of the three kingdoms – have very few sympathisers, even among their own sex.'[19] For 'strong-minded women' read crones. Mr Mill presented his petition to Parliament, reported journalists, amidst gusts of merriment and witty repartee – 'I am all for a petticoat government!,' roared one MP to cheers and laughter.[20] The whole thing was a joke.

One or two editors were gracious enough to publish the text of the petition and discuss its contention that the vote should at least be offered to single women who were independent householders on the same terms, more or less, as it was currently offered to men; several of them printed inaccuracies – principally that its signatories were exclusively middle- or upper-class 'ladies of Westminster'; but most, if they mentioned it at all, dismissed it as a brief episode of light relief in the usual dour round of parliamentary business.

Almost every editorial commenting on the possibility of giving a vote to women made the same point: that they didn't really want it. 'We say that the women – the wives, mothers and daughters of England – would not have the suffrage were it offered to them tomorrow.'[21] There were no secret ballots then; what decent fellow would allow his wife, mother or daughter to venture out to the polls on election days to make a public spectacle of herself, standing cheek by jowl with rabble-rousers and bawling out like a market trader her choice of a candidate above the din? It was unthinkable. Most journalists decided it would be better if this fantasy were immediately nipped in the bud. Silence was the best response: these women should be ignored. Telling them to go home and look after their husbands and children, though tempting, would only incite them to prepare indignant new petitions with which to bother Parliament and waste everyone's time.

Naturally, this is exactly what they did. In 1867, Mill moved an amendment to the Representation of the People Bill. The Bill was already set to widen the franchise for men by introducing more constituencies in the industrial areas of the north and lowering the qualification terms for eligible property-owners. It would also replace the term 'male persons' with the more generic 'man'. Seeing this as a possible loophole, Mill proposed that mankind should be understood de facto to include women: 'The two sexes must rise or sink together.'

Mill was no orator (he borrowed that phrase from Tennyson). A number of women witnessed his speech, crammed into the Ladies' Gallery, a hot little chamber high up behind the Speaker's chair and screened by iron grilles so thickly wrought that to squint through the spaces gave one a headache. 'Silence Is Requested', read a notice on the wall. They squirmed to hear Mill grind to a halt during his speech for almost two minutes; he seemed quite lost, and his eyebrows 'worked fearfully'.[22] At the division, there were 73 votes for the amendment, and 194 against.

None daunted, in 1868 Mill and his circle presented another mass petition to Parliament to try to counter some of the opposition to the first. You think it's only a fanatical little splinter group of metropolitan women who want the vote? This time there were some fifteen thousand signatures, men's as well as women's, and no one was going to laugh at it once they realized that the national treasure Florence Nightingale's was among them.

There was a certain amount of scuffling behind the scenes, incidentally, over Miss Nightingale's appearance. In March Mill wrote to Mary Somerville, a veteran of the first petition, to ask if she would do him the honour of being the first name on the new one. He had to write again when he discovered to his embarrassment that he had stupidly sent her the wrong sheet of paper to sign, but she cheerfully agreed to help anyway. The next month Helen Taylor wrote to Miss Nightingale to enlist her support. Mill must have been mortified: he had already promised top billing to Mrs Somerville. But he need not have worried. 'I do (in these things) exactly as Mr Stuart Mill bids me,' replied Miss Nightingale to Helen. 'If he bids me sign after Mrs Somerville, I do it. If he bids me sign a great deal lower down, which I think would be much more proper, I do it.'[23]

Despite her inclusion on the petition, it cannot be said that Florence Nightingale was an avid suffragist. She certainly believed in female activism, famously questioning in 1860 why women have 'passion, intellect, moral activity – these three – and a place in society where no one of the three can be exercised?'[24] But fighting for the vote was not a priority to her. She wrote privately to Mill that, though she acknowledged it was important that women should be classed politically as 'persons', it would surely be years before they got the vote, and in the meantime there were more important problems to be solved. A few years earlier she had admitted that she was brutally indifferent to the rights or wrongs of her sex,[25] so perhaps Mill counted his blessings that he managed to secure her signature at all.

Nothing obvious happened in Parliament as an immediate result of the 1868 petition. Rather than snuffing it out, however, Mill's failure ignited the women's suffrage campaign. By this time the original Petition Committee had inspired a network of organizations not only in London, where there were at least two separate societies, but in Manchester and Edinburgh. They were soon to be joined by similar societies in Birmingham and Bristol, Dublin, Liverpool and elsewhere, all supported by women and men with a single object in mind, the vote, but with varying opinions about how it should be accomplished and exactly which women should be first in the queue to use it.

Some, like Mill, thought universal suffrage was the answer: a vote for everyone over a certain age, men and women, married and single, provided they fulfilled a set of simple criteria. Or maybe it should just be single women householders, or women earning above a certain wage, or the wives of property-owners? The nature of the prize differed from suffrage society to suffrage society; even from member to member, which hampered progress. So did confusion over semantics. Women's Suffrage Society? Society for Woman [*sic*] Suffrage? Female Enfranchisement? Emancipation? Was there a difference?

In London, practising suffragists at this time tended to be middle-class and comparatively well educated. The London National Society for Women's Suffrage, formed in July 1867, had its roots in the Kensington Society, but strove to be more inclusive than the latter, which according to Emily Davies was for intellectuals only. Nevertheless, its executive committee was probably representative in its elitism. It included the writer and journalist Frances Power Cobbe; wealthy philanthropist, and friend of the Mills, Clementia Taylor (though it's true, she had once been a governess); Mary Lloyd, who was a sculptress and Power Cobbe's partner; the Temperance campaigner Margaret Bright Lucas, part of a dynasty of reforming politicians; and Caroline Stansfield, the wife of an MP and a seasoned activist, with Clementia Taylor, for 'Ladies' Emancipation'.

Meanwhile, Kensington Society member Elizabeth Wolstenholme had spread the word in Manchester, where another 'National Society' was joined by men as well as women, including a newly appointed barrister called Richard Pankhurst. It was run almost from its inception by Lydia Becker, a figure who soon drew instant recognition as a living caricature of the indefatigable spinster amateur. She was short, stout, bustling and bespectacled, a keen botanist and the founder of Manchester's Ladies' Literary Society, and, after she heard Barbara Bodichon speak on the subject in 1866, an utterly committed suffragist. Behind the cartoon image was a woman of great energy and imagination, who criss-crossed the country giving lectures, inciting support and generally rousing troops for the Cause. Those troops were as likely to be found among women at the pithead or in the cotton mill, she pointed out, as in a nice, well-spoken drawing room.

Edinburgh's National Society was founded soon after Manchester's by Margaret Bright Lucas's sister Priscilla Bright McLaren. They were a little more adventurous in their approach to women's suffrage over the border. By the end of 1868 they had dispatched some fourteen thousand signatures south in support of women's suffrage, and by 1876 a staggering two million.[26] Jessie Craigen was one of the Scottish campaign's most spirited evangelists. She was the daughter of a ship's captain and an Italian actress, and had some experience of the theatre herself, though she was built more like an opera-singer than an ingénue. This experience shone through when, from 1870 onwards, she started travelling around the United Kingdom holding meetings on such subjects as 'The Rights and Wrongs of Women', keeping audiences in thrall with her booming voice and huge stage presence. She must have covered thousands of miles with her dog, Tiny (who was probably nothing of the sort), between Cornwall and Cape Wrath. She usually employed someone to march ahead of her ringing a hand-bell to grab people's attention; then she would stride on to a makeshift platform, clamber perilously on to a chair, and begin the show.

Jessie's theatrical panache was a far cry from the more cerebral methods of the London Society or the earnestness of Manchester. But however they chose to go about persuading other people, most suffragists at this stage agreed on what the point of women having a vote was. It was not just a matter of natural justice: women were seeking political influence to change things that had too long remained unchanged. Child poverty, sweated labour, the white slave trade (prostitution and trafficking), liquor laws, inadequate medical services, desperate working conditions: all these were scourges affecting women and urgently in need of reform.

When Marjory Lees and her fellow pilgrims set out full of hope and excitement in their caravans, on their bicycles or on foot – somewhat in the spirit of Jessie Craigen – they were marching not just for the vote, but for a better world. Some of them were born into reforming families; others were inspired by the likes of Mary Somerville, Florence Nightingale, Emily Davies and Dr Elizabeth Garrett Anderson. Whether they had personal experience of it or not, there was a heritage of philanthropy behind them in the ethos of the Temperance Societies, for example; the anti-slavery campaign; in the nascent trades unions and co-operative societies of the north and various charities for distressed gentlewomen or street children in the south. The Pilgrimage was something of a moral crusade – just like the first wave of the suffrage campaign set in motion by Mill and his petitioners.

Mill lost his seat in 1868 and died in 1873, but that did not mean that the movement lost momentum. In a climate of change in almost every other sphere of life – industrial, technological, educational – and at a time when news spread quickly and travelled far, there was no reason to doubt that the fight for enfranchisement wouldn't end soon in success. Once the press got the jokes out of its system, that is.

It was occasionally the case that the laugh was on men, which was refreshing. The satirical magazine *Punch* often favoured the underdog, and began to champion the cause of disenfranchised women with scores of biting cartoons on the hypocrisy of anti-suffragists, particularly politicians. *Fraser's Magazine* published a sketch on the political situation on the planet Venus, where women are from, of course, and where all the MPs are female. A Bill for male suffrage has just been introduced into the House. 'The notion of admitting young cornets, cricketers and fops . . . to a share in the legislature, the prospect of Parliamentary benches recruited from the racecourse, the hunting-field and the billiard-room [proves] too much for the gravity of the Commons.' After the hilarity dies down a little, the very lovely leader of the opposition lets rip. It is glaringly obvious, she declares, that a female was made to rule:

> With finer natural perceptions than man, less ungovernable in her emotions, quicker and clearer in intellect, physically better fitted for sedentary life, more inclined to study and thought, everything seems to qualify her for legislation . . . It is a false mistake to try to turn men into women, to shut them up indoors, and set them to study blue-books and reports in their intervals of business, to enforce on them an amount of thought, seclusion and inaction so manifestly uncongenial to their physical constitution . . .[27]

Once the number of suffrage societies around the country began to increase, so did the number of new petitions winging their way to Westminster. The novelty soon wore off for those MPs who had found Mill's efforts such a hoot: in 1869 alone there were 255 petitions, some of them – like Edinburgh's – listing hundreds or thousands of names. Perhaps that's what moved Prime Minister William Gladstone to comment in 1871 that the intervention of women in parliamentary proceedings would be 'a practical evil of an intolerable character.'[28] He felt henpecked.

A few petitions to the House of Lords from this period have avoided routine destruction in the parliamentary furnaces. There is one from Bath suffragists enquiring politely if someone will receive a deputation; one from the inhabitants of Derby; and others from Horsham in Surrey, Dunfermline in Scotland, Beckenham, Bridport – all over. The number of signatures ranges from a modest fifteen to over a hundred, making these documents suggestive rather than representative of support. No doubt they were regarded in Parliament more as an irritation than an imperative to reform. Each one, however, took someone to organize it, someone to print the necessary forms, go out canvassing, collate the results and deliver them to London. And this is only a fraction of all the submissions sent over the years from across the United Kingdom.

One of the grandest of surviving petitions is dated a little later than the others – November 1884 – and signed by the headmistress and assistant mistresses of Dulwich High School. It was sent in response to the provisions of the Third Reform Act, passed that year, which extended the franchise to 60 per cent of the country's male population and none of its women. The petition is succinct in its demands, pointing out:

> That by this Bill two millions of the least educated section of the Community will be added to the electorate, while educated and intelligent women, who are heads of households, are excluded from the operation of the Bill, although they contribute equally with men to the taxation of the Country.
>
> That among the persons so excluded are women landowners, who form one seventh of the land proprietors in the country; women of means and position living on their own property, schoolmistresses and other Teachers, women farmers, merchants, manufacturers and shopkeepers, besides large numbers of self-supporting women engaged in other occupations.[29]

Twenty-three teachers signed it, neatly and with courage. None could be confident that the parents of their pupils would not consider this to be a vulgar and subversive exercise. They risked their livelihoods by showing their commitment to the Cause.

By then, however, an important step had been taken which went some way towards combining women's politicization with a measure of respectability. The Primrose League was formed in 1883 by Conservative Party supporters to encourage lay members of the community to raise money and public awareness of Tory candidates and their campaigns. Most of those lay members were women, and although the league was not supposed to concern itself directly with the suffrage question, there was an inevitable overlap of activists for both causes.

A Liberal equivalent was set up in 1886 as the Women's Liberal Federation, whose members did periodically discuss passing a resolution in favour of votes for women, finally managing to do so in 1890. The Women's Liberal Unionist Association followed in 1888 for those opposed to Irish Home Rule. A cynic might say that there was a direct link between the establishment of these three outfits and the passing of the Corrupt and Illegal Practices Prevention Act in 1883, which outlawed the payment of canvassers. In any case, they gave women of conviction a chance at least to influence the electorate, if not to join it.

Further sweetmeats were occasionally tossed to suffrage campaigners during the second half of the nineteenth century in the form of legislation, which that same cynic would consider to be merely diversionary, to quell the appetite or distract attention. But that would be unjust. It was largely thanks to the dignity and determination of those involved in the National Suffrage Societies formed in the wake of John Stuart Mill's brief tenure as an MP that women began to inch towards enfranchisement. It was a little like an incredibly long-winded game of Grandmother's Footsteps. When the opposition looked away for a moment, campaigners would quickly gobble up a concession here or a clause there, and gradually – *so* gradually – move forward.

The year 1869 was a momentous one. Wyoming became the first American territory to give women the vote; Emily Davies opened the first women's college at a British university (which later became Girton College at Cambridge); and the Municipal Franchise Act was passed, which might not sound quite as exciting as the other two events but was in fact crucial in the fight for women's suffrage. The Act included an amendment tabled by Jacob Bright – brother of National Suffrage Society pioneers Margaret Lucas and Priscilla McLaren – granting female ratepayers a vote in town-council elections.

This was the first time British women were formally enfranchised on a national scale, although a few had tried to slip through the net before. The case of Lily Maxwell of Manchester was famous. When the electoral register for her constituency was published prior to the 1868 General Election, for some inexplicable reason her name was on it. So, encouraged by Lydia Becker – who physically took her to the polling booth on the day – she cast a vote. According to Miss Becker, Lily was an elderly, unmarried lady; she is the only person I have ever heard of who sold crockery and red herrings for a living. She kept her own little shop; she had no husband, brother or son living with her to influence her choice of candidate; she paid her own rates and taxes and knew her own mind: the perfect pioneer.

Keen to capitalize on this serendipitous precedent, Manchester Suffrage Society's legal advisor Dr Richard Pankhurst quickly gathered the names of over five thousand similarly qualified women and took their case to the Court of Common Pleas, arguing (as their counsel) that if Lily Maxwell had been allowed a vote, then these ladies should be too. He lost on the unanimous verdict that all women are personally incapable of making a sound political decision. What Lily thought of this judgement is unrecorded. Dr Pankhurst went on to draft the empowering amendment to the Municipal Franchise

Act and in 1870 the (unsuccessful) Women's Disabilities Removal Bill – the first devoted to women's suffrage. This radical, anarchic and brilliant man was a great friend to the Cause.

Attempting to navigate the legislation concerning women's suffrage is bewildering. Because of all the Private Members' Bills, amendments, various clauses repealed and reinstated and successive readings passed or failed, identifying the milestones among the hair-pin bends en route to the vote is not easy. Dr Pankhurst's suffrage Bill was lost on its second reading in the House of Commons in 1871; the subject was debated again in 1872, '75, '76, '78 and '79; in 1884 (twice), '86, '87, '91 and so on – in fact, a total of eighteen times between 1870 and 1904. On several occasions further petitions were drawn up to back the suffragist argument: over 186,000 signatures were submitted in 1871, and nearly 328,000 in 1873. The strength of this campaign speaks volumes of the various suffrage societies' organizational skill and, most of all, their persistence.

The 1869 Act may have locally enfranchised single women rate-payers – ignoring married ones, as they didn't yet have any legal autonomy from their husbands – but it didn't entitle them to stand for election as councillors themselves. This is why another of the Act's clauses, giving them the right to stand as Poor Law Guardians and School Board members, is so significant. In a limited way women could now act as candidates as well as voters. Poor Law Guardians were responsible for supervising all aspects of workhouse life and could therefore directly influence the future of thousands of disadvantaged people. School Board members built and managed elementary schools and administered scholarships and bursaries. This was heady stuff.

Again, there are a few instances of maverick women being elected to office historically, particularly at parish level. When Sarah Bly was appointed sexton of her local church in London in 1733, presumably through sheer force of personality, her rival took his complaint to the Lord Chief Justice and had her dismissed on the grounds that 'such a choice requires an improved understanding which women do not have.'[30] In 1843 a dogged West Yorkshire woman became church-warden by default simply because she had bothered to turn up to the relevant meeting. A local paper picked up the story:

> At the time appointed, the *wife* of the assistant overseer entered the Vestry with the parish book in which the usual entry is made on such an occasion, and after waiting nearly an hour and no person making his appearance, either lay or clerical, the good dame took her departure and budged home with the book under her arm. On entering her dwelling, her husband eagerly enquired who was appointed warden, to which she replied, why *me* to be sure – *thee*, ejaculated the astonished official, yes, *me*, reiterated the wife, for there was not another living soul at the meeting, therefore, I suppose, I must be the churchwarden.[31]

It wasn't until the Local Government Act of 1894 that women were legally allowed to elect and stand as parish and district councillors. The previous year, New Zealand had become the first entire country to enfranchise women.

It is a disingenuous exercise, especially given the dedication and determination of those who went before them, but if one were to single out the two most important names in the history of the women's suffrage campaign, they would be Millicent Garrett Fawcett and Dr Pankhurst's wife Emmeline.

Suspicious though he was of celebrity – in spite of being something of one himself – John Stuart Mill realized the value of charisma in this campaign. From the very beginning, individuals were singled out and promoted, or promoted themselves, as figureheads. In London, one of the first and most enduring was Millicent Garrett Fawcett (1847–1929), the younger sister of Dr Elizabeth Garrett Anderson. Being under twenty-one, Millicent was too young to

have signed the 1866 petition herself and, though she did remember
hearing Mill talk at a meeting in 1865, perhaps it isn't surprising,
given his reputation as a public orator, that she could not quite recall
exactly what he said. She was eighteen then, the daughter of a pawn-
broker turned maltster and ship-owner, brought up in a Liberal Suffolk
household and educated at an 'Academy for the Daughters of Gentlemen'
in Blackheath, London, which she left at the age of fifteen.

Millicent Garrett Fawcett as a young woman.

It cannot have been a shock to her parents that Millicent turned
out to be a firm believer in women's rights. Her eldest sister Louisa
(who died in 1867) lived in London and was involved with the
Langham Place ladies. Millicent used to stay with her on visits to
the capital, when Louisa, who was married, chaperoned her to lively
political meetings. The next eldest Garrett girl, Elizabeth, shared

her struggles with the medical establishment with her sisters. Her triumph in 1865, when she was grudgingly admitted to the Society of Apothecaries, was inspirational. Elizabeth's friend Emily Davies is said to have recognized in Millicent the promise of a great leader, who combined an endearing sense of the down-to-earth (she was a terrific knitter, for example, and gleefully learned to ride a bicycle as soon as they came into fashion) with a clear-headed ability to prioritize issues, manage people and express herself engagingly and with authority.

In 1867 she married Henry Fawcett, who was a Cambridge professor, a Liberal MP, and blind. They met at a party at Clementia Taylor's house in London when Millicent was eighteen and he thirty-two. It was a memorable occasion on several counts, being the night the news of Abraham Lincoln's assassination reached London. Apparently Henry had already proposed to at least two Langham Place ladies – Barbara Bodichon's friend Bessie Rayner Parkes and Millicent's own sister Elizabeth; the latter is said to have refused him on account of his blindness. Perhaps she thought her own career would be compromised by facilitating his. In any case, it's unlikely that Millicent ever knew that she was not Henry's first choice, even within her own family, and the marriage was a happy one.

Henry had an interesting history as well as an interesting love-life. Like Millicent, he was born into a politically aware, Liberal family. He was, naturally, better educated than she was, going up to Cambridge in 1852 to read mathematics. He was elected a fellow of Trinity in 1856, while training as a lawyer, and hoped to enter Parliament as soon as he felt suitably qualified. In 1858, aged twenty-five, Henry joined his father, William, on a country shoot. Henry strode ahead of the main party; William didn't notice him, aimed at some partridges, and shot his son full in the face.

With extraordinary stoicism, Henry made a conscious decision not to allow his blindness to hold him back, and it did not. He left Lincoln's Inn to return to Cambridge, where he was appointed

Professor of Political Economy in 1863; two years later he was elected MP for Brighton. It was Henry who seconded Mill's amendment for women's suffrage in 1867, and who eventually became Postmaster General, showered with honorary doctorates and a favourite of Queen Victoria. He died in 1884.

Even without his disability, Henry's success would have been remarkable. He owed a great deal to his wife, who – unlike her sister – was happy to mould her ambitions to his. Millicent flourished as an academic wife, a political amanuensis, a campaigner for higher education for women, and a social secretary. Married life also gave her the opportunity to become a skilful administrator and an accomplished public speaker, though she always got what she called 'cold spasms' beforehand. When the Petition Committee morphed into the London National Society for Women's Suffrage, she served on its first executive, ultimately becoming the president of the National Union of Women's Suffrage Societies. She wrote a couple of novels too, and gave birth to a daughter, Philippa, who followed her father to Cambridge and sensationally became the most successful candidate in Part I of the Mathematical Tripos. Not just the most successful woman (no great honour, as there were so few): she got the highest exam marks that year of *anyone*.

The first ever public suffrage meeting in London was held in 1867 and Millicent was a speaker. It was her debut. She was attractive in an arts-and-craftsy kind of way, described as having a mass of auburn hair and a silvery voice; she spoke with humour, humility and complete conviction on the absolute necessity for women to have the vote on the same terms as eligible men.

Numerous lecture tours followed, though she did slow down when Philippa was young. Her attitude to motherhood was original, though not – as we shall see – as alarming as Emmeline Pankhurst's. Millicent is more than likely to have left Philippa in the care of Oddo, their beloved Dandie Dinmont terrier, if she was too busy to look after her herself. This was logical, because she trusted Oddo and Oddo loved Philippa. The little girl often tottered out on her own to play. 'I have told her not to get run over,' Millicent assured concerned friends, 'and she won't.'[32]

In this and other aspects of her private and public life, Millicent Garrett Fawcett was an optimist. She supported successive amendments proposing to offer enfranchisement exclusively to single women on the premise that anything is better than nothing and you have to start somewhere. This concessionary attitude created tensions within the London National Society, which split in two for a while. Many campaigners – Elizabeth Wolstenholme, who in 1874 became Mrs Elmy, among them – were not prepared to compromise, believing that the only way to victory was to fight all out for universal adult suffrage. But compromise was at the heart of Millicent's creed. She was excellent at playing Grandmother's Footsteps, salvaging advantage whenever she could till she had accumulated success. She didn't storm any citadels, nor did she lead her followers into battle. Instead she tried to persuade the opposition to work constitutionally. For her, women's suffrage was not a matter for fiery revolution, but an evolutionary certainty.

Emmeline Pankhurst (1858–1928) thought differently. Although they shared the same ultimate goal, she and Mrs Fawcett were quite unalike. She was provocative, volatile; she combined almost ethereal beauty and fierce strength in a figure lacking Millicent's Edwardian plumpness. She inspired passionate adulation, even infatuation, while Millicent's devotees were calmer and more assured (though no less loyal). Emmeline has been described as being like a mistress, Millicent like a wife.

Emmeline's heritage was a little earthier than Millicent's. Her activist grandfather was said to have barely survived the Peterloo Massacre and her grandmother was a member of the Anti-Corn Law League, agitating against the artificially high price of bread in the 1840s. Emmeline's mother took her to her first suffrage meeting when she was a young teenager. Lydia Becker was the speaker, and though there does not seem to have been a Damascene moment of enlightenment at this point, the experience at least familiarized the girl with the Cause that was to occupy her entire adult life.

It is probably her husband who kindled the flame. Emmeline married him in 1879, at twenty-one. He was twice her age, with a pedigree of activism in women's suffrage. Richard Pankhurst was born in Staffordshire, educated in Manchester at school and university and then in London, where he was awarded a doctorate in law with a gold medal. He became a solicitor first, before being called to the Bar in 1867.

After his marriage, Dr Pankhurst stood for Parliament as an independent radical Liberal, feeling himself out of sympathy with traditional Liberal policies on colonialism. His platform rather startlingly included universal suffrage, the abolition of the House of Lords, Home Rule for Ireland, the disestablishment of the Church of England, and a free and secular education for all. This highly flavoured fare was too strong for the electorate to stomach and he lost. His politics by now could hardly be called Liberal at all. By 1886 he had joined the Fabian Society, drawn increasingly towards socialism. In 1894 he became a member of the new-born Independent Labour Party (ILP), formed the previous year by his friend Keir Hardie.

Dr Pankhurst's comparatively extreme political views damaged his law practice. His readiness to oppose the powerful Manchester establishment as a matter of honour – when they planned a scheme to dump raw sewage in the River Mersey, for example – lost him influential friends, and when he died of a perforated stomach ulcer in 1898, intestate, his wife was left with less than nothing.

Emmeline had had five children by then, four of whom would play their own part in the fight for the vote. Christabel was the eldest; then came Estelle, better known by her second name, Sylvia; then Francis Henry, who died in 1888 at four years old; then Adela; and finally Henry Francis, nicknamed Harry. Christabel was the nicest to look at (according to Sylvia), the cleverest, the best-behaved and the only one not to be consigned to a nanny. In other words, she was her mother's favourite.

For the rest of the brood, Sylvia tells us, life was pretty grim. Emmeline was not exactly maternal. The children often appear to have bored her and she lost patience with them whenever they displayed what she considered to be weakness. The young Sylvia was forced to grieve for her beloved little brother in secret, and learned never to cry when she was hurt. She was once tied to her bed all day for refusing a dose of cod-liver oil. Harry was practically ignored, not being a boisterous lad. Theirs was not a blissful childhood. Strangely, Emmeline revisited motherhood in her late fifties when she adopted four more children, all 'unwanted' war babies, but it was a short-lived project, all of them being re-adopted by other people within about ten years.

Emmeline Pankhurst.

In 1880, the year Christabel was born, Emmeline joined the committee of the Manchester National Society for Women's Suffrage; five years later, the Pankhursts moved to London, where Emmeline combined running the house and family with further political work. Much of her time was taken up by the Women's Franchise League, founded in 1889, which campaigned exclusively for universal suffrage. The Pankhursts hosted meetings in their house on Russell Square in Bloomsbury, when the girls were given the job of arranging the chairs beforehand and collecting donations in pretty little brocade bags. Sylvia was appointed official sign-writer. She was seven years old, an artist in the making.

Emmeline was also a businesswoman, though not a particularly good one. She ran a home furnishings shop she called 'Emerson and Co.', which was supposed to resemble a miniature Liberty's, full of beautiful and useful things oozing the spirit of the age in a William Morris, John Ruskin style. In reality Emmeline's taste was a tad fussy – a legacy of happy times spent at a school in Paris – and a great deal of the stock failed to sell.

The exigency of widowhood in 1898 meant that Emmeline must earn a living. The family had returned to Manchester five years earlier, where she was now appointed the city's first female registrar of births and deaths. She also resurrected Emerson and Co. for a while. It was always important to her to feel she was paying her way in life, and she abhorred having to accept charitable handouts from a testimonial fund set up in memory of Richard. Sadly, she couldn't earn enough to refuse.

During the next few years she worked with astonishing energy for suffrage societies, the Women's Franchise League, the ILP and on the local School Board, as well as maintaining her day job. The ILP kept her busiest, and she was thrilled when told that a brand-new meeting hall built for the party in Salford in 1903 was to be named in honour of her late husband. Imagine her frame of mind, then, when it was announced that Pankhurst Hall would not be open to women. Not even Pankhurst women.

Emmeline's outrage marked a turning-point. She was forty-five years old. Her eldest daughter was already a seasoned suffrage campaigner and had just enrolled (aged twenty-three) at Owen's College, Manchester, to read law. Sylvia was now an award-winning artist who had, ironically, been commissioned to paint murals for Pankhurst Hall. They were both assets to the family and the Cause. Adela was only eight, still at school in Manchester, and Harry was barely more than a toddler: both were too young to worry about. Fired by personal indignation and an acutely frustrating sense of impotence – and exasperated by the apparent complacency of suffragists like Mrs Fawcett – Emmeline decided enough was enough. She must do something extraordinary. On 10 October 1903 she called a meeting of her closest allies in the ILP, all women, and invented the Women's Social and Political Union, later to become infamous as the home of the suffragettes.

Meanwhile, back in London, Millicent Fawcett's mind was on other things. In 1897, following a joint conference at which she had presided the previous year, twenty different National Societies for Women's Suffrage around the country resolved to affiliate and form the NUWSS. Its headquarters were in central London (where its Telegram address – usually a single word – was 'Voiceless'). This new arrangement made lobbying for cross-party support in Westminster much more efficient, and the resulting economies meant there was more money to spend on public awareness of the suffrage campaign, on salaries for officials and advisors, on publicity and on establishing new branches.

At this stage Millicent was living at 2 Gower Street in Bloomsbury, where she remained for the rest of her life, sharing the house with her sister Agnes, who was an interior designer, a suffragist (naturally) and a Poor Law Guardian in Holborn. For a short period, Millicent and Emmeline Pankhurst were thus almost next-door neighbours. The Fawcetts' social circle included government ministers, medical pioneers, academics and intellectuals, all of whom appreciated Millicent's gravitas and good sense. But in 1901 she left all this behind, having been asked to head a commission of inquiry into social activist Emily Hobhouse's accusations, after the Second Boer War, that the British had run atrociously inhumane concentration camps for interned Boer women and children.

Miss Hobhouse was a suffragist herself, employed by the Women's Industrial Council to investigate working conditions for women and children. She was a professional whistle-blower; someone who sought out iniquity and tried to bring the powers-that-be to book. She offered practical help whenever she could, travelling to the United States to support Cornish emigrant tin-miners (being a Cornishwoman herself) or to the Cape Colony to investigate rumours of what would now be called war crimes by the British. When she returned from South Africa, the government refused to accept her criticisms, or her hysterical first-hand evidence, and commissioned Millicent with five other calm and respectable ladies to form an official committee and leave at once for the camps to uncover the 'truth'.

Off went Millicent to South Africa, prepared to live for the next four months in an empty railway carriage and to travel the veldt on a bicycle, witnessing God knew what kind of horrors. She was fifty-four, with no great experience of travelling abroad, and certainly not the kind of person likely to make concessions to the heat like the leaving-off of stays or a warming flannel petticoat. 'You have no right to go about Africa in things you would be ashamed to be seen in at home,' wrote the explorer Mary Kingsley in 1897; no doubt Millicent concurred.

Miss Hobhouse had claimed that thousands of Boers died in the camps as victims of malnutrition, enforced poverty, avoidable illness and the wanton brutality of their British captors. The government hoped Mrs Fawcett would prove her wrong. It would be tricky to argue that Millicent was an impartial judge. She was something of an imperialist, linking the potentially civilizing influence of enfranchised women with a wider mission to civilize the Empire. Her opposition to Irish Home Rule was well known, and her patriotism absolute. She was a child of her time, in many ways a Victorian relic who believed in women's innate *politesse* and moral strength. Making a fuss was vulgar. But it is a mark of her character that she did not hesitate to express her support for Miss Hobhouse, even though the government decided to publish its own 'findings', in what Miss Hobhouse nicknamed the Whitewashing Report, before they had heard a word from Millicent. The official line was that the Boers had been treated with humanity, and that most of their woes stemmed from their own insanitary habits. Millicent repudiated this, maintaining that the British had caused the deaths of 27,927 women and children – one in four of all the camp inmates – through starvation, disease and exposure. Nor had they treated the survivors honourably.

The reaction of a Baptist minister in Liverpool to the Fawcett Commission's findings was typical of many members of the public at home in Britain: 'Great Britain cannot win . . . without resorting to the last despicable cowardice of the most loathsome cur on earth – the act of striking a brave man's heart through his wife's honour and his child's life! This cowardly war has been conducted through methods of barbarism . . . the concentration camps have been murder camps.'[33]

Millicent never spoke much about her South African experiences, except to say with rather shocking pragmatism that they probably helped the cause of women's suffrage. Look what a mess men made when left to their own devices. They didn't just leave the world untidy and grubby: they were lethal. And look what a transformation there might be when the compassionate voice of a woman is heard and understood. Especially should the voice belong to that most oxymoronic of creatures, a woman of authority.

When Millicent settled back in Gower Street after her unexpected adventure, few could have denied that she was now a woman of authority. She was on the parliamentary committee of the NUWSS, which she had helped to found; she was chairman of her local branch, the London Society; vice-chairman from 1902 of the International Woman Suffrage Alliance; and involved with the Women's Liberal Unionist Association. Her name was honoured as an early supporter of the women's colleges at Cambridge (where she helped to run the city's own suffrage society) and as the widow of a much-admired government minister.

She had interesting friends and relations, too. The relations we know about, though Elizabeth Garrett Anderson (1836–1917) deserves extra attention. 'Hard and Godless' she may have been, with a bedside manner described as at best brusque (it's said she once emptied a vase of flowers over a recalcitrant patient), but she was also one of British history's most enduring pioneers. She became the first woman to qualify in this country as a medical doctor. She went to the same school as Millicent; then, aged eighteen, she met Emily Davies. In the following years, between them they managed to force, persuade, charm or shame open the three main barriers to women's social progress, accessing higher education, the medical profession and finally the vote. For nineteen years Elizabeth was the only woman member of the British Medical Association. She taught medical students at the London School of Medicine for Women, opened in 1874. She worked tirelessly for various different suffrage societies, on School Boards and in local government, and her activism spanned almost the entire campaign, from the signing of the first petition in 1866 to the passing of the Representation of the People Act in 1917 (made law the following year). There could not be a truer pedigree of devotion to the Cause in its widest sense, as something to empower women to maximize their own potential for the good of society.

So much for her sister. Millicent's friends were scarcely less impressive. They included some of the most spirited women of the day. Emmeline Pankhurst was never a close ally, but Katherine Russell, Viscountess Amberley – the woman Queen Victoria said deserved a 'good whipping' for her suffrage views – was. What agitated the queen so much was Kate's distressing habit of standing on public platforms and addressing the hoi polloi. This is not what Ladies did. It must be said that Kate's extra-marital relationship with her son's tutor didn't exactly enhance her reputation, nor did her promotion of birth control, but one gets the impression that politics rather than promiscuity were at the heart of the royal disapproval.

Novelist Thomas Hardy added his much-revered name to the list of Millicent's supporters. He wrote a letter assuring her that he had 'for a long time been in favour of woman suffrage . . . because I think the tendency of the women's vote will be to break up the present pernicious conventions in respect of . . . customs, religions, illegitimacy [and] the stereotyped household '.[34] A writer of similar celebrity, Robert Browning, was her erstwhile schoolteacher's nephew and an ally of Elizabeth; George Eliot moved in the same circles as she, as did Sir Hubert Parry, composer and royal favourite, whose wife, Maud, was an ardent suffragist and joined the 1913 Pilgrimage.

Another friend, Margaret Ashton, was of less opulent stock, but still a pioneer. She became Manchester's first woman councillor, after chairing Withington Urban District Council for years. She was also a pilgrim, as was Sarah Lees of Oldham – Marjory's mother – who in 1910 became England's second ever woman mayor. (Perhaps predictably, Dr Elizabeth Garrett Anderson beat her to it.[35]) Selina Cooper, whom we shall meet later on, worked in a cotton mill from the age of twelve; she was one of Millicent's favourite suffrage speakers. Ground-breaking journalist and feminist Vera Chute Collum thought the world of her, as did members of the famously radical Bright and Cobden dynasties.

The point of all this is that Millicent, though privileged, was not a snob. Nor did she assume that civilization petered out beyond the Home Counties. Historians are apt to characterize the NUWSS as a southern and slightly spineless outfit, and Mrs Pankhurst's WSPU as full of northern grit. In fact, Millicent Fawcett inspired the most democratic episode in the whole of the suffrage campaign – the Pilgrimage – while the Pankhursts were accused at the height of their militancy of being explicitly *un*democratic, both in terms of who the majority of WSPU members were, and how the organization was run.

One of Mrs Fawcett's greatest strengths lay in recognizing other people's talents, developing them not just for the good of the Cause but of the self. Once the NUWSS got going, its officers were often young university-educated women unable to find employment elsewhere, so wary was the workplace of involving itself with unpredictable and probably unstable 'bluestockings'.[36] Either that, or they were working women, like Selina Cooper, whose education might have been scant but whose life experience and common sense were invaluable. Enthusiasm and new ideas were constantly being fed into the union. A good deal of fresh air circulated round Millicent Fawcett, much sound thinking and plain speaking. Paradoxically, as well as being an obvious asset, this was her besetting problem. At an early suffrage meeting to which the organizers, eager for publicity, had managed to entice the press, a journalist was overheard as he turned for the door before the end. 'I shall go,' he declared. 'These women are only talking sense. There's no copy in that.'[37]

3

DEEDS AND WORDS

1903–1909

Woman is denied the rights of citizenship. She is an outlaw. Thus logically and justly she ought to be a rebel.[1]

EMMA SPROSON NOTED the time as she gently unlatched the baby from her breast. It was six o'clock on the morning of Thursday, 7 February 1907. Before she left the house in Wolverhampton, she handed her son to his grandmother with a kiss, buttoned her coat, pulled down her hat and turned to face the dark street outside. She had to hurry to catch the 6.55 a.m. train to London – and she was already exhausted. 'The baby was strong,' she remembered later, 'but I was weak.'[2] Emma had only a few pence in her pocket but was confident her friend Mrs Pankhurst would help her once she arrived in the capital. Emma was on a mission.

Women like her did not habitually make friends with people like Emmeline Pankhurst. As a child she had worked 'half-time' (sharing her days with school) delivering milk, mangling heavy, wet laundry and then as a shopgirl. But despite her interrupted education she was quick-witted and filled what little spare time she had with reading and thinking. In 1896, when she was nearly thirty, Emma married Frank Sproson, a local postman who was also the secretary of Wolverhampton's Independent Labour Party. She was happy to share her husband's political activities. When Frank booked the increasingly high-profile Mrs Pankhurst to come and speak on women's suffrage one evening in 1906, Emma chaired the meeting and confidently invited Mrs Pankhurst to stay overnight with them. Soon afterwards – no doubt inspired by the great lady – Emma joined the Women's Social and Political Union.

Emma Sproson.

She had been what she called 'a keen feminist' ever since attending an election meeting a few years ago at Southport, where Lord Curzon (of anti-suffrage fame) was standing as the Tory candidate. When the floor was thrown open for questions at the end, Emma stood up – to a gasp of incredulity from the assembled gentlemen – and efficiently began to quiz the candidates. They refused as one to answer her because she was a woman, therefore had no vote, therefore had no right to address them or even to be there at all. That, at the time, was unimpeachable political logic.

When the train steamed into Euston station on that day in 1907, Emma apprehensively made her way a mile and a half south to 4 Clement's Inn, where Mr and Mrs Frederick Pethick-Lawrence lived. It was one of a range of impressive-looking red-brick buildings, rearing up at least five storeys and filled with offices and apartments. The Pethick-Lawrences had hosted the headquarters of the WSPU in their suite of rooms there since the previous summer. Emmeline Pankhurst was spending an increasing amount of time in London by then, to the extent that the Manchester Registrar General had asked her to question where her loyalties lay: with her job, or with the WSPU.[3]

Emma Sproson was tired and hungry; her breasts ached, mortifyingly leaking milk for her distant baby, and among the bustling, strangely accented women she must have felt like an alien. But not for long. There was too much to do. The official opening of Parliament was five days away. Despite regular promises made by the Liberal government since 1905 that a serious debate would be timetabled to settle the question of women's suffrage, nothing constructive had happened so far. The patience of all those agitating for the vote was wearing thin, and the officers of the WSPU had decided that if there was still no provision in the upcoming session, they would stage a protest. This wouldn't be an exclusively London-based event; working women would be sponsored to come down from the north and join the fray, including Emma.

On 11 February the WSPU drew up plans for two hundred of its members to be organized into fourteen groups, each with a nominated leader. They would march in two columns on the 13th, the day after Parliament opened, if the King's Speech ignored them yet again. Caxton Hall had already been hired for a grand meeting at 3 p.m. on the afternoon of the 13th; tickets had sold out ages ago. Perhaps this would be a celebration instead of a council of war? It was a perfect venue: large, slightly tucked away near St James's Park, yet only a few minutes' walk from the House, within earshot of Big Ben. With suitable ambition, they called the meeting the 'Women's Parliament'. There would be speeches and a resolution put to the vote, either applauding the government's long-awaited conversion or deploring its repeated dismissal of women's suffrage. They would then march the results of that resolution up the road to Westminster, in triumph or in anger. Most of them must have realized triumph was unlikely.

Emma met other WSPU sympathizers on the morning of the 13th at Essex Hall, next to a Unitarian church not far from Clement's Inn, where they had been asked to gather for singing practice. To the tune of 'John Brown's Body' they learned a rousing new anthem:

Rise up, women! For the fight is hard and long;
Rise in thousands, singing loud a battle song.
Right is might, and in its strength we shall be strong,
And the Cause goes marching on.

Glory, glory Alleluia; Glory, glory Alleluia;
Glory, glory Alleluia; the Cause goes marching on.[4]

After lunch the suffragettes, as they were now becoming known, filed along the Strand past Parliament Square to Caxton Hall, where the Women's Parliament duly opened and the appropriate resolution was passed. Sure enough, the King's Speech had not mentioned women's suffrage at all. At Mrs Pankhurst's surprisingly raucous cry of 'Rise up, women!' the fourteen brigades of protesters (including a few men) mustered behind their leaders in two separate battalions to launch their assault on Westminster – these are the military terms in which the *London Daily News* reported the 'riot' the following day. Even though WSPU leaders claimed this was originally designed as a peaceful protest, the meeting at Caxton Hall had been frenziedly emotive. No one there can have forgotten the shocking occasion the previous October when ten suffragettes had been arrested for breaching the peace at the House of Commons and imprisoned. Peace, the police and the WSPU were never easy bedfellows.

As they approached the Palace of Westminster the protesters found their way barred by police. So, 'very gently,' remembered Emma, 'we bowled some of them over.'[5] Scores more policemen arrived, on foot and mounted on horseback. Some formed a cordon outside the Houses of Parliament while others charged into the crowd of demonstrators to break it up. According to the press, there were thousands of onlookers by now. News travels fast on the streets of London. Emma and her companions tried to make their way to St Stephen's Hall, part of the complex of parliamentary buildings where the monarch's subjects may traditionally petition their MPs. The two battalions took different routes to baffle the enemy. Only fifteen individuals made it to St Stephen's, however. Emma was seized on the way by two police officers who used her 'very roughly' and was promptly arrested.

There was a brief lull in the excitement when most of those arrested were allowed to stumble back to Caxton Hall on bail. Anyone injured or in shock after the fracas was patched up and given a cup of tea. Many of the women had fallen, knocked to the ground by men or horses, or had been hit; most were muddy by now, dishevelled and thoroughly frightened. After another meeting at 8 p.m., at which Emma was asked to speak, a second attempt was made to reach Parliament. There were more riots, more arrests; by ten o'clock some sixty people had appeared, like Emma, at Cannon Row police station just around the corner, summoned to attend the next day at Rochester Row Court. They came from London, Lancashire, Leicestershire, Yorkshire, Staffordshire, Cardiff and Glasgow. Their ages ranged from eighteen to fifty; there was a nurse among them, a shopkeeper and a schoolteacher, a weaver and a brass-moulder, a servant and several housekeepers, a couple of typists and an actress.

Emma Sproson's occupation was simply noted as 'married'.[6]

When she took a late omnibus home to her lodgings that night, Emma disingenuously asked the driver what all that trouble earlier on had been about. He answered with disgust, 'It's them suffragettes. They come here, upsets the traffic, upsets Parliament, upsets London. They wants to get in Parliament. They wants to get a husband, and if they got a husband, they couldn't cook a dinner. They couldn't cook an egg . . . If I had my way, I'd tie 'em back to back and chuck 'em all in the Thames.'[7]

Next morning, Emma saw her picture on the front page of a newspaper; she felt half proud, no doubt, and half mortified. After appearing in front of the magistrate Mr Curtis Bennett (a name she remembered all her life), she was charged and sentenced to a fine of £1 or two weeks' imprisonment. Of all those arrested on 13 February, only two – a married couple – decided to pay the fine. The rest were bundled into Black Marias and driven an hour up the road to Holloway Prison. There they were brought undrinkable cocoa and inedible bread in a filthy tin while waiting to be paraded – humiliated – in front of the prison doctor.

Another suffragette arrested at the same time as Emma, Mary Ann Rawle, described what happened next in a diary she kept secretly on smuggled sheets of lavatory paper. In her own untutored words, she was told to 'pull of my boots pull my hair down undo my blouse take all my money and pawn tickets out of my pocket, these along with my hair comb and hat pins was taken of me.'[8] She and Emma were inspected, weighed and measured, instructed to wash, given ill-fitting shoes – a random size for each foot – a coarse grey dress branded with broad arrows and a disgusting under-petticoat, which in Emma's case drooped an inch below the hem of her dress. No other underwear except scratchy black stockings. Wearing once-white caps over their loose hair and a jolly blue-and-white checked apron, they looked like lunatic country housewives.

They were then provided with two stiff sheets and a towel, and led to their separate cells, which measured about six by nine feet. The bed in Emma's was nothing but a wooden plank four inches above the floor. She was given a Bible and a pamphlet called 'The Narrow Way', an extended sermon by a Mr Pink all about striving and selflessness. Mary Ann Rawle had a little volume with the mocking title *A Healthy Home*. In their cells they found various bits and pieces: a wooden stool and a tiny shelf; a piece of tin the size of a table-knife and a wooden spoon for cutlery; a brush, comb, salt cellar and slop pail; and a dustpan with a coconut-fibre brush for doing the housework. 'What a mixture!' sighed a confused Mary Ann.

Each day began at 6 a.m. when the women were awoken by a bell, though in reality most were awake already and had been for most of the night. They were expected to make their meagre beds, wash their pint mugs and empty the slops. There was a chance to visit a lavatory after breakfast, but if you missed it – too many people, not enough time – there would not be another opportunity until after lunch at 1.30 p.m. Chapel was every morning (twice on Sundays) before exercise, which lasted half an hour or an hour and involved traipsing round a melancholy clump of scrub in the yard, which marked the burial spot of the last two women to be hanged at the jail.

Emma hated the food, which consisted of bland, gelatinous soup, occasional suet dumplings or lumps of fatty boiled bacon and once in a while an egg. They were allowed to bathe once a week unless they were menstruating. The prisoners were not supposed to speak to anyone, even during exercise, and were allowed to send only a single letter, receiving none. The chaplain came to visit one day, but was hardly a conversationalist. Mary Ann remembered her chat with him well. 'Are you going out in the morning do you come from Lancashire Yes that will do.'[9]

To help pass the dismal hours and quell her yearning for her baby, Emma tried to decipher the cobwebby scratches made by successive prisoners with illicit hatpins in the wooden door of her cell.

Some of them were so faint she had to rub in dust to read what they said. This palimpsest of misery and hope fascinated her.

Her one prison letter, written to her husband Frank, still survives. 'Arrested at 5 p.m. this afternoon,' she informed him. She imagined the 'cruel criticisms' Frank must be suffering now that word of her arrest had reached Wolverhampton, and worried about their son, so suddenly weaned and now without his mother. 'Watch baby carefully. Get Mrs Mitchell to make trousers for [him] from an old uniform coat of yours . . . If he should become irregular in his bowels give him fluid magnesia.'[10]

Frank answered in a message Emma did not receive until after her release. He confessed that he was not surprised to hear she was in Holloway. 'Now whatever you do, don't fret and worry about us, we are all right . . . baby takes his food like a man! . . . I still sing to him and he still laughs; so all is well here.' He didn't let her rabid reputation as a suffragette get him down. 'I am having the usual sneers but am sufficiently thick-skinned enough to take no notice of such childishness. I am quite proud of you and admire your courage, so don't be down hearted.'[11]

Ever the pragmatist, Emma took her husband's advice. There is a photograph of her in the Museum of London crouching on a city pavement chalking slogans on the flagstones with a couple of sister suffragettes, one of whom is looking cheerily up at the camera. Emma is intent on her work, wearing what looks like a borrowed astrakhan coat and hat (it's early spring) and watched by a little crowd of bemused men and boys.[12] By the end of March 1907, presumably not having gone home in between, she was in Holloway again, this time on a charge of disorderly behaviour and resisting the police. Because she was now a repeat offender, her sentence was doubled. WSPU officials wrote to Frank while she was inside to report on her

health and spirits, and when she was released she was invited – as a
speaker as well as a guest – to a 'Public Luncheon' held in prisoners'
honour at the Holborn Restaurant near Clement's Inn. She recorded
the menu in mouthwatering detail: tomato soup, turbot, lamb and
'Macedoine des fruits Holborn': essentially, a fresh fruit salad.

Emmeline's highly charismatic eldest daughter Christabel
Pankhurst had visited Emma in Holloway. She ran the WSPU at the
time with her mother and the Pethick-Lawrences. No doubt Emma
was given the usual award of an enamelled suffragette brooch in the
shape of a portcullis designed by middle Pankhurst daughter Sylvia;
the youngest, Adela, had been among the ten women imprisoned in
October 1906 and young Harry bravely sold suffrage literature on
the streets. It would be tempting to think of the WSPU as a family
concern. In fact, from its conception that autumn day in Manchester
in 1903 to the moment it ceased hostilities on the outbreak of the

Sylvia Pankhurst.

First World War in 1914, it was a more or less benign autocracy under Emmeline Pankhurst. The organization never had a working constitution and relied for its impact on creating an intensely emotional link between its leaders and its followers, on celebrity and heady sensationalism rather than the prosaic art of persuasion. Persuasion patently didn't work, especially when used by suffragists whom Sylvia described witheringly as tame and prim, with nervous high-pitched voices and an apologetic air. Women like Emma Sproson and Mary Ann Rawle were restless, deeply frustrated by the political status quo both locally and nationally, and passionately responsive to the WSPU's ideal that, despite their unfortunate gender, they held the power to change history.

The WSPU never raised as much money as the NUWSS, nor did it have as many members, but their commitment to the Cause – and

Christabel Pankhurst (left) and Adela Pankhurst.

to their charismatic figureheads – was unparalleled. Their devotion burned bright; bright enough, sometimes, to blind. Inspired by Emmeline's extraordinary presence and oratory, they left meetings full of missionary zeal. Well-publicized heroines like Annie Kenney (1879–1953), a Pre-Raphaelite mill girl from Marjory Lees's home town of Oldham, encouraged the young and the working-class; the dignified novelist and social reformer Charlotte Despard (1844–1939), who looked like a Victorian relic, became a role model for older gentlewomen; Anne Cobden Sanderson (1853–1926), the daughter of the famous free-trade campaigner Richard Cobden, represented the old-school radicals; Lady Constance Lytton (1869–1923) was an aristocrat through and through with an acute social conscience. Frederick (later Lord) Pethick-Lawrence (1871–1961) was a prominent lawyer and newspaper publisher who acted as financial secretary to the WSPU, while the pioneering Labour politician Keir Hardie (1856–1915), who left school at seven and worked down the mines, was a suffragette favourite and champion. In other words, there was somebody in the WSPU for everyone.

A *Daily Mail* journalist writing on 10 January 1906 coined the term 'suffragette'. It was meant to be disparaging, the diminutive suffix not only suggesting a frivolous, girlish attitude, but a sham. Just as leatherette was sham leather and cashmerette sham cashmere – both current terms at the time – a suffragette was a sham campaigner.[13] Members of the WSPU chose not to take the hint. Their slogan – 'Deeds Not Words' – had been in place ever since Emmeline established the organization, signifying a new age of proactivity in women's politics. The Women's Social and Political Union was designed to stir up and rejuvenate the suffrage campaign, as what we would these days call a ginger-group. Three years later, when its headquarters transferred to London, it had developed into a far more substantial thing: an engine for change, fuelled by the conviction of its officers and members. Now 'Deeds Not Words' was not an aspiration, but a threat.

In October 1905 a meeting had been held in the Free Trade Hall
in Manchester by Liberal politician Sir Edward Grey in advance of
the General Election in December. It seemed clear that the Tory government would not be returned to office, so the WSPU wrote to ask
Sir Edward if he would receive a local deputation of members, in the
hope of initiating a fresh approach to women's suffrage. Recklessly,
he failed to reply. Christabel Pankhurst and Annie Kenney decided
to turn up at the meeting anyway – much as Emma Sproson had
done in Southport – and ask the man in person why he and his party
persisted in ignoring half the country's population.

The WSPU had designed a rather prolix banner for the event.
It read 'Will the Liberal Government Give Votes for Women?', but
according to Emmeline Pankhurst all those words made it too heavy
for Christabel and Annie to carry, so they decided to cut the length
of the banner to the last three words, without the question mark.
Thus was born one of the most enduring political slogans in our
history. Up went the banner when the time came and, getting to
her feet (energetically propelled by Christabel), Miss Kenney called
out her question to Sir Edward. It was the same question posed by
the original banner, and was ignored. People tried to pull her down
to her seat again, to tell her to shut up, to cover her face with a hat;
when she refused to be silenced the chief constable of Manchester
came down and politely asked whether she would be prepared to put
her question in writing. If so, he said he would take it to Sir Edward
himself. When he delivered it to the platform, it was passed from
speaker to speaker but no one attempted to address it.

Annie Kenney's decision to stand on a chair and shout her protest
during the vote of thanks at the end of the meeting was the last straw.
Stewards hauled her and Christabel from the hall, Miss Pankhurst
screaming that if they threw her out she would assault them: 'I shall
spit at you!' And so she did. Eventually both women were arrested
and sentenced, Christabel to seven days in Strangeways Prison and
Annie to three. Winston Churchill had been at the meeting and,

feeling chivalrous (though not a committed suffragist), he went to the jail the next day to pay the women's fines – which would have mortified them – but the governor refused to take his money.

That incident marked the beginning of the WSPU's policy of militancy. Eight months later, on 21 June 1906, the first three London suffragettes were imprisoned after disturbing the peace during a deputation to the home of Chancellor of the Exchequer Herbert Asquith. One of them was a Lancashire teacher, Teresa Billington, in her late twenties; the second was Jane Sparboro, a sixty-four-year-old seamstress from East London; and the third was Ada Knight, the disabled wife of a black sailor, Donald Brown, who took *her* name when they married and supported her wholeheartedly. The organization's appeal was wide and far-reaching at this stage, and the courage of its individual members, who were acting entirely without precedent, was remarkable. Millicent Fawcett, arch-suffragist, admired them. In a letter to *The Times* on 27 October 1906 she wrote of the ten suffragettes arrested while attempting to storm Parliament that month that, in her opinion, 'far from having injured the movement, they have done more during the last twelve months to bring it within the realms of practical politics than we have been able to accomplish in the same number of years.' In *forty* years, in fact. She even held a banquet at the Savoy that December for the offending suffragettes, now released, inviting the inconveniently vegetarian Mr George Bernard Shaw and his wife as special guests.

Towards the end of 1907, however, things began to change. Emmeline Pankhurst declared that she was cancelling that year's annual general meeting of the WSPU, and all such meetings in the future, intending instead to continue running the union autonomously via a committee of her own choosing. This was in response to a plea from Teresa Billington, Charlotte Despard and others that the WSPU should be organized along democratic lines like the NUWSS. It was supremely ironic that an outfit demanding fair representation for women failed to practise what it preached. So

Teresa and Charlotte left to set up an alternative suffrage society, the Women's Freedom League (WFL). The WFL repudiated violence, though still claimed to be a militant organization: another departure from the ethos of the WSPU.

During the following year, the Women's Anti-Suffrage League and the Men's League for Opposing Women's Suffrage were both founded – more about them later – and in 1908 the first window-breaking campaign began. By then Emma Sproson had left the WSPU. On her return to Wolverhampton after her second release she had been met with abuse and a squall of vitriolic poison-pen letters, which would have been tolerable had she still believed in Emmeline's ideals. But recently it had become apparent that Mrs Pankhurst, as Emma put it, was 'out for a Dictatorship'. This did not sit well with Emma's socialist principles. Someone else described Christabel as 'cynical and cold at heart',[14] and Sylvia was deeply unhappy at this time, both personally and professionally. All was not well in the Pankhurst camp, which inevitably damaged the WSPU, since the two entities were essentially symbionts.

The suffragists, or constitutional campaigners, meanwhile, were in something of a quandary. It was increasingly obvious that in order to win the hearts and minds of the British people, something would have to be done to persuade the public that the idea of giving women the vote was neither dangerous nor distasteful. All this unpleasantness on the streets of London and Manchester was becoming counter-productive. 'No-one endowed with an ordinary amount of common sense would deny that women have a right to vote,' wrote a political observer, 'but no-one will be found to admit it while her manners are so obviously odious.'[15] Here was the core of the suffrage problem. Members of the WSPU had attracted more publicity for the Cause than ever before: the papers were writing about them; people talked about them in their homes, factories, out shopping, at school, even at church; cartoonists satirized their opponents (in *Punch*, for example) or their leaders (almost everywhere else). They were news. But it was impossible for any supporter of women's suffrage to capitalize on the publicity by making progress. Despite Mrs Fawcett's qualified support of their achievements, the suffragettes were increasingly cast as comic pantomime villains, bit-part players in the parliamentary Punch and Judy show, fighting over votes as if they were a string of toothsome sausages. The long game played by the patient suffragists since 1866 was in danger of ignominious defeat.

Mrs Fawcett and her followers had lobbied Parliament, canvassed on behalf of sympathetic candidates at elections, held meeting after meeting after meeting, tried to show empirically what women could achieve in public life as local government officials, councillors, academics, professionals and philanthropists. They had been responsible, unbelievably tactful, trying to keep their dignity while desperate for change. Yet sometimes it felt as though they had got nowhere. Gone backwards, in fact: people were accusing the whole movement of self-immolation. It was hard to know what to do next.

The answer came in a stroke of genius, when in 1907 members of the NUWSS hit upon a completely novel idea. To rehabilitate their diseased image, they too would take to the streets, but not in a combative spirit, not as protesters. Instead, they would *demonstrate* belief in themselves and in the power of democracy with a vast celebratory parade. They would raise up banners proclaiming the virtues of suffragism, like 'Gentle but Resolute', 'Justice not Privilege'. This would be a spectacle, a show, something people would come to marvel at, admire, enjoy and, most of all, remember.

It went wonderfully well. On 7 February – the very day Emma Sproson set out from Wolverhampton – three thousand NUWSS members from around the country gathered at Hyde Park Corner and marched to Exeter Hall in the Strand, where speeches were made and bands played rousing tunes. It may have been cold, wet and foggy, the women's skirts may have dragged heavily at their heels (hence the procession's nickname of the 'Mud March') and the feathers in their hats drooped damply, but this was a joyful occasion.

'I am real glad that the weather is bad,' confessed one of those taking part, 'because this great procession tramping through the mud shows that we are not mere fireside advocates of our cause. The wet and the mud have not kept at home a single woman who had promised to join our cause.'[16] Participants wore red-and-white rosettes – so did some of the policemen on duty, given them by smiling suffragists – and carried posies of winter blossom tied with red and white ribbons. Just as they would during the Pilgrimage six years later, all sorts of suffragists marched together, with women from different places, classes and backgrounds side by side. A reporter from the *Tribune* was amazed at the women's solidarity:

> Not one class of women alone was represented in this great procession of voteless citizens who had come to plead at the bar of public opinion for the right to representation . . . There were the brilliant women of the London world, high-born dames with their Girton and Newnham daughters, there were literary and professional women by the hundred – the woman doctor, the high-school mistress, the woman artist – and there were the women of the great industrial north – women who had left their factories in far-away Lancashire to take part in the march.[17]

This was a pageant, as spectacular for its appearance as for its obvious sincerity. Most newspapers, incidentally, called the members of the NUWSS 'suffragettes' – something that still impacted on suffragists during the Pilgrimage; this was the cross they would have to bear for the duration of the campaign and well beyond. Few appreciate the difference even now. For the moment, however, the confusion worked in the suffragettes' favour, for here was a large group of women willing to show by example why they should have the vote, and to look as though they deserved it. The *Manchester Guardian* understood the significance of the Mud March: 'That old ladies and delicate ones, and timid ones to boot, should have done this quite simply and bravely argues at least a good deal of quiet conviction and a resolution not likely to be easily broken.'[18]

The Mud March was the first planned, public demonstration (rather than public protest) held by massed women in the cause of suffrage. Those who took part did not do so blithely. They were unsure how the police would react, or whether bystanders or nay-sayers would try to incite trouble. According to suffragist Ray Strachey, there was no need to worry:

> [The] vast majority of women still felt that there was something very dreadful in walking in procession through the streets; to do it was to be something of a martyr, and many of the demonstrators felt that they were risking their employments and endangering their reputations, besides facing a dreadful ordeal of ridicule and public shame. They walked, and nothing happened . . . Crowds watched and wondered; and it was not so dreadful after all.[19]

The crowds were kind. Women waved handkerchiefs, men raised their hats; at the end of the day everyone was tired, but proud.

WSPU members were not included in the Mud March unless they happened also to belong to the NUWSS or other suffragist organizations. Plenty of people *did* belong to both the militant and non-militant branches of the campaign, including – perhaps surprisingly – the 1866 suffragist pioneer Dr Elizabeth Garrett Anderson, who joined the suffragettes in 1908. Perhaps they felt moved to cover all bases. Well aware of its own need to engage more popular support, however, and impressed by the popular success of the Mud March, the WSPU decided to organize another procession – bigger and better – in the summer of the following year. They advertised it as a 'monster' march, to take place on 21 June 1908, christened 'Women's Sunday' for the occasion. Like the Mud March, it would centre on Hyde Park but this time there would be 'hundreds of thousands' of amazed spectators and some thirty thousand participants.

First, however, the WSPU needed to work on its image.
Emmeline Pankhurst decreed that suffragettes – a name she astutely
embraced[20] – should at all times strive to appear as feminine as
possible. Annie Kenney was dressed by the artistic Sylvia Pankhurst
in picturesque shawls or wistful pale-green gowns from Liberty's.
Dowdy coats and skirts were discouraged in favour of expensive
dresses and 'picture hats', and nothing masculine or eccentric was
allowed (except in the case of composer Ethel Smyth, who invariably
looked both masculine and eccentric). For the monster march,
everyone was to wear white, with a sash in the WSPU colours, unless
they were in academic gowns or some other appropriate costume.
Mrs Emmeline Pethick-Lawrence chose the colour scheme in May
1908: green for hope, white for purity and violet for dignity.
The colours' initials stood as a convenient acronym for 'give women
the vote'.

Ethel Smyth.

Now things got a little ridiculous. No sooner had the WSPU announced its plans for Women's Sunday than the NUWSS started working on yet another demonstration of its own, to be held the week before. Both projects formed a response to Herbert Asquith's explicit request for proof that the majority of British women actually wanted a vote. He succeeded Henry Campbell-Bannerman as prime minister in April 1908 and, after a series of failed Private Member's Bills and suffrage amendments in Parliament, his support for the Cause was a prize worth having. But there must also have been an element of tit for tat in this battle of the marches.

The WSPU embarked on a publicity campaign involving truly enormous posters with life-sized photographs of twenty prominent suffragettes' faces on them, and a steam launch on the Thames decorated with banners, from which doughty WSPU officer 'General' Flora Drummond bellowed through an inadequate megaphone at bemused MPs enjoying tea on the terrace of the House of Commons. The centrepiece of the NUWSS advertising strategy was an image created by artist Caroline Watts known as the Bugler Girl: 'a woman trumpeter, standing on ramparts, flag in hand, and blowing an inspiriting call to the women of Great Britain to come out and stand by their sisters in this fight.'[21] Posters featuring the Bugler Girl were distributed all over the country, along with handbills explaining that this procession was not for militants, but for 'homemakers'. These were ordinary women who longed to make the world a better place, who needed a vote not so that they could boast equality with men, but to help 'homeless women, and the thousands of little children whose homes are sad, by . . . putting right such things as these which women understand.'[22]

The WSPU and the NUWSS each had a number of 'suffrage shops' around the country at which they displayed and sold propaganda and coordinated regional plans. Local organizers booked trains and arranged places to stay, to get changed, to eat and use the lavatory; everyone had a job to do, and did it well. That was all part of their plan: to demonstrate that women were capable of carrying off a highly complicated enterprise with aplomb.

Both the suffragettes and the suffragists realized how important it was, from the point of view of press and public, to emphasize the essential femininity of their campaigns. The WSPU did this by requesting those white dresses for everyone on such a scale that an entire new fashion movement was born: a sort of suffragette *chic* with lots of white lace, accented and endlessly accessorized in 'the colours'. (Later on, the 'gists would have their turn when it became all the rage after the Pilgrimage to raise skirt hems by a daring four inches – the length suggested by the Pilgrimage organizers to prevent the sort of clogging experienced during the Mud March.)

The NUWSS concentrated instead on the ethos of the undertaking, stressing the 'homemaker' narrative and showcasing the traditional feminine accomplishment of needlework. As their procession flowed from the Embankment to the Royal Albert Hall on 13 June, six abreast and two miles long, it looked like a brilliant, silken river with almost a thousand embroidered banners dipping and bobbing through the wide streets, their colours glancing in the sunlight and constantly changing. This was arguably the most spectacular pageant London had ever seen. Most of the banners represented the occupations of women involved. And at this stage it should be explained just how many dedicated suffrage societies there were. It is often suggested that the campaign for women's votes was essentially a two-pronged attack on the government by the WSPU and the NUWSS. Certainly, most campaigners were either militants or non–militants, but within those two camps, affiliated to them or quite independent, were scores of different organizations operating in slightly different ways, with different focuses and plans of action. The following list gives an idea of their number at this time, give or take a month or two, and of their scope. It's a surprisingly long one – and plenty more followed later on.

Among the biggest groups was the Women's Freedom League, founded by Charlotte Despard and others in 1907 to promote civil disobedience rather than physical violence in the fight for the vote. Different political parties had their own societies, as did different religious groups. The Actresses' Franchise League (AFL), established in 1908, worked a little like a concert party in wartime, its members performing suffrage plays around the country as propaganda and to raise morale. The Artists' Suffrage League, set up in 1907 by Mary Lowndes, designed artwork and banners. Writers and musicians had their own suffrage networks, as did teachers, local university students and women's colleges, pharmacists, women sanitary inspectors, nurses, clerks, civil servants, 'business women', cyclists, even gymnastic teachers (a particularly fine body of women, according to the press). Sympathetic trades unions included the textile workers', mill workers', cigar-makers', clay-pipe finishers' and – if an unwieldy banner hefted aloft during the Mud March is to be believed – the union of 'Patent Cop Winders, Hawk and Bobbin Winders, Gassers, Doublers and Reelers'.

On their June parade, Mrs Fawcett's constitutionalists were joined by members of other supportive groups, including the National Union of Women Workers, Liberals, Fabians, Conservatives, Unionists and the Women's Co-operative Guild. Not only did the array of banners they all carried represent those who were marching, and where they came from, but they also commemorated heroines of the movement. Thus, included among those taking part, at least in spirit, were Florence Nightingale, Queen Elizabeth I, Charlotte Brontë, Joan of Arc, the American suffragist Lucy Stone and Josephine Butler. Music swirled around from various brass bands along the way and the audience (for this was definitely a performance) cheered and clapped. There were a few who jeered, of course; there always would be. When one of the marchers paused to give some coins to a beggar-woman with a baby, someone shouted, 'There you go! Spending your father's money!'[23] But overall the atmosphere was one of pride, admiration and affection. Millicent Fawcett had spent months planning this; at the end of the day at the Royal Albert Hall, when

GREAT VOTES FOR WOMEN DEMONSTRATION IN HYDE PARK, SUNDAY. JUNE 21, 1908.

Crowds gather for 'Women's Sunday', 21 June 1908.

everyone was exhilarated and exhausted and sang 'For she's a jolly good fellow' to her, she wept with gratitude and relief.

The WSPU's Women's Sunday event was just as successful. It wasn't quite as breathtaking a spectacle as the previous week's march, according to the papers, but more energetic. It was more complicated, too, involving seven separate routes through London which converged on Hyde Park, an idea stolen a few years later by the Pilgrimage organizers. Holding the culmination of the day here, in open space, was an inspired idea: there was almost no limit to the number of onlookers. Indeed, *The Times* estimated that between a quarter and half a million people turned up on that gorgeous midsummer afternoon to see the 'shrieking sisterhood' on its best behaviour. No doubt many were hoping for some trouble, some ugliness, but the monster march was impeccably organized – a triumph. The *Daily Mail*'s comment about NUWSS marchers on 13 June applied to the WSPU too: 'What you are doing today will be in the history books.'[24]

Surely Asquith and his colleagues would be convinced by now that most women did indeed want the vote and would use it wisely? What better proof could they desire than the peaceful participation of tens of thousands of wives and mothers, sisters and daughters from all over the country, in such magnificent demonstrations of shared intent? Twenty different speakers had addressed the crowds in Hyde Park at the end of Women's Sunday, and at each of the twenty platforms formal resolutions were passed demanding women's suffrage. Christabel Pankhurst sent a record of the resolutions to Asquith without delay. And without delay he replied: he had nothing to add to previous statements. Although the Liberal government was considering introducing a new Reform Bill capable of amendment, or tweaking, to include a limited number of women in the franchise, it could not guarantee that this amendment would become law. That remained 'a contingent question in regard to a remote and speculative future'.[25]

This response bitterly disappointed Millicent Fawcett and members of the NUWSS. It incensed the WSPU. Just before Women's Sunday, Christabel had warned in *Votes for Women*, the suffragette journal, that 'if the Government still refuse to act, then we shall know great meetings, though they are indispensable for rousing public interest, fail as a means of directly influencing the Government. We shall then be obliged to rely more than ever on militant methods.'[26]

These words delighted anti-suffrage campaigners, led by the prolific writer Mrs Humphry Ward, almost as much as Asquith's statement. There had been a flurry of 'anti' activity following the success of the Mud March the previous year, and the positive publicity surrounding the processions during the summer of 1908 was worrisome to them. The news that the WSPU was returning to its old antics meant an increase in support from those who regarded suffragettes as terrorists, and perhaps – once and for all – a stop to all this nonsense about women's rights.

The anti-suffrage movement may have gained numbers, but it lacked originality. The same old arguments were still bandied about at meetings of the Men's League for Opposing Woman Suffrage, the Women's National Anti-Suffrage League, or the delightfully named Middle Class Defence Organisation, that women were physically, mentally and emotionally incapable of using a vote responsibly; that suffragism appealed only to the frigid and the unlovely ('women's rights are men's lefts') and that the power of women was best wielded in its proper sphere, at home and in the nursery:

> *The rights of women, – what are they?*
> *The right to labour, love, and pray;*
> *The right to weep with those who weep,*
> *The right to wake when others sleep;*
>
> *The right to dry the falling tear,*
> *The right to quell the rising fear;*
> *The right to smooth the brow of care,*
> *And whisper comfort in despair . . .*
>
> *The right to live for those we love,*
> *And suffer much that love to prove;*
> *The right to brighten earthly homes*
> *With pleasant smiles and gentle tones;*
>
> *Are these thy rights? – Then use them well,*
> *Thy holy influence none can tell;*
> *If these are thine, why ask for more?*
> *Thou hast enough to answer for!*[27]

Suffrage societies were patronizingly accused of holding waspish 'political mothers' meetings' or 'henpecks' with speakers who lacked gravitas. The novelist Marie Corelli wrote a pamphlet in 1907 with the title *Woman, or – Suffragette? A Question of National Choice.* 'Shall we sacrifice our Womanhood to Politics?' she asked ominously. 'Ten thousand times no! "Votes for Women" is the shrill cry of a number of discontented ladies who somehow seem to have missed the best of life . . . Woman was and is destined to *make* voters rather than be one of them.' Lady Griselda Cheape, president of the St Andrews branch of the Scottish Anti-Suffrage League, said she had heard that the WSPU paid poor women a guinea each to go out and get themselves arrested – political mercenaries, if you like – and it was her opinion that having women walking the streets looking for trouble was never going to end well.

When it had the time and the inclination, the NUWSS addressed the arguments of the anti-suffragists with good-humoured ridicule. To the astounding charge that women had no right to a vote because politics were invented by men, a witty suffragist replied, 'This is splendid! We now know why [the antis] opposed the higher education of woman. Man invented the alphabet . . . And all Mrs Humphry Ward's novels, written in the alphabet . . . Is it not bewildering?'[28]

The antis' ire may not have bothered Mrs Fawcett seriously, but the government's obstinacy certainly did. She did her best to think round the problem, supporting suffragist parliamentary candidates, building up the education and propaganda programmes in NUWSS branches around the country and trying to come up with the ultimate statement of faith in the power of ordinary women to change the world for the better. But for the WSPU, who tended to ignore the antis altogether, the time for talking and thinking was over. Direct action was considered a justifiable last resort.

From now on the number of suffragette arrests mounted alarmingly. Some resulted from stunts, like the 'rushing' of the Palace of Westminster by WSPU members in October 1908, which landed both Emmeline and Christabel Pankhurst in Holloway for incitement, or the sensational lowering of a banner demanding votes for women from the Ladies' Gallery in the House of Commons in the same month by members of the Women's Freedom League, who subsequently chained themselves to the grille and had to be cut free. The window-smashing campaign gathered pace and attracted much press attention. Though embraced by women who felt they could do their bit by hiding a toffee-hammer in a fur muff and striking at the commercial heart of the West End, window-smashing was not a universally popular activity. The composer Ethel Smyth thoroughly enjoyed it, selecting just the right rocks to hurl at politicians' windows, and some women took great pride in their stone-bowling. But to members of the public who might have been wavering in their support for suffrage, this was a crass way to make a point. Journalists latched on to it, gleefully portraying the perpetrators as female Jekyll and Hydes, simpering in drawing rooms one minute and frenziedly causing criminal damage left, right and centre the next. As a weapon of war in the battle for the vote, it was not a great success.

On the other hand, it did occasion perhaps the most powerful image of the whole campaign for women's votes: the forcibly fed hunger striker, pale and courageous, refusing food for the sake of her political beliefs and assaulted by a system intent on breaking her in spirit and in body. Most of those who went on hunger strike did so because the authorities refused to class them as political prisoners. Had they been regarded thus, they should have been able to keep their own clothes and enjoy certain privileges in terms of extra visitors, letters and food. It would have implied a measure of respect. Instead, like Emma Sproson and Mary Ann Rawle, they were treated as common criminals, even if they had inflicted no damage to either property or persons.

Marion Wallace Dunlop (1864–1942) is thought to have been the first suffragette hunger striker. She was an artist, arrested in June 1909 for stencilling on the wall of St Stephen's Hall in the Palace of Westminster a passage from the Bill of Rights: 'It is the right of the subjects to petition the King and all commitments and prosecutions for such petitioning are illegal.' Though sentenced to a month in Holloway, after refusing food for three and a half days she was released.

The first hunger striker to be forcibly fed, however, was a stone-thrower: Mary Leigh of Manchester. On this occasion, she threw slates rather than stones. It was September 1909 and Asquith was making a visit to Birmingham. Mary perilously climbed on to the roof of the building where he was speaking and tore off slates to slice at the ground in protest. Sentenced to a month's hard labour as a non-political prisoner in Winson Green, she refused to eat or drink anything. The decision was taken to feed her forcibly, first by trying to jam a spoon through her clenched teeth, and then through a nasal tube. In the end she was defeated, and agreed to take a little nourishment each day from a feeding cup.

Soon, brave women in prison cells around the country were not only hunger-striking, but enduring forcible feeding. Many described the experience as utterly barbaric, akin to rape and grievous bodily harm. It could (and did) lead to pleurisy, infections, sepsis and heart trouble, as well as broken teeth, internal tearing and bowel problems. One of the most shocking accounts of it is by Kitty Marion (1871–1944), the stage name of German-born actress Katherina Schafer. She freely admitted to being 'inclined to violence'; when she was imprisoned for stone-throwing she said, 'the mere going without food for a principle did not excite me very much' – although she did it anyway.[29] To make as much trouble as she possibly could, she also stuffed a handkerchief in the little window in her cell door so that the warders couldn't see her, then barricaded the door with her bed, which she would not move, she said, until women had won the vote. Someone had to chisel away the hinges and lift the door away to end the siege. In every way she could think of, she made a nuisance of herself.

The establishment retaliated. After two days without food or water Kitty was taken to a room where three doctors, two in operating aprons, awaited her.

One asked me to drink some milk. I refused and was seized and overpowered by several wardresses, forced into an arm chair, covered by a sheet, each arm held to the arm of the chair by a wardress, two others holding my shoulders back, a doctor holding my head back.

I struggled and screamed all the time. Not knowing the procedure of forcible feeding and thinking it was done through the mouth, I clenched my teeth when they had me in position and helpless, when suddenly I felt something penetrate my right nostril which seemed to cause my head to burst and my eyes to bulge.

[I was] choking and retching as the tube was forced down to the stomach and the liquid food poured in, most of which was vomited back especially when the tube was withdrawn. There are no words to describe the horrible revolting sensations. I must have lost consciousness for I found myself flat on the floor, not knowing how I got there. When wardresses were picking me up to carry me back to my cell, I heard one say, 'Eh, but she's heavy!' I said, 'Of course I am, put me down, I'll walk back, they would leave work like this for you women to do.'

I called the doctors a lot of dirty, cringing doormats to the government to lend themselves to such outrageous treatment to women. As I was half dragging myself and being assisted by wardresses up the stairs, I suddenly saw the prison doctor on the other side of the banisters. I stopped and with all the force and venom possible I cried 'You brute!'[30]

Kitty slapped the doctor's face with the back of her hand, and when she was returned to her cell she broke one of the tiny glass panes in her window and screamed, 'Down with tyranny!' to the outside world in protest (a group of little boys obligingly screamed it back, every night), before gnawing a hole in her paltry mattress so that she could pull out the fibre stuffing and make a fire of it, blasphemously fuelled by pages from the Bible.

On her release, Kitty was awarded a medal by the WSPU to

mark her imprisonment, with bars across the green-white-and-violet ribbon listing the dates of her hunger strikes (she lost 36lb in five weeks and now looked seventy, as if she had aged about thirty years). The enamelled bar at the bottom of the ribbon signified that she had been forcibly fed – in her case, a staggering 232 times.

Emma Sproson had a medal, too. When she got back to Frank and the children in Wolverhampton after the momentous spring of 1907, she continued to work for women's suffrage, despite deciding to leave the WSPU. As a member of the Women's Tax Resistance League, founded in 1909, she even went on hunger strike herself, imprisoned in Stafford jail not for bowling over policemen or chalking on pavements this time, but for refusing – for the sake of the vote – to pay for a dog-licence.

4

FOOT SOLDIERS

1909–1912

We may not be quite angels – had we been we should have flown –
We are only human beings who have wants much like your own;
And if sometimes our conduct isn't all your fancy paints,
It wasn't man's example could have turned us into saints![1]

WHEN MARJORY LEES'S mother, Sarah, was sensationally elected
Mayor of Oldham in 1910, a visiting journalist asked her what she
thought of those who had voted against her, probably hoping for an
unlovely display of triumphalism. The answer he got from this small,
stout and forthright widow in her late sixties – given with a twinkle
in her eye – suggests she was a suffragist through and through.
'Men have a perfect right to their opinion,' she assured him. 'They
also have a perfect right to change it.'[2] Sarah believed in the power of
political persuasion, and of leadership by example. There were not
many opportunities for women to lead by example in 1910, but what
few there were, she grasped. Not only was she Britain's second ever
female mayor, she was the first woman councillor to be elected in
Lancashire, the first woman freeman of the Borough of Oldham,
and a stalwart supporter of local charities and welfare institutions –
with time as well as money.

Local newspapers in places like Oldham regularly reported what
was going on among suffrage campaigners in London during the

Sarah Lees.

ten turbulent years between 1903 and 1913. Among hair-raising reports of neighbourhood disasters – 'cold weather causes havoc with tomatoes', 'boy falls into boiling fat', 'cut pimple causes death' – are columns on meetings, demonstrations, protests, imprisonments, varying in length and tone according to the publisher's sympathies.

Most branches of the NUWSS and the WSPU around the country had a press correspondent on the committee, responsible for alerting papers to forthcoming meetings, inviting journalists to events and writing letters to the editor. There are endless epistles about the importance of differentiating between 'gettes and 'gists, all virtually ignored. This one from Mary Ward, who was secretary of the Cambridge Association for Women's Suffrage, highlights another perennial problem: unfair tactics from the opposition.

> Sir – will you allow me to give expression in your columns to the indignation which was felt by a large body of suffragists who

attended the anti-suffrage meeting in the Guildhall on Wednesday
at the very questionable way in which a majority of votes for the
resolution [*against* votes for women] was secured? After the show of
hands for the resolution – a very moderate show so far as the body
of the hall was concerned, and for which full time was allowed – the
Chairman dropped his voice and murmured 'Contrary' in a tone
that did not reach the back of the hall, where most of the suffragists were seated, and then hastily – scarce two seconds I think had
elapsed – declared the resolution carried, this being the first intima-
tion that a number of those present received that a 'contrary' vote
had been called for.[3]

Other committee members were appointed to organize speakers, arrange missionary work, liaise with HQ in London, look after
the subscriptions, make suffrage literature available in leased suffrage shops or elsewhere, and build up the membership. A single
meeting could involve weeks of work. Among the records of the
Birmingham Women's Suffrage Society there is a notebook full of
frenzied reminders of everything that needs to be done in advance
of a public suffrage meeting in the Town Hall.[4] At least a month
before the date in question, the Lord Mayor must be asked for permission to use the building; someone has to be persuaded to chair
the meeting and speakers must be engaged. The NUWSS helpfully
kept a register of speakers, circulated to its branches, including their
names, specialist subjects and all the various riders attached should
you wish to book them. It lists 156 women and 32 men. They naturally expect travel expenses, but otherwise they are a mixed bag.
Comments in a special column for personal preferences include 'only
indoor meetings', 'an audience of women only', 'educated audience',
'working-class audience', 'cannot stay the night', 'will not travel
alone', and 'prefers a fee as time is valuable'.[5]

Once you know who the speakers will be – and they usually
include local men and women as well as visitors – the printing must

be tackled. You need posters of various sizes, handbills, tickets in different colours for different areas of the hall, programmes and press releases. You might also need an anti-heckler device: a postcard-sized piece of paper printed with the legend 'If anyone interrupts do not turn round. TAKE NO NOTICE.'[6]

For Birmingham Town Hall you'll need at least fifty-two stewards, all wearing sashes, to direct people to their seats and keep order. Each of them requires a plan of the hall. The stage should be decorated with plants, flowers and ribbons in the colours, and some sort of musical entertainment always goes down well. Once, the guest musician saved the day when a suffrage meeting of the Women's Liberal Federation at the Royal Albert Hall nearly descended into chaos. Members of the WSPU in the audience interrupted so relentlessly that the rest of the audience mutinied and tried to shout or even drag them out of the building, the stewards having been given strict instructions by the organizers not to prevent anyone having their say. According to someone who was there, mass fisticuffs threatened to break out, with people almost tumbling out of the galleries and jumping up and down on their seats – until the mighty organ started up with a loud rendition of 'Oh dear, what can the matter be?' Happily, this reduced everyone to fits of laughter, even the earnest suffragettes – 'and oh, how deadly earnest the suffragettes could be!'[7]

Finally you embark on the publicity campaign for the meeting, putting notices in the papers, asking restaurants and shops whether they'll display posters for you, engaging men to parade about in sandwich boards and asking the members of your society to deliver flyers house to house. You'll need to let the chief constable know when the meeting is to be held, so that he can arrange whatever police cover he thinks advisable; you should invite him, along with the head of the fire station, to be special guests.

You should also invite the men who run the local adult education schools, along with officials from the university, nearby factories, working women's associations and girls' clubs. If the meeting is at night, make sure those who will be sitting on the platform – guests of honour, suffrage society committee members and speakers – are aware that some colours look more becoming by gaslight than others. Buy pies and buns for refreshments, from the Co-operative bakery if possible.[8] Tip anyone who has had to work extra hard for you: sixpence for the postman and perhaps something for the delivery boy. And make sure the visiting speaker knows what train they are supposed to be catching, that there will be someone to meet them at the station, and that they have somewhere to stay overnight if necessary. Oh – and if you have any cardboard handy, you might think of slipping it under your bodice in case things get out of hand and people start throwing things or manhandling you. Cardboard makes surprisingly sturdy body armour, especially if moulded to your body in the bath first and then allowed to dry. It was certainly better than the material the visiting American suffragist Alice Paul used to protect herself on a march in London. According to an onlooker, her buttons tensed over the padding 'like hounds on the leash':

> and when a few minutes later, under the excited gaze of an expectant crowd, the rough-handling began, the buttons (strained beyond endurance) broke from their moorings in swift succession, and the padding like the entrails of some woolly monster emerged roll upon roll. She must have looked rather like the Michelin tyre advertisement coming undone; for the material she had chosen for a chest-protector was an unending coil of black cotton-wool, wound round and round her body, times without number; and when the outside coil slackened and gave down, the rest followed, loop upon loop. The crowd was, of course, highly diverted. 'Oh! Look at the stuffing!'[9]

Kate Frye (1878–1959) was a paid organizer for the New Constitutional Society for Women's Suffrage, founded in 1910 for those who agreed with the WSPU's politics but repudiated its

militant methods. As such, she knew just about every trick of the
trade. Not only was it her job to organize meetings, she was also
expected to help set up whole new suffrage societies and to canvass
for support in places where officially there was none. Kate had been
on the stage before becoming a professional suffragist; she went to
acting school in 1902 and worked in the theatre – on and off – until
1908. At first she had no need to earn a living: her father was a fashionable grocer with a town house in West London, a country one in
Buckinghamshire and a set of conveniently wealthy relations. From
1892 to 1895 he served as the Liberal MP for Kensington North. But
he was not an astute businessman and by the time Kate started as an
employee of the New Constitutional Society, the fortunes of the
Frye family were in sharp decline.

Kate Frye.

Kate already had a suffrage pedigree. She had taken part in the Mud March in 1907 and carried the banner of the North Kensington Women's Suffrage Society in the June 1908 march with the NUWSS. In 1910 she helped garner 280,000 men's signatures to present to Parliament in a petition for women's suffrage (which made no deeper impression than any of the other petitions – some the size of garden rollers – rumbling into the Palace of Westminster with monotonous regularity since 1866). Young enough to be energetic, but at thirty-two too old to be flighty, she was the perfect choice for the organizers of a small outfit hoping to extend its influence beyond the Liberal drawing rooms of London.

Fortunately for us, Kate was an inveterate diarist. Her official journal is an exhaustive account of her work for the society in 1912. Another record – much longer and fuller – is a delicious personal narrative of her life as an attractive, opinionated, self-confident and slightly dissatisfied woman.

The journal first.[10] It opens in April with Kate visiting the London HQ of the New Constitutional Society for her instructions. She knows she is to be sent on a mission to faraway Norfolk, where she worked the previous year, but needs to collect the names and addresses of a few key people to visit there, and the times of her trains. The next day she leaves for East Dereham, a small town between Norwich and King's Lynn. The day after that she spends canvassing, calling at likely-looking houses and asking whether any ladies who live there – or gentlemen, indeed – might think of joining a mid-Norfolk branch of the New Constitutional Society if it were established in the area. It's also her job to enlist new 'country' members of the London society, collecting a shilling's subscription from each.

She pounds the streets all morning, with no companion or chaperone, and then entertains a possible secretary of the putative local branch to tea. The following day she writes letters until 3 p.m. Then she's back on the streets till 7.30 p.m. She manages to capture a single new member, on average, each day. After a week she moves on to Fakenham, about twelve miles away, to scout for possible venues for meetings. The secretary of the Drill Hall, she notes, is not averse to the idea of hosting suffragists, but the man who runs the Assembly Rooms is 'not so friendly'. Then it's back to canvassing. She calls on a solicitor's wife, who is 'slightly in sympathy' but who thinks rather querulously that her husband would disapprove of her joining the society. She lines up visits to another solicitor's wife, a doctor's wife and a schoolmistress before the day is done, and extracts a promise from the vicar to chair a meeting, should enough people ever be found to attend it.

Kate is a true foot soldier of the women's suffrage movement, independent and almost shockingly modern in her approach to work. Her next stop is King's Lynn, where she is told not only to survey potential venues (listing them with their capacities) but to find out who the best and/or cheapest printers are; what are the political leanings of the local newspapers; whether vicars there are sympathetic to the Cause – a clergyman is always an influential person to have on your side; and where are the best places to stay for organizers like her and for visiting speakers. In King's Lynn, she reckons Mrs Plowright's boarding house is the best, as it has a back bedroom available away from the noise of the street, a shared sitting room and the luxury of inside sanitation.

And so it goes on. From King's Lynn she returns to Fakenham, then to Burnham Market (where she seeks out the name of the local policeman, should it ever come in useful) and Hunstanton. She does manage to arrange the odd meeting. The one at Fakenham is not a great success: there are too few people and too many speakers. In Hunstanton she and two other organizers take part in a poster parade for publicity, but only attract a solitary new member. The following day in Snettisham she persuades teachers and parents to allow local children to march along for women's suffrage with trumpets and a bell. She declines to comment on how successful that little venture was.

Every spare minute Kate has during the two months she spends in Norfolk is devoted to canvassing. She returns to London on 17 June. On the 18th she is allowed a single rest day before returning to the fray, organizing fundraising events for the New Constitutional Society and liaising with officials of the NUWSS and WSPU. She even spring-cleans the office. At the end of September she is sent to Kent for a few weeks to do the same sort of work she had done in Norfolk, and by the following spring she's back tramping the sleepy streets of Fakenham.

Even though she doesn't often articulate how she feels in this journal, which was kept for the benefit of her employers, it is obvious that she must have been exhausted most of the time. For proof of that, we can read her personal diaries, which are gloriously indiscreet. Here's the entry for Saturday, 11 March 1911. She's staying in East Dereham with two other New Constitutional organizers, Alexandra Wright and Helen Ogston:

A most bitterly cold day – a lot of wind – no sun but hardly any rain. To the Hotel by 10 – then till 12 o'clock canvassing the shops again. Then an hour's waiting while the others were out – back to lunch at 1. Roast chicken, stuffing & sausages – new potatoes, greens, gravy, bread sauce, rice pudding, stewed prunes, Camembert cheese, standard bread.[11] The [land]lady is being very kind to me. I think she likes me and is sorry I am going . . . [She] is a sad little widow – come down in the world. Went back to the Hotel soon after two o'clock. It was crowded with football players. Alexandra & I went out paying calls – so amusing – some people are quite nice. The Minister nice but so quaint – the district nurse quaint – but with us [i.e. supportive of the Cause] – and the Minister's wife most annoyed with us – and the doctor's wife shaking with rage. It was funny – she did so want to be rude – but we weren't quite the sort. I came in to tea – then back to the Hotel to find a Mrs Caley having tea in the Coffee Rooms while her husband and brother or cousin were with the defeated Cup Tie folk next door having a frilled ham tea. It seems they are the chocolate people who live near Wymondham, where we go after here to get up a meeting. She is a most sweet little woman and has promised us introductions and help and her husband too was nice. I came back 7.30 for dinner – wrote letters and diary after, though I felt very tired . . . Mrs West came in to know if I would join in a card game. The message came from Mr Moon, the teacher who is a permanent lodger here. I have noticed he has kept his door open to have an eye on me.[12]

Spooky Mr Moon was not the only gentleman with Kate in his sights. When she was twenty-seven she had become engaged to a fellow actor, John Collins, only consenting to marry him ten years later, after he had served his apprenticeship as a faithful suffragist. Meanwhile she enjoyed the attentions of several other men, some welcome, others not so much. Sidney, whom she came across in Lowestoft in Suffolk, was one of her keener admirers. He held the keys to the hall where Kate was organizing a meeting, which meant frequent visits to his office. He embarrassed her, being the sort of man 'who cannot get away from Sex.' Kate realized he was trying to behave well, but finding it a struggle. She didn't blame him: she was looking particularly bonny at the moment – positively blooming. Maybe she should try to capitalize on his obvious attraction to her by persuading him to join the New Constitutionals? She certainly wasn't averse to a bit of mild temptation. 'I suppose it helps the Suffrage, but it shouldn't. But it is hard to live up to Suffrage. In some moods I could flirt with a Broomstick.'[13]

Sometimes it is difficult to imagine that the campaigners for such a lofty cause as women's suffrage were ordinary people; people with feelings, adrenaline, who got excited or irritated, exasperated and exhausted by everyday life just like us. Kate Frye brings the movement down to earth. Her diary emphasizes how frustrating a business suffrage campaigning could be, yet how essential it was to work as hard as one possibly could to achieve the prize – which should not, of course, have been a prize at all. Kate considered it her *right* to vote. It was preposterous that she couldn't. And she was not the sort to sit and wait for things to happen, because too often they simply didn't.

People like Kate were beavering away all over the country: both militant and constitutional activists. London may have been the backdrop to the most dramatic events during the campaign for women's votes, but from the Channel Islands in the south to Shetland in the north, and from East Anglia to Ireland, busy societies of men and women agitated their communities to join the crusade. Each did what he or she could. Kate Frye's long-suffering fiancé carried heavy processional banners which bruised his neck and made his arms stiff when gusts of wind unsteadied them. Someone had to do it: many of the banners were far too weighty for women. Ladies whose families were supportive but who didn't have the energy or courage to go out campaigning themselves offered to host what were called 'drawing-room meetings' – sort of suffrage 'at homes' – while others, used to public speaking, volunteered to help with open-air gatherings. Perhaps they were teachers, or councillors like Sarah Lees.

Some women had very particular talents. They did not necessarily have to belong to dedicated associations like the writers' or athletes' or secretaries' suffrage societies to make their contribution. No doubt Kate's experience on the stage helped her perform her role as a New Constitutional Society evangelist, and her vivacity was an asset with which she could convert men like Sidney to suffragism. Mary 'Murdie' Murdoch had different attributes. She was a hugely popular doctor in Hull, affectionately remembered even today for her commitment to the city and its people, her indefatigable nature, her open-topped carriage drawn by two horses flamboyantly done up in the suffrage colours, her faithful dogs who followed her absolutely everywhere, and her complete inability to suffer fools gladly.

Her energy in support of the suffrage cause is legendary; she even offered to drive (male) voters to the polling booths during pre-1918 elections for the vicarious thrill of *almost* changing the world. She was a stupendously dangerous driver. Murdie understood her popularity and had full confidence in her own irresistibility, putting both to good use for the Cause.

Writer Laurence Housman, after whose name it is obligatory to add 'brother of the more famous A. E.', not only published suffrage propaganda, he also designed and stitched his own banners and hosted a workshop, the 'Suffrage Atelier', where scores of other craftsmen and -women did the same. He also wrote, among many other pieces of suffrage literature, a biting pastiche of Rudyard Kipling's poem 'Tommy' called 'Woman This and Woman That'. This is the opening verse:

> *We went up to St. Stephen's with petitions year by year.*
> *'Get out!' the politicians cried; 'we want no women here!'*
> *M.P.s behind the railings stood and laughed to see the fun,*
> *And bold policemen knocked us down, because we would not run.*
> *For it's woman this, and woman that, and 'Woman, go away!'*
> *But it's 'Share and share alike, ma'am!' when the taxes are to pay!*
> *When the taxes are to pay, my friends, the taxes are to pay*
> *O, it's 'Please to pay up promptly!' when the taxes are to pay!*[14]

Florence Stevens was a musical suffragette from Manchester; her special contribution to the fight was to learn to play the fife so that she could march with the WSPU's fife-and-drum band, formed in 1909. The drum major of the band, which included some sixty members in frogged jackets, skirts of shocking brevity and peaked caps, was stone-thrower Mary Leigh. Perhaps the most esoteric skill of all belonged to the Hon. Evelina Haverfield from Dorset. She was a horse-whisperer, able to sidle up to police horses during demonstrations and, most inconveniently for the rider, make them sit down.

Actually, 'horse-whisperer' is putting it a little too whimsically: her fearless method was to rap the horses' hind legs smartly in just the right place to make them buckle.

One of the most important skills of any suffrage organizer, anywhere in the country, was to recognize and encourage the potential of others. Selina Cooper (1864–1946) was a local heroine of the suffrage movement, whose prowess as a speaker was nurtured by militants and non-militants alike. She worked in a cotton mill in Barnoldswick, Lancashire, half-time (like Emma Sproson) from the age of eleven and then full-time at thirteen. When she was eighteen she was forced to leave the mill to care for her sick mother, taking in laundry to help keep the family afloat. It was when her mother died in 1889 that Selina's political life began. She went back to work and joined the Nelson Cotton Workers' Union, where she campaigned for what would appear to us to be very basic rights. Why were there no doors on the lavatories at work? Why was nothing done about sexual harassment?

Selina attended evening classes at the local Women's Co-operative Guild and began to read widely, informing her instinctive sensitivity to the injustices of the workplace and the world beyond. She joined the local branch of the NUWSS, collecting a staggering 800 signatures towards the total of 29,359 on a petition sent by women textile workers like her to Parliament in 1900. By now she was involved in local politics too, elected on to the Burnley Board of Guardians in 1901 as the joint Social Democratic Foundation and Independent Labour Party candidate. She was married to Robert Cooper, a fellow socialist and suffragist.

It was obvious to both the NUWSS (of which she was an affiliated member) and to the WSPU that Selina was an enviable asset. She was a brilliant speaker, an intuitive politician and naturally charismatic, without any of the spurious gloss of celebrity. Never one to be swayed by others against her will, Selina chose to refuse the overtures of the Pankhursts and remain with the constitutionalists. As one of Mrs Fawcett's most radical and engaging disciples, she joined the London procession on 13 June 1908 and toured the north-west of England and beyond, interpreting the meaning of suffrage for people across class and cultural divides. She was fearless and compelling.

She was also – like Kate Frye – endearingly human. Her papers, deposited in the Lancashire Archives, reveal someone whose political ideals were obviously the guiding light of her life, whose sense of humour and lack of 'side' – of airs and graces – shone through, and whose handwriting and spelling were cheerfully atrocious.[15] She was obviously a practical woman, well aware that she had a house to run while out changing the world. There is a tiny, well-thumbed book among her things full of hints for the home. Two cloves in a cup of tea cures a headache, it says. Keep a little muslin bag by the sink for eggshells and scraps of soap. Tie it tightly on washing day and you'll need neither powder nor bleach. Put white pepper in your pocket to keep the midges away on a walk.

There are several entries in her diaries about domestic worries. Selina and Robert had two children. Their son, named John Ruskin Cooper after the artist and social revolutionary, died at four months, but daughter Mary survived and obviously needed to be cared for while Selina was away on suffrage business and Robert was at work. It's a mark of her reputation that the NUWSS agreed to pay for a housekeeper.

Most of her archive, however, concerns her political interests. It is a treasure trove. There are postcards of marches and deputations, including one of Selina with a group of Lancashire suffragists standing on the station platform all dolled up and ready to catch the train to London to join the Pilgrimage in 1913. Another shows a cartoon anti-suffrage campaigner on a beach trying to sweep back the waves of progress with a ridiculously dainty little broom. A letter from future Prime Minister Ramsay MacDonald (whose wife Margaret was an active suffragist) offers to draft a resolution in favour of women's enfranchisement for her to present to the Nelson Women's

Textile Suffrage Society. Militant Preston suffragette Edith Rigby, a doctor's wife, addresses her as 'Dear Comrade'; Selina herself signs off her correspondence 'Yours fraternally'.

Train tickets and programmes of meetings flutter out from the pages of her notebooks; there are maps and diagrams of the Pilgrimage and processional routes; brightly printed suffrage envelopes with pictures of banner-waving ladies on the outside; a note asking her to accept the enclosed cheque, since the editors of the *Common Cause* understand she's been ill and might like to 'buy some comfort'. There is also a lovely photograph of her at the age – I suppose – of about forty, dressed in velvet and lace with an agate brooch at her neck, her thick hair simply pulled back and coiled on top of her head, and her face unlined and graceful.

Selina Cooper.

The portrait might suggest that Selina was unworldly, but her diary proves otherwise. She describes a trip to the Lincolnshire port of Grimsby in November 1909. She had been asked by Mrs Fawcett to try converting the unconvertible: a group of dockworkers. The fish auction was in full swing when she arrived, and she was escorted to a platform on the quayside by crowds of bidders suspiciously pleased to see her. The platform looked like a large box; after ten minutes, the top of it started lifting from below and Selina heard an ominous thumping. It turned out to be a vast storage tank full of live, writhing cod, waiting to be delivered to local hotels. All doughty Selina could do was hold her ground – 'I stuck it,' she wrote – standing widely astride so the lid was held down by her skirts. 'They were very much disopoentid [*sic*] that I did not scream.' Everyone clapped like mad when she finished. She won a good many people's hearts that day.

It didn't always end so happily for her. In Norfolk, the lorry she was using this time for a platform was hijacked and driven, while she was still aloft, into the village pond. She had to wait till a policeman arrived to deliver her back to dry land. In Oldham, where she stayed with Mayor Sarah and Marjory Lees, her coat and dress were badly torn in the fracas during a meeting. What a good thing she had a petticoat on, commented the mayor mischievously, otherwise . . .

The glimpses of life on the road as a suffrage speaker offered by Selina's notebooks are tantalizing. We want to know more. 'Slept in the same bed as Lloyd George!' 'The man who took me to the Burnly bus [after a meeting] never had a woman's arm on his for 20 years.' 'Staying with Henry Nevenson. The great War Corespondent roasting Bloaters [and] loseing the key of his Home.'[16] The artist and suffragist Laura Knight comes up to her after a meeting and says she would give a great deal to impress an audience like that. Ethel Smyth's compliment is slightly less convincing, but welcome all the same. She explains that because she's deaf, she hasn't been able to hear a word Selina has said: 'But I know you have spoken wonderful because I have watch the people's faces.'

Two entries in the diary stand out as special moments of triumph. The first records an occasion in Newcastle when she was one of several people speaking on separate platforms at an outdoor meeting. 'I had Mrs Pankhurst as my competitor. I could not get a crowd so I took my hat of and my hair tumbled down my back so I soon got a crowd.' Her hair, her crowning glory, fell to below her waist; not only was the audience captivated by its beauty (presumably), but by the shocking fact that she had unleashed it in public. Here's my favourite entry:

> When I was working at Cambridge I was staying with [a] Professor . . . I was addressing a meeting in the Market Square the undergrads came to break my meeting up when they made a noise I carried on speaking they got very vexed and at last they said I was a <u>Brick</u> [a brick is a good thing to be: they admired her for carrying on]. Next morning when I was leaving for London they came to Professor's House about 100 of them and escorted me to the Station stood each side of the door in equal number. I march through they waited for the train open the carriage door lifted me in carriage and as the train started stood at attention.

Pure show business.

Important though they were, suffrage society meetings and speakers' tours were not the only means of raising public awareness of the campaign. There were many different methods of spreading the word, apart from the demonstrations and processions already mentioned. The simplest thing was to tramp the streets knocking on doors and talking to people, as Kate Frye did. Suffragettes wore sandwich boards with messages on them which hurt their knees as they walked. They were not allowed to obstruct the pavement, so were forced to dodge the traffic and horse droppings in the gutter. Occasionally women selling copies of the *Common Cause* or the WSPU paper *Votes for Women* (later renamed the *Suffragette*) would pin posters to their clothes and rustle along as mobile billboards, dreading the rain.

The more adventurous rode bicycles decorated with appropriate ribbons and shouted through megaphones. One of the reasons suffragists were and are so often confused with suffragettes, incidentally, is because the photographs taken at the time were all monochrome, so it's not easy to tell what colours trim sashes and rosettes – or bicycles. Most people assume they are green, white and violet because that's the best-known combination. But if you belonged to the Women's Freedom League, for example, you wore green, white and gold. The Actresses' Franchise League wore pink and green, the Church League for Women's Suffrage a rather papal yellow and white, members of the Civil Service Suffrage Society chose blue and gold, the Jewish League purple and 'celestial blue', the Men's League for Women's Suffrage black and gold, and Kate Frye's New Constitutional Society green, white and silver. The Women's Tax Resistance League was perhaps the dullest of the lot, with black, white and grey.

In March 1908 the WSPU commissioned someone to construct a huge kite advertising a forthcoming meeting, with the slogan 'Votes for Women' on it in large black letters. It was flown, no doubt with considerable difficulty, near the Houses of Parliament. The most adventurous publicity campaign of all happened the following year. On 16 February when Parliament opened, Muriel Matters of the Women's Freedom League took to the air. The *Hull Daily Mail* – among scores of other papers – reported the stunt the following day. One can imagine local Dr 'Murdie' Murdoch's excitement when she read it.

A Lady Who Cannot Be Kept Down

Miss Muriel Matters, known to fame as one of the ladies who chained herself to the Grille in the House of Commons gallery, chartered an airship – or, to be accurate, a dirigible balloon – on which she intended, armed with a megaphone, to travel the route of the Royal procession at the opening of Parliament yesterday, and entertain the crowd with exhortations to support the demand for 'votes for women.'

In its fulfilment, this ingenious programme fell somewhat short of expectation. At half-past one Miss Matters was duly hoisted into the basket of the balloon at Hendon, in the presence of a large crowd. She was surrounded by parcels of Women's Freedom League flags and 56lb of handbills, and attached to the car were streamers 40ft. in length, with the ubiquitous inscription 'Votes for Women.'

Things went wrong at the start, however. For almost half an hour the engines refused to work, and it was after two o'clock when the balloon, which was under the direction of Mr H. Spencer, rose into the air. The flight towards London was rapid, but the wind was so strong that Westminster was passed at an altitude that caused Miss Matters' streamers to go unseen and her megaphone unheard. She alighted at Coulsdon, near Croydon.

Miss Matters said she was not nervous at all – not nearly so much as during the 'grille' incident. 'I think we can say now we are well up to date,' she observed. 'If we want to go up in the air, neither the police nor anyone else can keep us down, and if we could throw handbills we could easily throw anything else.'

Miss Matters is an Australian.[17]

It is unclear how the trip was financed. Muriel Matters is reported as having hired the dirigible herself, but as an aspiring actress and musician who had been in England only for a few years, it seems unlikely that she could have afforded this extravagant gesture on her own, even though she charged a whole guinea – 21 shillings – to speak at public meetings. Perhaps the WFL sponsored her, though like all the suffrage societies it was hardly awash with money. (An exception was the National League for Opposing Woman Suffrage (NLOWS), formed in 1910 when the separate men's and women's anti-suffrage leagues amalgamated, and heavily subsidized by the likes of Lords Rothschild and Curzon.) Alongside the need for propaganda, the requirement for funds was a constant preoccupation for both militants and non-militants. Income from subscription fees was not enough to run a high-profile national campaign.

Supporters rattled tins and sold suffrage literature. The NUWSS instituted a type of associated membership scheme, the Friends of Women's Suffrage, whereby people could sign up for a lesser fee and fewer commitments. The minute books of suffrage societies around the country record a relentless number of bazaars and sales of work. A blouse sale in Cambridge raised an astounding £33 – that's equivalent to about £3,000 today – while Leeds market had a regular 'suffrage stall' selling all sorts of bits and bobs. An advertising flyer for a similar stall listed 'Clothing New and Clothing Old (great bargains); Tempting Knitted Goods and Infants' Garments; Boots and Shoes; Eatables, Savoury and Sweet; Country Produce of All Kinds; Furniture for the House; Plants and Bulbs for the Garden; Visit the Livestock Stall if you want an Engaging Pet'.[18]

The most imaginative fundraising ideas of all were dreamed up by university students. Flushed with the developing success of their own campaign for access to higher education, many of Britain's first female undergraduates were eager supporters of the sister campaign for women's enfranchisement. Not only were there suffrage societies at women's colleges and halls of residence, but several ran what they called 'Parliaments' too, peopled by staff and students in the roles of prime minister, leader of the opposition and so on, and holding debates mirroring what was being discussed at the time in the Palace of Westminster. They didn't shy away from unglamorous subjects. Somerville College's Parliament in Oxford debated the Liquor Traffic (Local Control) Act and prison reform, as well as various Representation of the People Acts and – on one frivolous occasion – 'A Bill to Limit the Prevailing Extravagance in Fashion of Women's Dress', decreeing that no one was to wear more than £100-worth of jewellery at once, and no hat should measure more than twenty inches (about half a metre) across.[19]

It was also at Somerville that some of the jolliest fundraising events were held. During 'Suffrage Self-Denial Week' – a period highlighted by suffrage societies every year to encourage extra donations – students came up with a dizzying array of services. A couple opened a pop-up milliner's shop, where for threepence you could have the scarf on your summer hat washed, ironed and re-tied. They also shampooed hair and gave 'lessons in coiffure'. Someone offered for sale a recently acquired and apparently fully transferrable proposal of marriage. Elsewhere you could order bespoke rude verses or personalized nicknames for a fee; you could get your Sunday-afternoon letters home written for you; your coat brushed, your stockings mended, your collar washed, your cycle cleaned or your fortune told. Fortune-telling was something to which Kate Frye also turned her hand to raise funds for the New Constitutional Society. She even had business cards printed, advertising her skills as a clairvoyant.

Back at Somerville, an elaborate enterprise was dreamed up by the Red Hand Gang, consisting of two first-years or 'freshers', who kidnapped a valuable clock and left in its place a ransom note. They demanded payment for the return of the clock at a rendezvous that night at 10 p.m. on the tennis courts. When the time came, the thieves were ambushed and locked in a cupboard until they agreed to forfeit 'treasured hair-combs &c.' which were auctioned the following day for the Cause. It was a 'glorious rag', according to their suffrage society report, 'of a kind too seldom seen in College.'[20]

The grandest fundraising effort of the whole campaign was the Women's Exhibition held by the WSPU at the enormous Prince's Skating Rink in Knightsbridge (no longer there) during a fortnight in May 1909. It was partly a vast bazaar, with all the crafts and produce stalls you would expect from such an event, and partly a pageant of all things to do with women's achievements and aspirations. It was a deliberately feminine affair, advertised on the streets of London by little girl suffragettes doing maypole dancing and immaculately turned-out women riding side-saddle on noble-looking grey steeds. This was a public-relations exercise as well as a fundraiser, building on the success of Women's Sunday the previous year and designed to emphasize the fact that suffragettes were not in fact monsters but wives, mothers, daughters and sisters who excelled at domestic accomplishments and responded to beauty.

There were stalls selling exquisitely decorated cakes or bonnets and local delicacies brought down from the provinces, like Yorkshire parkin; you could meet famous women artists and authors; visit waxworks of various heroines; watch a mannequin fashion show of modern art nouveaux gowns; cast a vote in a mock polling booth on some fairly uncontentious issue of the day like daylight saving. You could also visit a reconstructed prison cell with a real-life ex-prisoner sitting in her broad-arrowed uniform; or take ju-jitsu classes for self-defence: not everything was kittens and knitting.

Everyone wore their prettiest clothes and hats to the exhibition. The WSPU colours were everywhere, with banners and tableaux designed and gorgeously painted by a harassed Sylvia Pankhurst, and appliqué mottoes like 'It's Dogged as Does It' and 'Set the Pace for Those Behind' (was this a jibe at the constitutionalists?). The whole event was a celebration of green, white and violet. Suffragette souvenirs were specially commissioned for the occasion: tea sets and jewellery, embroidered blouses and embellished stationery. The fife-and-drum band marched around outside, and inside the euphonious Aeolian Women's Orchestra played to the crowds.

Every day someone famous performed an opening ceremony – Mrs Fawcett's illustrious sister Dr Elizabeth Garrett Anderson, newly appointed Mayor of Aldeburgh and recent convert to the WSPU, was the first – and hordes of men, women and children came to visit: suffragettes, suffragists and sceptics. The exhibition raised £5,664 (about £500,000 today). Only 250 new members were signed up to the WSPU, but the image of the suffragettes did temporarily improve, aided by a series of wonderful pictures taken and sold as

postcards by professional photographer Christina Broom[21] and by a
lull in militancy for the duration.

According to her introduction to the exhibition programme,
Emmeline Pankhurst had organized it to help 'the most wonderful
movement the world has ever seen. A movement to set free that half
of the human race that has always been in bondage, to give women
the power to work out their own salvation – political, social and
industrial.'[22] She considered it a great success.

It was a policy decision on the part of the WSPU to welcome
men as well as women to the exhibition. Men could be members
of NUWSS branches, but they couldn't formally join the WSPU,
and Mrs Pankhurst appreciated that a 'them and us' mentality was
unhelpful to the public. Inevitable too, as her campaigning tactics
increasingly (and unfairly) came to be reported in terms of a 'sex
war'. In 1910 the militant suffrage campaigner Victor Duval established a masculine equivalent of the WSPU, the Men's Political
Union for Women's Enfranchisement (MPU). Duval had been an
accomplice of the first hunger striker, Marion Wallace Dunlop,
when she stencilled her extract from the Bill of Rights on the wall
of St Stephen's Hall, and was twice imprisoned for suffrage-related
offences. He was also a supporter of Kate Frye's New Constitutional
Society, highlighting the fluency of membership between different
organizations at this time.

The press quickly picked up on the news that other men had not
only been imprisoned but had gone on hunger strike themselves.
Hugh Franklin was first arrested in 1910, when as a passionate young
man of twenty-one he had attempted to assault Home Secretary
Winston Churchill with a dog-whip in a railway carriage. He felt
no personal animosity towards Mr Churchill, he insisted, but he
did hold him responsible for the state's barbaric treatment of suffragettes. Two months later he found himself back in jail after throwing
rocks at Churchill's windows. The third time, it was for arson. On
all three occasions he went on hunger strike and was forcibly fed

over a hundred times. When he was at liberty, he actively protested against the force-feeding of another man, William Ball, arrested in December 1911 for window-smashing.

Mr Ball's case became something of a cause célèbre. He was sentenced to two months' hard labour in Pentonville, and in protest against not being classed as a political prisoner – which a number of women offenders now were – he immediately refused all food. He was forcibly fed in the hospital wing for five weeks, his physical and mental condition gradually deteriorating until he was certified insane and, without any consultation with his wife, committed to a public lunatic asylum. As soon as she heard, his wife had him discharged into private care and questions were asked in the House about whether his treatment had caused his mental breakdown and whether he should have been sentenced to hard labour in the first place. A Home Office investigation published its findings the following May: 'Ball was from the first treated with the utmost consideration. The one mistake seemed to have been that his wife was not informed of the earliest symptoms of this mental disorder.'[23]

Non-militant men played their own part in the struggle. Many NUWSS demonstration marches had a 'men's section' and constitutional suffrage societies around the country welcomed male members, though rarely on to the committee. They were specially targeted by propagandists among the antis. 'Votes for Women, Never!' booms one of the National League for Opposing Woman Suffrage handbills. 'Men of England, your interests and those of your families, and the welfare of the country are in danger. Rally to prevent it . . . Don't make yourselves and your country the laughing stock of the world, but keep political power where it ought to be – in the hands of the men.'[24] They, too, suffered for their beliefs, though not as violently as Messrs Franklin and Ball. Laurence Housman, whose unrealized ambition it was to be imprisoned, was proud of the fact that he managed to convert two antis to the Cause simply by having rotten eggs thrown at him. He was on the Pilgrimage at the time;

the fact that he had made the effort to march miles and miles did not impress them, but as soon as the missiles found their mark, the sceptics immediately signed up as suffragists, outraged at this treatment of a fellow gentleman. 'It's nice to think that chickens gone wrong can sometimes be of more use in the world than ourselves,' commented Housman wryly. 'Thus we find our right place in the universe.'[25]

Housman was famously supportive of his suffragist sister, Clemence, with whom he lived in London. Selina Cooper had her Robert, Kate Frye her faithful John and Emma Sproson her Frank. But some campaigners were not so fortunate. There are stories of women having to keep their allegiance to the WSPU secret from the men of the house, wearing coded jewellery in peridot, crystal and amethyst as a signal to those with eyes to see, and stockings with a tiny 'votes for women' slogan stitched into them, or pinning a ribbon in the colours to their petticoats. A man in Guildford proudly told his friends that if he ever found his wife taking part in a suffrage demonstration he would 'lay her out on her bed.'[26] One girl's grandfather locked her and her mother in the larder to prevent them from taking part in a suffrage parade.[27] These men may have been bullies, or genuinely afraid for their wife's safety and reputation (and their own); it cannot have been easy for those brought up in conservative, traditional households to acquiesce to this subversion of good order. What's more, according to suffragette Letitia Fairfield, an astonishing number of reasonably educated men had no idea of the facts. Friends of hers – and she was a doctor – knew nothing of the country in which they lived. They had never heard of sweated labour. One said that he thought women were paid less for doing the same jobs as men because 'their underclothes were cheaper.'[28]

It was harder for working-class men and women to cope with the exigencies of having an activist in the family. Hannah Webster was born on a farm in the Peak District in 1871. She spent a resentful childhood darning her brothers' socks or picking feathers for pillows while they read and played dominoes. She went into service, then worked as a seamstress before clambering on to what she called the 'domestic treadmill' on her marriage to Gibbon Mitchell. Her personality and circumstances combined to politicize her and by 1904 she was campaigning for socialism and suffragism with equal vigour.

Hannah had joined the WSPU by then. Her autobiography, *The Hard Way Up*, describes how mercilessly she was heckled by men for the whole of her career as an activist. One man taunts her for having only one child. She should get herself home and make more. Hannah retorts that she's glad she has only one: it is an awful thing for children to be brought up in the belief that their mothers are classed with infants, imbeciles and criminals. Some smart alec questions what she would do with a vote if she had one: '"I expect you would take it home and put it in a mince pie, wouldn't you?" "No," I said angrily. "Perhaps I might do as you do, take it to the Town Hall and make a 'hash' of it."'[29]

Hannah's husband did not overtly object to her suffrage activities. But he didn't understand. She was furious when he paid a fine to release her from Strangeways Prison, where she had been sent with Adela Pankhurst in 1906 for obstructing the police. And though he may have paid lip-service to her feminism, she was not convinced that he appreciated its implications: 'No cause can be won between dinner and tea, and most of us who were married had to work with one hand tied behind us, so to speak. Public disapproval could be faced and borne, but domestic unhappiness, the price many of us paid for our opinions and activities, was a very bitter thing.'[30]

5

BAD NEWS

The height of militancy

Give me Dignity or Give me Death.[1]

THE DARKEST DATE in the whole suffrage campaign was Friday, 18 November 1910. It has gone down in history as 'Black Friday'. Everyone involved in the campaign for the enfranchisement of women received a blow that day. Things had been looking comparatively hopeful during the previous few months. A cross-party committee was formed after the General Election in January (which resulted in a hung Parliament) to unite all pro-women's suffrage members in the House of Commons in support of a brand-new Reform or 'Conciliation' Bill. Proposed legislation would include an amendment to enfranchise all women householders and occupiers of business premises with a minimum rateable value of £10. The Bill was introduced in Parliament on 14 June and passed its second reading by a majority of 110 votes. The government vowed to allow enough parliamentary time to negotiate all the different stages necessary to pass it into law, as long as the Liberals remained in power. This was great news for suffragettes and suffragists alike.

The WSPU called a truce, which lasted until November 1910 when Asquith suddenly declared that he was *not* prepared to accommodate the Bill after all. When the bad news came through, Emmeline Pankhurst and hundreds of members of the WSPU were holding another Women's Parliament at Caxton Hall, like the one Emma Sproson attended in 1907. Immediately Mrs Pankhurst heard of the prime minister's decision, she mobilized a deputation of three hundred furious suffragettes to march up the road to Parliament Square and protest. The ceasefire they had maintained during the deliberations of the Conciliation Bill was forgotten.

They were met by crowds of policemen, some of them brought in from the rough neighbourhoods of the East End where they were used to dealing with miscreants rather more pragmatically than 'up West'. For six hours the women were subjected to the most brutal treatment, summed up in a photograph that appeared on the front page of the *Daily Mirror* the following morning. It shows Ada Wright, a veteran protester in her late forties, crumpled on the ground at the feet of a gentleman in a top hat, obviously concerned; at least five policemen are there, one of whom has his arm outstretched towards her with something in his fist, while a boy laughs in the background. Ada has her kid-gloved hands over her eyes; her black hat is still firmly affixed but she looks completely vulnerable and broken.

According to Ada, the government tried to prevent the *Daily Mirror* from printing the photograph, and even attempted to seize the negatives. On being shown the image, the Chief Commissioner of Police insisted that Miss Wright had probably collapsed from exhaustion or over-excitement – she was just a little tired and emotional, in other words – and that she was obviously being helped rather than threatened by those friendly bobbies. But members of the Conciliation Committee were so appalled by the first-hand accounts they were hearing of what *really* went on that they lobbied for an official inquiry. The committee's honorary secretary was the journalist Henry Brailsford; he and pioneering psychoanalyst Dr Jessie Murray were tasked with collecting witness statements. Their report, or 'memorandum', makes harrowing reading, especially if one can imagine the shocked voices of the women giving evidence.

They took statements from 135 people in all. Some agreed to

their names being used, others preferred only initials, and the rest remained anonymous. Florence Sotheran, daughter of a prosperous bookseller, sounds as though she had stepped from her drawing room straight into hell:

> For hours one was beaten about the body, thrown backwards and forwards from one [policeman] to the other, until one felt dazed with the horror of it . . . Often seized by the coat collar, dragged out of the crowd, only to be pushed helplessly along in front of one's tormentor into a side street, while he beat up and down one's spine until cramp seized one's legs, when he would then release one with a vicious shove, and with insulting speeches, such as 'I will teach you a lesson, I will teach you not to come back any more. I will punish you, you ----, you ----.' This took place over and over again, as, of course, each time they released one, one returned to the charge . . . The chest bruises one received while pushing forward were, of course, inevitable, but it was this officious pummelling of the spine . . . when they held you helpless which wore you out so, and left you so shaken . . . Once I was thrown with my jaw against a lamp-post with such force that two of my front teeth were loosened . . .[2]

Another woman's arms and wrists were wrenched; she was shaken, pushed, and flung to the ground. Desperate, she asked for help to reach some railings and while she lay against them trying to recover her breath, a policeman grasped her head, twisted it round and rubbed her face against the railings, back and forth. Someone was thrown under a passing motor car; the wheels ran over her skirt but miraculously missed her body.

Miss Henria Williams was a former teacher and a member of the WSPU and the Tax Resistance League who travelled up from Essex to take part in the Women's Parliament. She was frail enough to be described by onlookers as elderly and weak, though in reality she was only forty-three. Her testimony makes her sound like a quavery old lady:

The police have such strong large hands, that when they take hold of one by the throat, as I saw one man do, but not to me, or grasp one's sides or ribs, which was done to me, they cannot possibly know how tightly they are holding and how terribly at times they are hurting. One policeman after knocking me about for a considerable time, finally took hold of me with his great strong hands like iron just over my heart. He hurt me so much at first, I had not the voice power to tell him what he was doing. But I knew that unless I made a strong effort to do so he would kill me. So collecting all the power of my being, I commanded him to take his hand off my heart. I think he must have read from my face that he had gone too far, for a look of real fear immediately came on his face . . .[3]

It was hardly a nice thing to talk about, and it may be that some of the women interviewed by Brailsford and Murray preferred not to dwell on it at all, but there were several accusations of sexual assault – commonly known as 'sex filth' – in the report. Miss H. told of one particularly violent policeman putting his arm around her and groping her left breast, 'nipping it and wringing it very painfully, saying as he did so, "You have been wanting this for a long time, haven't you?"'[4] Miss C.'s skirt was tugged up above her head while a policeman tried to lift her off the ground by raising his knee, presumably between her legs, though she doesn't articulate that detail. 'This he could not do, so he threw me into the crowd and incited the men to treat me as they wished. Consequently several men who, I believe, were policemen in plain clothes, also endeavoured to lift my dress.'[5] Miss Elizabeth Freeman was gripped by an officer on the thigh: 'I demanded that he should cease doing such a hateful action to a woman. He said, "Oh, my old dear, I can grip you wherever I like today!"'[6]

Mrs Mary Earl, a visiting suffragette from Dublin, was quite happy to put her name to her statement:

I went out as one of the party of eight women who were to try to reach the House by an underground passage. The scene down there was terrible, but the most terrible part to me was the disgusting language used by the police, who were, I understand, brought specially from Whitechapel. In the struggle here the police were most brutal and indecent. They deliberately tore my undergarments, using the most foul language − such language as I could not repeat. They seized me by the hair and forced me up the steps on my knees, refusing to allow me to regain my footing. I was then flung into the crowd outside.[7]

The Conciliation Committee presented its memorandum to the Home Office on 2 February 1911 with a formal request for a full public inquiry into the treatment of the women's deputations, not just on Black Friday itself but on two further occasions a few days later. But Home Secretary Winston Churchill refused to take the matter any further. His opinion was the same as it had been back in November, immediately after Black Friday. He believed the police had acted under instructions

. . . that they should avoid, as far as practicable, making arrests. The result was that some of the ladies who desired to be arrested, made repeated efforts, and no doubt a few of them exhausted themselves and may have required medical treatment. Several used a good deal of force, as six of the police were reported injured . . .[8] I cannot conclude without reaffirming my conviction that the Metropolitan Police behaved on 18th November with the forbearance and humanity for which they have always been distinguished, and again repudiating the unsupported allegations which have issued from that copious fountain of mendacity, the WSPU.[9]

Allegedly, two women died as a result of Black Friday. One of them was Mary Clarke, Emmeline Pankhurst's younger sister, who passed away suddenly on Christmas Day 1910, two days after her release from prison. There was no direct evidence to link Mrs Clarke's death with her arrest on 23 November (after a separate spate of window-smashing), but the implication was that the violence of Black Friday and its aftermath had weakened her constitution beyond repair. The other fatality was that of Henria Williams, who had so feared for her life when the policeman clutched at her chest. She died of a heart attack on New Year's Day 1911.

Despite the horrors of Black Friday, there was a moment during the summer of 1911 when Millicent Fawcett almost believed the two wings of the suffrage campaign might be reunited. Following the general election in December 1910, an amended Bill was introduced by a re-formed Conciliation Committee and again passed its second reading, with an increased majority. Again Asquith promised to grant the facilities to debate it in the next session. And again – perhaps in desperation – most suffragettes and suffragists believed him.

On 17 June, huge numbers of militant and non-militant campaigners came together in a new spirit of optimism to celebrate the coronation of King George V. A programme was published by the Woman's Press, a printing firm associated with the WSPU, explaining what was going to happen. This procession ran along the same lines as the events held during the summer of 1908, except that this time some forty thousand people were involved, marching in a seven-mile column extending from the Embankment in London via Trafalgar Square, Pall Mall, Piccadilly and Knightsbridge to the Royal Albert Hall and Kensington Town Hall.

The list of those taking part proves just how widespread and imaginative the suffrage campaign had become. Right at the front rode 'General' Flora Drummond, WSPU organizer extraordinaire, aboard a sturdy horse. This was possibly the unfortunate bay mare found in the stables just before the 'off' being whitewashed to make her smarter,[10] in which case Mrs Drummond must have been praying for fine weather. Joan of Arc appeared next, also on horseback and in armour, followed by a Prisoners' Pageant representing seven hundred convicted suffragettes, an Historical Pageant, and a Pageant of Empire. The prisoners were all dressed in white, like holy martyrs. Those who followed them were not so much the famous heroines of British history, although Abbess Hilda of Whitby was there; rather they were groups of influential women from the past, such as members of medieval guilds, lady freemen of the City of London and matriarchs of aristocratic families, many of whom possessed a right to vote.

At the core of the procession, drawn by two suspiciously white horses, was an enormous float, the 'Empire Car', on which a *tableau vivant* symbolized the part played by women in Imperial Britain. Then came home and colonial suffrage campaigners in national dress; a ten-strong column of queens from British history; and representatives of just about every suffrage group in the British Isles and beyond. They were all dressed in the appropriate colours, with gilded banners and flags fluttering in a light breeze and sparkling in the broken sunshine.

Kate Frye was there with her sister, Agnes, and fiancé, John, who had been deputized to carry a banner for the WSPU. She marched not with the New Constitutional Society but with the Actresses' Franchise League, to which she also belonged.

> I was a Group Captain and had the announcement round my arm and much enjoyed the dignity. Was not with any very interesting people but it didn't matter as I was so taken up with myself . . . I was the 3rd section behind the 3rd Floral Arch – very pretty it all looked but some of the walkers of the AFL looked very dowdy. But it was all simply magnificent – 70,000 of us [she over-estimated], five abreast, and some of the Sections were just wonderful – a real pageant and I enjoyed myself tremendously. It started at 5.30 and it was not much after 6 when we were off – we were in a splendid position. The end had not left the Embankment before we started the meeting [at the Royal Albert Hall] at 8.30 – 7 miles, 1000 banners 70 bands. We were just behind one and it was quite lovely marching to it. We all kept time to it and at least walked well. Several of the onlookers

I heard say that ours was the Smartest Section . . . Such crowds – perfectly wonderful – there couldn't have been many more and they must have waited hours for a good view . . . hardly a rude remark and constant applause all the way for us.[11]

When they got to St James's, Kate noticed a few grumpy old men looking balefully at them through the windows of their gentlemen's clubs, but they didn't worry her. Also at St James's, veteran Elizabeth Wolstenholme Elmy – whom Kate called 'the dear old Suffragette of over 40 years' work' – stood to attention and was saluted by everyone in turn as they passed. She was seventy-eight. In the lull between reaching the Royal Albert Hall and the final meeting getting under way, Kate and Agnes ate sandwiches and chocolate, which revived them enough to make a good fist of singing 'March of the Women' in the hall later on. Ethel Smyth's rousing anthem had been premiered in March that year at the same venue. On that occasion, although a WSPU choir had been rehearsing for ages, the first performance did not go entirely to plan. They were so nervous that the pitch – already lofty – crept even higher and, to be frank, 'it became rather a shriek.'[12] Now, however, everyone was used to it. In fact, Kate was so delighted by the sound of her own voice that for a moment she considered having it professionally trained.

John turned up at the end of the meeting and escorted the two women, still singing, to Kensington High Street; then they had a lemonade with ice in a bar near Paddington Station, caught the 11.15 p.m. train home to Buckinghamshire and eventually got to bed 'in the broad day light' at 3 a.m. This was better than canvassing endless curates in Kent, any day.

It was the perfect time to hold a show like this: London was full of visitors from around the country and the world, ready to celebrate the coronation in a few days' time. Everyone was in a good mood – apart, possibly, from a little girl standing outside the Ritz Hotel in a straw hat decorated with life-like daisies. When Selina Cooper's eminent friend Henry Nevinson processed by, very slowly, at the head of the Men's Political Union, his horse spied the hat and, bored and hungry, proceeded to eat it. That cost Nevinson half a crown, he remembered ruefully.

Seating had already been erected along parts of the route, it was a holiday weekend, the weather was fine, and who knows? There might even be some trouble to witness and enjoy. Suffragettes were notoriously dangerous, even when dressed in white chiffon and carrying wands. There was no trouble, however. Everything went entirely according to plan. Despite the reservations of old-style suffragists like Emily Davies, who warned Millicent Fawcett beforehand of any association with the suffragettes, it was a shiningly happy and hopeful (if exhausting) day. Several of those who joined the Pilgrimage, like Marjory Lees and Selina Cooper, remembered it with fondness. They tried to recreate something of its celebratory spirit in the summer of 1913 when, given what had happened later in 1911 and 1912, hardly anyone associated the suffrage campaign with joy and unity any more.

The coronation procession may have gone well, but nothing changed afterwards. For members of the WSPU, it was merely a fleeting shaft of sunshine on a long, dark day. The institutional violence they suffered only strengthened their resolve to commit to what was fast becoming a guerrilla war. There was more window-smashing, more arson, more criminal damage. New rules were drawn up at WSPU headquarters: now it was officially permissible to destroy the contents of letterboxes with various flammable materials or substances like paint pigments, varnish, jam, tar, or potassium permanganate, which left a vivid and appropriately purple stain when mixed with water. Phosphorus was a favourite, although dangerous to handle. A 'false alarm' policy was introduced to distract the emergency services. In 1912, twenty-seven convictions resulted from a total of 425 hoax calls; the numbers rose even higher in 1913.[13] Arson was encouraged, although no one was expected to put lives at risk. Property was fair game, however, whether private – especially politicians' houses – or public, like stations and churches. So were national treasures in the form of works of art and historic relics.

Militants were encouraged to use their initiative. Mrs Pankhurst did not relish the idea of paid WSPU organizers risking arrest, as they were more useful out of prison than in it. Nor did she condone suffragettes with young families putting themselves in harm's way. But everyone else was to do whatever they could to raise the profile of the Votes for Women campaign, with the result that newspaper columns began to specialize in stories of maverick protesters armed with hammers, hatpins, even – in the case of two Manchester suffragettes – sausages and polonies. They used the charcuterie as missiles, firing them at an unhappy (and vegetarian) Keir Hardie as he left a Labour conference in early 1913. This is puzzling, since Hardie was a suffrage supporter himself.

When the police raided artist Olive Hockin's studio flat in Notting Hill in March that year, after an incriminating copy of the *Suffragette* was found at the scene of an arson attack with her name and address scribbled on it, they were aghast at what they found.[14] Here was a veritable 'suffragist arsenal', according to newspaper reports, littered with 'the munitions of war'. They uncovered several wire-cutters fixed to poles of wood or iron; bags of stones; tins and bottles of paraffin; a fake number-plate for a motor car; and 'a large quantity of combustibles'. Olive denied they were hers; they belonged to friends, she insisted. Nevertheless, she was charged with conspiracy to set fire to a croquet pavilion at Roehampton Golf Club and with damaging a glasshouse at Kew Gardens. She had been under police surveillance for a while, and unfortunately her comings and goings from the flat tallied exactly with the time of the crimes.

The authorities were becoming less and less enthusiastic about sending suffragettes to jail now. Winston Churchill was correct to suggest that the police were instructed on Black Friday to arrest as few people as possible. The militants were in danger of clogging up the country's penal system, and once they were sentenced, their antics were causing as much disruption as the original offence. Janie Allan – scion of a fabulously wealthy ship-owning family from Glasgow – was trouble right from the start. She was arrested for taking part in one of many window-smashing campaigns on the streets of London's West End, working in partnership with a wheelchair-using suffragette, May Billinghurst, who concealed a supply of choice

May Billinghurst.

stones under the rug on her knees. At her trial Janie made a speech about the iniquity of sending idealists like her to jail while those who condemned women to a life of sweated labour, who made money from human trafficking or who abused little girls were treated with risible leniency. Once installed in Holloway, like Kitty Marion before her she barricaded herself into her cell. It took three men with crow-bars nearly an hour to break down the door. She went on hunger strike, naturally, and was forcibly fed. She said that what she craved more than anything for when she was freed, and could eat and drink again, was alcohol. 'I used to lie awake between three and six in the morning and say that if ever I got out I would take Green Chartreuse.'[15] But when it came to it, she wisely decided to forgo the liqueur and drink black coffee instead, just in case she became addicted.

Lady Constance Lytton was another thorn in the Establishment's side. All militants were thorns in its side, of course, but some ran deeper than the rest and caused more mess. Lady Constance was a reluctant suffragette at first, earnestly interested in prison reform for female convicts and social welfare for working girls, but unsure about the tactics of the WSPU. However, she met Emmeline Pethick-Lawrence and Annie Kenney in the course of her work with a girls' club in 1908 and was charmed by them. Almost on impulse one day, she threw a stone at a politician's car and went on to be imprisoned four times for violent acts of protest. Usually, as soon as the prison governor found out that she was the daughter of an earl and was said to suffer from a heart condition, she was safely stowed in the prison infirmary and then released early.

This was extremely vexing. Determined to do her bit for the Cause and her comrades, 'Conny' came up with a plan. 'I decided to write the words "Votes for Women" on my body, scratching it in my skin with a needle, beginning over the heart and ending it on my face . . . My skin proved much tougher than I had expected.'[16] She substituted a rigid hatpin for the bendy sewing needle; even so, it took twenty minutes just to carve the 'V' and she never managed to complete her graffito. The next time the occasion arose, she thought of a more efficient way to prove her mettle. She adopted a pseudonym

– Jane Warton – and the disguise of a poor, deliberately ugly working woman, having noticed that unattractive prisoners fared far worse inside than pretty ones. When she was arrested this time there was no hurried remission of the sentence and no anxious tutting about the state of her health when, having refused to eat, she was forcibly fed. Indeed, after the briefest of examinations, the doctor whipped away his stethoscope with the cheerful cry, 'Oh, ripping, splendid heart!'[17]

A cartoon of forcible feeding from the WSPU paper the Suffragette, *January 1913.*

Afterwards, Conny was proud she had duped the authorities and experienced what other less socially exalted women had endured in the feeding chair. But it was barbaric. She kept being sick over the doctor, who slapped her face in exasperation. He sat astride her knees and tried to ram the food down her throat. She sobbed and sobbed, violated, and the weight fell from her insubstantial frame like hot wax from a candle. When she was released, she couldn't even sit down, her bones were so close to her skin. There were grotesque blisters on her feet (the shoes she had been given were far too small) and she had cellulitis and oedema. She went on to suffer two strokes, resulting in partial paralysis, and for the last ten years of her life could manage only words, no more deeds. She wrote her memoirs laboriously, with her left hand. Her days as a suffrage activist were over.

Suffragettes have been accused in the past of using hunger strikes more as a publicity tool than as a genuine and last-ditch attempt at protest. Antis claimed that they chose not to eat so that they would then be forcibly fed and could claim to be victimized by a heartless and depraved system. In fact, being forcibly fed was rarely a choice and always horrific. Interviewed in 1961, suffragette Mary Richardson said she still shook with fear when she heard slow footsteps outside a door or window (she was then in her late seventies), dreading the arrival of doctors and wardresses with their ghastly paraphernalia. She went on secret hunger strike when she was imprisoned, hiding her food so the authorities would think she had eaten it and collecting old nails and pebbles from the exercise yard to sew into her hem and so increase her weight.

Another popular misconception is that prison was invariably hateful. There could be a camaraderie, a sisterhood among suffrage campaigners that many found precious, whether or not they joined a hunger strike. Moments of kindness, dignity, even happiness glint through their memories. They smuggled encouraging letters and poems to one another's cells, sang songs, told stories, talked endlessly while they sat and sewed. They were resourceful, playing cricket in the exercise yard, if the wardresses were sympathetic enough to allow them to do so, using a rolled-up sanitary towel as a ball and a piece of packing case for a bat. One of them recalled a team from the neighbouring Lyons Corner House coming in to cater for them while they waited in court for the Black Maria, and another sent out for baskets of fruit to be dispatched from the local grocer at home.

Phyllis Keller was arrested on 5 March 1912 for breaking

the windows of arch anti-suffragist Lord Curzon and was sent to Holloway. The letter she wrote home to 'dearest old Mum' a fortnight later is teeming with news.[18] First of all she gets practical matters out of the way. She's sending all her dirty washing home and requests some clean handkerchiefs, a nightgown and her 'tidy blue coat and skirt' in return. There's a new rule about food: as long as it's not sent by post she is allowed any amount; she'd like Mum to arrange for two whole days' supplies a week, please. Make sure there's some liquid honey, a pot of marmalade and a bottle of Camp coffee essence. Potted meat is especially welcome, much better than the collapsible pieces of pie sent previously. She'll manage on the prison food for the rest of the time. When she's released in a week or so, can there be a taxi waiting to collect her? She can hardly be expected to walk across London with all her bags . . .

The most exciting thing that's happened recently is that Mrs Pankhurst has moved into the next cell but one to Phyllis, and next to Mrs Pankhurst is Dr Ethel Smyth. Mrs P. is 'far nicer than she looks. She's ripping' and Dr Smyth plays the organ in chapel, making the services there slightly more bearable than usual. The main trouble is that there's no ventilation in the prison. When everyone is packed into the same room, as they are at prayers, it's impossible to breathe and people are routinely carried out, having fainted. Dr Garrett Anderson is also an inmate at the moment. She's such a dear. Phyllis used to think she would never want a lady doctor, but if there are any more like Elizabeth Garrett Anderson, then she can't think why you would ever want a man to attend you again.[19]

She tells Mum how she's spending her leisure time (of which there is, admittedly, a little too much). They play rounders or hockey; they are permitted to sit outside as long as they like, within reason, provided they are doing prison work. Phyllis is sewing a shirt. And then there's housework. She polishes her boots with banana skins, which works a treat, and is perfecting the art of having a bath in a pudding basin. A friend of hers has a big white mackintosh which she spreads on her cell floor; then she pours her scant allowance of bathing water on to it, undresses, lies down and squirms about. Phyllis has to content herself with trying to get clever with a nugget of sponge.

No doubt Phyllis's cheerfulness was assumed, in part, to comfort family and friends at home. And she does seem to have been a particularly resourceful suffragette, regaling her grandson in later life with tales of how she and her friends used to go to West End restaurants, have a meal, then climb up on to the tables shouting 'Votes for Women!' and making such a disturbance that they were thrown out without having to pay for the meal. But she was not alone in admitting that life in prison could have its compensations. She learned a great deal there.

Barrister Frederick Pethick-Lawrence was legal advisor to the WSPU until he and his wife Emmeline were 'let go' by Emmeline and Christabel Pankhurst in 1912. The Pankhursts were becoming increasingly autocratic at this stage, and resented not only the influence of the Pethick-Lawrences but their wealth and, in the case of Frederick, his gender. They had always wanted the WSPU to be an entirely female organization and while Frederick's expertise and money had been useful, his presence in the top rank of the WSPU administration was no longer welcome.

Frederick never wavered in his support for and admiration of those who, like Phyllis Keller, were incarcerated for their political beliefs. He articulated how he felt about them in his autobiography, describing the occasion he was asked to defend three suffragettes in court. Before the proceedings began he noticed the dock was grubby, and immediately took out his handkerchief to polish the railing clean in honour of the arraigned women.

> Ridiculous as it may seem, this single act, which I performed out of courtesy to my wife's friends, made a greater demand on my courage and resolution than anything I did later in the campaign, not excluding my own prison sentence and forcible feeding. By it I

testified that in this matter of the women's revolt I had taken sides
with the dock against the bench; and I accepted the full implication
of all that that entailed.[20]

Nineteen twelve was a shadowed year, notorious for bad news. The
sinking of RMS *Titanic* was perhaps the most shocking disaster of
all, followed by the failure of national hero Captain Robert Scott to
reach the South Pole and his death, with a handful of brave companions, in a blizzard just a few miles from food and salvation. Closer to
home, coalminers held their first national strike in February, which
spread from Derbyshire to the entire British coalfield and lasted for
thirty-seven difficult days, disrupting industry and transport. In
May, thirteen thousand immigrant workers in London's East End
also went on strike and in September Norfolk was inundated by
floods, leaving thousands homeless. Across the Irish Sea, Belfast and
Dublin bubbled and spat over the question of Home Rule (this caul-
dron of unrest was soon to boil over), while Irish farmers struggled
to cope with an outbreak of foot-and-mouth disease.

And women still had no vote in Parliament.

A Birmingham suffragette called Bertha Brewster, writing to
the *Daily Telegraph* in February 1913, did not pull her punches:

> Everyone seems to agree upon the necessity of putting a stop to
> Suffragist outrages, but no-one seems certain how to do so. There are
> two, only two ways in which this can be done. Both will be effectual.
>   1. Kill every woman in the United Kingdom.
>   2. Give women the vote.[21]

It is interesting that Bertha, as a militant, gave everyone fighting for
the vote the umbrella term 'Suffragist': it made the 'outrages' for which
she and her sister suffragettes had been imprisoned sound more reasonable. Her point was that, despite the impassioned determination

of hunger strikers, political debates and popular engagement, active and passive protest of every conceivable kind, women remained impotent dependants with no more political influence, nationally, than an infant or an imbecile. It wasn't just one hand they had tied behind their backs, as Hannah Mitchell claimed, but both hands. George Bernard Shaw wrote a letter to *The Times* to protest in his own inimitable way. He noted that Herbert Asquith had yet again declined to enfranchise women, apparently on the grounds that they were a different species from men – like small, furry animals, perhaps. As a responsible citizen, how can he be expected to follow 'a Prime Minister who places one's mother on the footing of a rabbit?'[22]

The implied insults and rank injustice of Asquith's treatment of 'the woman question' were now too much to bear. While the suffragist crusade for hearts and minds was conducted between 1908 and 1913 in muted colours, but with increasing intensity, the militants turned to shock tactics, to flames and uproar. 'The argument of the broken pane is the most valuable argument in modern politics,' declared Emmeline Pankhurst.[23] At this stage it must have seemed to her like the only argument left.

Nestling in an archive box in a library in North Carolina is a wonderful scrapbook.[24] Nothing I have come across speaks with more immediacy of the militants' struggle during this fervid period before the vote was won. We don't know who compiled it – there is no name inside the front cover – but she, or conceivably he, was obviously a suffragette of the deepest dye. The book is beautifully bound. It was produced by the WSPU as a postcard album, and is decorated in the colours with stylized silver art nouveau trees framing a medallion designed by Sylvia Pankhurst. Stepping towards us, as though she is breaking free of the medallion, is an angel-like girl surrounded by a drift of doves. There are broken shackles at her ankles and an open prison gate behind her. A banner streams around her shoulders, printed with 'Votes for Women' all along its length.

Inside the book are random cuttings and photographs. There are not many notes – the odd comment, that's all – but a glance through its sugar-paper pages is enough to suggest the bewildering scope of the militant campaign as the country sped towards global conflict. There is little wonder that most people were shocked when the Great War began in the summer of 1914: there was so much else to occupy their attention that it crept up on them almost unawares.

The scrapbook is full of colourful characters, each glimpsed with tantalizing brevity before we move on to the next. There is a tiny woman in academic dress being hauled along a Manchester street by two unfeasibly tall policemen. The strange little party is surrounded by men in flat caps with a couple of smart young lads in suits and hats playing to the camera in the foreground. This is Dora Marsden (1882–1960), a graduate of what used to be known as Victoria University in Manchester. She grew up in West Yorkshire; her father was a dealer in woollen waste who went to seek his fortune in America when Dora was eight and never came home. Dora became a teacher and a suffrage activist with the WSPU. When this photograph was taken in October 1908, she had recently been released from Strangeways, where she had contrived to be as awkward an inmate as she possibly could. Not only did she go on hunger strike to protest against her categorization as a non-political prisoner, but she refused to wear prison clothes, brazenly tearing them off to go naked instead. The authorities even tried strapping her into the dreaded 'canvas dress' – a straitjacket – when she was found to be 'unwell' (the usual euphemism for menstruation), but she was so minute that she wriggled out of it. Strangeways was glad to see her go. On the occasion of the scrapbook photo she was in the process of being ejected from a meeting at her old university, where she had made a nuisance of herself yet again by loudly agitating for votes for women. The WSPU was mightily proud of Dora Marsden.[25]

On another page, Christabel Pankhurst is standing on a platform next to one of Landseer's lions in Trafalgar Square, dressed from head to toe in luminous white and obviously in full oratorical flow.

Christabel Pankhurst addresses the crowds in Trafalgar Square.

A row of bored policemen stands at the bottom of the platform. One appears to be picking at the skin on his finger. Presumably she has not yet uttered the words that were to condemn her to Holloway that day, otherwise the police would be looking rather livelier. She boldly invited the audience to come with her and 'rush' the House of Commons – try to invade it, in other words – and was promptly arrested for incitement to riot.[26]

Elsewhere four suffragettes scull by in an elegant rowing boat with an impromptu sail printed with the WSPU slogan. They are haranguing spectators at the Torquay Regatta as they go and are soon to be attacked, the caption tells us, by a similar boat 'manned by four male scoffers'. We don't know who won. There's a photo of Marion Wallace Dunlop gazing at the inscription she stamped on the walls of St Stephen's Hall in Westminster. Apparently it took two men over two hours to erase the violet ink-stains with pumice stone, soap and water. Next, Janie Allan's friend Rosa May Billinghurst (1875–1953) smiles knowingly at the camera from the seat of an elaborate five-wheeled chair, her hands on its powerful levers ready to propel herself into the thick of the action.

May Billinghurst was known as 'the cripple suffragette'. She came to the campaign by way of social work. The misery she witnessed while volunteering at her local workhouse was profoundly depressing. She was convinced that if women had more political power, there would be no need for such places, and the morale of society – as well as its morals – would therefore improve immeasurably. May's options were limited. At five months old she had contracted an unnamed disease – perhaps polio? – which resulted in paralysis from the chest down. With her legs in iron callipers and using crutches she could shuffle along for short distances, but otherwise she relied on her invalid chair. The suffrage movement gave her comparative freedom. Where ideals were the currency, she was rich, and whatever she could do practically to further those ideals, she did.

May founded and helped run a branch of the WSPU in Greenwich, and included herself in the number whenever there was a protest to be made. She was arrested and even imprisoned more than once, and used her popularity with the press, who liked to picture her sentimentally as one of life's victims, to draw attention to the Cause. To vilify the authorities, too: how could our dastardly government sanction caging up this poor little bird with broken wings in a prison cell?

Although police officers claimed that they tried to wheel May Billinghurst out of danger whenever there was violence on the streets, she viewed things differently. She described being dangerously manhandled during a suffragette protest at Westminster in 1910:

> At first the police threw me out of the machine on to the ground in a very brutal manner. Secondly when on the machine again they tried to push me along with my arms twisted behind me in a very painful position . . . Thirdly they took me down a side road and left me in the middle of a hooligan crowd, first taking all the valves out of the wheels and pocketing them so that I could not move the machine.[27]

May refused to be parked on the sidelines. On several occasions she is said to have extracted her crutches from their cradles at each side of the wheelchair and brandished them in front of her before charging at policemen like a human battering ram. This was a risky manoeuvre, as she might easily be tipped out of the vehicle and left helpless. 'Of course,' commented a sister suffragette, 'she took the risk with her eyes open and when this happened, as it did on occasion, made full and unscrupulous use of her infirmities so as to obtain the maximum publicity for the cause.'[28]

Turning another page of this serendipitous scrapbook we find Ethel Smyth staring sternly into the middle distance from beneath the brim of her tweed cap, dressed in a jacket, shirt and bow-tie. Members of the working women's deputation who visited Lloyd George in January 1913 (see Chapter 1) pose outside HM Treasury in the uniform of their professions, looking proud, spotless and somewhat self-conscious. That's a happy image, and there are others: Vera Holme (1881–1969) beams at the wheel of a splendid, shiny motor car. She is wearing a chauffeur's cap and behind her, stifling a giggle, is Emmeline Pankhurst.

Vera – often known as 'Jack' – seems to have been indomitably cheerful. She was a chorus girl with the D'Oyly Carte Company when she joined both the Actresses' Franchise League and the WSPU in 1908. Sylvia Pankhurst affectionately considered her 'a noisy and explosive young person, frequently rebuked by her elders for lack of dignity.'[29] On the evening of Saturday, 1 May 1909, she and a friend staged a brilliant performance of 'noises off' during a po-faced meeting of the League for the Taxation of Land Values in Colston Hall, Bristol. The principal speaker was Augustine Birrell, a member of the Cabinet and, like Asquith, an anti-suffragist. No sooner had he started speaking than a disembodied woman's voice was heard floating around the rafters, repeatedly demanding 'Votes for Women'. Nobody could work out where it came from, until one of the forty stewards on duty that night had an inspired idea. 'She's in the organ!' he shouted, and several minutes later Vera and her companion were found and turfed out of the building. The audience by now was in fits of laughter. Vera wrote a suitably Gilbert-and-Sullivan-esque ditty about it afterwards, based on the popular song 'The Lost Chord' and published in *Votes for Women*:

Seated one day in the organ,
We were weary and ill at ease;
We sat there three hours only,
Hid, midst the dusty keys.
We knew not if they'd be playing,
And to us what would happen then,
But when we heard Mr. Birrell,
It was then we protested, then.

Our voices rang out from the twilight,
But nowhere could we be found;
They looked from the floor to the ceiling—
Then stewards came searching round.
We asked for Votes for Women,
And that justice should be done;
But Birrell he could not answer,
And the audience made such fun![30]

The following year, Vera was appointed Emmeline Pankhurst's *chauffeuse*, which called for skills not just as a driver but as a mechanic, for motor cars at this time were notoriously unreliable. No doubt her sense of humour came in useful, too. In 1911 Vera and horse-whisperer the Hon. Evelina Haverfield set up home together, surely a formidable team with their joint mastery of four wheels and four legs.

The scrapbook continues the musical theme with its next photograph, showing a highly amused woman – bare-headed and with sleeves rolled up – holding a page of sheet music for a large man playing a minute cornet. It is accompanied by the following caption:

> Bow-street's serenity was somewhat disturbed yesterday, for when the suffragettes were answering for the previous day's misdeeds a man stood on the balcony of a house overlooking the police court and obliged with a cornet solo, the air being 'The Marseillaise.' An elderly sympathiser held the music-score and smilingly encouraged him.

The most surreal illustration of all features two men grappling with one another, thigh-deep in water. A delighted crowd looks on from dry land. 'Ducking the Suffragist Clergyman', runs the headline. 'The hand-to-hand fight in the lake at Mr Lloyd George's meeting on Saturday. The clergyman is on the right of the picture.' The reverend gentleman still has his jacket on, while his opponent is in his shirtsleeves. Each has hold of the other's shoulders and looks perfectly prepared to fight to the death.[31]

Finally, the owner of the scrapbook has mounted a double-page spread of scenes from the Great Pilgrimage. It's the only cutting in the whole book to relate exclusively to non-militants. And here, unusually, something has been added. Written in the margin is the simple, scathing comment, 'Pore dears.'

For all its variety, the North Carolina scrapbook only hints at the activities occupying British militant suffrage societies during these restless years. So much violence was inflicted by and upon them; every day there were reports of some new outrage, another tranche of arrests, further moral degeneracy. Although fully realizing that the more offensive the militants were, the harder it would be to persuade the government – *any* government – that women should have the vote, many of the non-militants privately sympathized with them. 'My heart goes out greatly to the suffragettes,' wrote NUWSS member Alice Clark wistfully, 'and I often wonder whether it is cowardice that still keeps me from joining them.'[32]

While their angrier sisters were involved in direct action, the constitutionalists doggedly persevered with attempts to capture the country's imagination through theatrical shows written and performed by members of the Actresses' Franchise League, rallies and exhibitions, printed propaganda in words and pictures, or even by way of flirtation, like Kate Frye. Sometimes the 'gettes and the 'gists joined forces. The Tax Resistance League, to which Henria Williams belonged, encouraged members from across the political spectrum to withhold their income tax on the grounds that there should be no taxation without representation, and if they had no income tax due, to default on other government levies – as Emma Sproson did, for example, when she refused to pay for a dog licence. Perhaps slightly less effective than all this was the formation in 1910 of a Women's Silent League of Freedom dedicated to winning the vote through meditation – a refreshing antidote to the suffragette approach; there was also a sort of moral crusade, publicized amongst a few devoted suffragists as the Guild of Honour, to deny their husbands conjugal rights until the vote was won.

In 1911 there was an inspired campaign across several different suffrage societies to boycott the national Census. The Women's Freedom League came up with the idea. Members and sympathizers were asked either to spoil their Census returns with some suitable slogan, or to avoid filling them in altogether. Both courses of action were illegal and liable to attract a £5 fine, though in the event no one was ever charged. The mildest form of protest in this campaign involved the writing of 'suffragist' in the space for 'occupation'; more militant souls left messages for the Census enumerators such as 'No vote no census return. Those who do not count in the nation cannot be <u>counted</u>',[33] or they simply entered 'no-one' in the list of names, explaining that as women were not legally 'persons' then how could they exist?

The bravest of all became temporarily homeless over the night of Sunday, 2 April, making themselves ineligible to be included. Crowds of evaders – suffragettes and suffragists – slept in offices and public buildings all over the UK; an all-night skating session at the Aldwych roller-skating rink was particularly popular. One group drove a caravan round London all night, eventually coming to rest in the early hours on Putney Heath, where they snatched a few hours' sleep before trundling blearily to Whitehall to deliver Mr Asquith a complimentary copy of *Votes for Women*. Evaders in Edinburgh cruised from café to café, specially opened by supportive owners. Artist Georgina Brackenbury shut herself up in a furniture van, and several ladies slept in barns, outhouses or, in one instance, in her cycle shed, wrapped up in a thick fur coat.

The most famous Census evader of all was a graduate from London by the name of Emily Wilding Davison (1872–1913). She managed to smuggle herself into the Houses of Parliament with the intention of remaining hidden there for forty-five hours, from Saturday, 1 April until the following Monday morning.

The adventure began at 4 p.m. on the Saturday afternoon. Emily must have disguised herself to pass into St Stephen's Hall: as an active suffragette she was certainly well known there, and an extremely unwelcome guest. She made her way down to the chapel crypt and found a little cupboard, only just big enough to accommodate her tall, slender frame. She had food and drink with her, and the plan was to rush out on Monday and surprise the House of Commons. 'I had got my message for Mr Asquith all ready,' she said. On Monday morning she was almost discovered by an MP escorting a lady visitor around the Palace.

> He pushed open the little door of my hiding-place and peered in. I was standing bolt upright behind the door. I scarcely dared breathe. 'Here's where Guy Fawkes was found,' he said [it wasn't].
>
> 'Most interesting,' murmured the lady, 'and do you think there are any ghosts here?' she added.

If I had bobbed out at that moment what would have happened? I should have given them a rare shock, for I was black as a sweep.

Hardly had I got over that shock when someone else came into the crypt. It was an old man. He was sweeping the chapel and drawing nearer and nearer. As he came past he gave the door a vigorous push. It flew back, and bumped against one of [my] boxes. He then peered cautiously round the door and saw me. He drew back with a start, and then said, 'Come along out of that.' I begged him not to turn me out. But he said he must do his duty, and well, of course, he had to do it.[34]

Emily refused to give her name when they brought her to Cannon Row police station, but the officers there recognized her. She was a veteran offender, already having been imprisoned several times in Holloway and Strangeways in Manchester, and was well known for her readiness not only to damage property for the Cause but to sacrifice her own well-being. There *was* no well-being for women without the vote, she insisted.

History has always assumed Emily was a Census evader, but actually she had already filled in a form at home with the words 'Rebellion against tyrants is obedience to God'. According to a letter she wrote to a newspaper in Northumberland, where her family came from, this whole adventure was orchestrated 'simply to show in a practical way that people cannot be governed without their own consent.'[35] In the event, she was enumerated twice, once at her own address and again somewhat retrospectively by officials at the House of Commons. There must have been a certain satisfaction for Emily in being noted for posterity as an inhabitant – if only for a night – of the Palace of Westminster.

Emily had enjoyed a comfortable childhood; she was educated by a governess at home and then at Kensington High School before entering Royal Holloway College – part of London University – to read English in 1891. When her father died in her final year, and was found to have left very little money, Emily was forced to leave. She worked as a governess herself until she had earned enough to finance a term at St Hugh's Hall in Oxford, where she finished her degree course in 1895 and was nominally awarded first-class honours, though no formal qualification, since Oxford did not officially confer degrees on women until 1920. She carried on teaching, and went back to London University as an external student to take another course, this time in modern languages. She graduated in 1908.

That year, Emily joined the WSPU. She was something of a loose cannon in the organization. She was striking to look at, red-haired and green-eyed; she was dramatic, highly religious, and utterly single-minded in her quest to shock the public and the powers-that-be into taking the suffrage cause seriously. She made no pretence about using violence symbolically, to highlight women's political oppression; she threw her stones and lit her fires, cracked her dog-whip and lobbed her bombs (which were actually iron balls with helpful labels on them saying 'bomb'), not just to cause physical damage to politicians and their property but as a warning to the general public of the personal risk they ran if they condoned certain government ministers' behaviour. The WSPU leadership did not always endorse her idiosyncratic tactics.

Emily was arrested and imprisoned multiple times. The most newsworthy was the previous occasion on which she had concealed herself in the Palace of Westminster, perched on a ladder in a ventilation shaft from about 3 p.m. on a Saturday until she was discovered by a PC Thorndike on his rounds at 6.30 p.m. the next day. Shocked, he asked her what she thought she was doing. She simply answered, 'I am a Suffragette and my ambition is to get into the House.'[36] Once in prison she usually went on hunger strike and was forcibly fed, after which – as was common with hunger strikers – she was released early. During her time at Strangeways she barricaded herself in her cell. The authorities were not content with breaking down her door. Instead they set a firehose on her, poking it through the window and drenching her with pressurized water for some fifteen minutes until the cell was almost full.

It was possibly a hint of things to come when in June 1912, during a long stretch in Holloway, Emily threw herself from a balcony on to some stone steps below. She had made her will before going into jail: possibly this was a suicide attempt. She was injured, but not gravely so, and told the doctor who examined her afterwards that she had done it because it had become obvious to her that a tragedy was wanted to draw attention to the barbarism of forcible feeding.

Given all this, did Emily really mean to martyr herself at Epsom on Derby Day in 1913? Mary Richardson had been detailed to sell copies of *Votes for Women* at the racecourse on that fine Wednesday afternoon, and recognized Emily. Mary claimed afterwards that, beforehand, Emily had discussed her plan to disrupt the race with Mrs Pankhurst (who had been concerned for the jockey) and that a few sister suffragettes knew what was going to happen. It wasn't a suicide, Mary insisted; just the gesture of a fanatic, horribly mis-judged. As the horses came thundering round Tattenham Corner – you can see it on the newsreel[37] – Emily darted under the railings and raised her arms, supposedly to drape a 'Votes for Women' banner on the king's horse, Anmer, as it galloped past her. But she had no idea how fast the horses were travelling, nor that Anmer was likely to try to leap over any obstruction in his way. Emily was felled in a split second. Her skull was fractured by the horse's hooves and she died four days later without regaining consciousness. They found two WSPU flags in her pocket when she was taken to hospital, along with a race card and a return ticket to London.

Emily's slow funeral procession from Victoria Station to St George's in Bloomsbury was a full-blown pageant, with thousands of WSPU members, mostly dressed in white, wearing black arm-bands, sashes in the colours and each holding a single lily stem, an iris or a crimson peony. They carried banners freshly stitched for the occasion: 'Give me Liberty or Give me Death', 'God Will Give Victory' and many others. As brass bands played melancholy music, carriages laden with hundreds of wreaths inched along in front of the

horse-drawn hearse. Emily's coffin was covered by a flag decorated
with the broad arrow of a prison uniform. Men doffed their hats in
common decency as it passed.

This occasion was filmed under the title 'The Woman who
Dared', prefaced by a decorative little text box informing avid view-
ers that 'this learned lady lost her life in trying to stop the Derby
Race at Epsom, she believing that the Suffragette cause would
benefit thereby.'[38] Whether this is deliberately disingenuous is hard
to know. The faces of women in the procession look remarkably
modern. May Billinghurst is there in her complicated wheelchair;
somewhere in the crowd is Kate Frye watching in a new black hat
specially purchased for the occasion. They are grieving, all of them,
and obviously shocked. Emily Davison may not have brought political freedom any closer to women, but by her final act she defined the
entire campaign as a violent struggle for death or glory.

Millicent Fawcett and the members of NUWSS-affiliated societies around the country were deeply saddened by Emily's death.
What a waste. They could appreciate her passion, but it was hard for
them to understand her motives. Even the passive resistance involved
in the Census campaign was difficult for true constitutionalists to
stomach. Such showmanship missed the point, which was to prove
that women were capable of taking part sensibly in every civilian
duty asked of them, and anxious to play the same responsible part in
society as the best of men. Many people in Britain thought Emily
Davison's act extravagant, hysterical and in very poor taste. That's not
an opinion the NUWSS necessarily shared, but they acknowledged
that now it was even more urgent that some definitive demarca-
tion should be made between the militants' approach to suffrage and
theirs. With the plans for it already in place, it was time for their
grandest gesture, dramatic enough to capture the attention of both
the public and the Palace of Westminster, and to convince the world
once and for all that women were worthy of the vote in every way.

6

A BECKONING ROAD

The suffragists' response

You speak, Mr Asquith, the suffragist said,
Of the will of the People wholesale;
But has the idea never entered your head
That the People are not wholly male?[1]

THE FORTUNES OF the suffrage campaign had ebbed and flowed over the years, its setbacks and triumphs shared between the militants and the constitutionalists. If the suffragettes claimed success it was often at the expense of the suffragists, and vice versa. Despite the apparent co-operation over the coronation parade in 1911, each group grew increasingly exasperated by the other. Though Millicent Fawcett never publicly criticized Mrs Pankhurst's methods, others in the NUWSS did. One called the WSPU 'a dictatorship movement of the sort that drives democracy out' and its members' devotion to Emmeline and Christabel 'idolatrous'.[2] And the non-militants were frequently described by WSPU members as unattractive and ineffectual. Sylvia Pankhurst thought them 'staid, so willing to wait, so incorrigibly leisurely',[3] and even Kate Frye characterized a typical specimen as a 'very large plain horsey looking woman'.[4] She spoke of people having suffrage like a disease, not so contagious that it spread like an epidemic, unfortunately, but just unpleasant enough to keep everyone cautiously at arm's length. Even though the press and therefore the public still failed to differentiate between the two political wings, they were increasingly aware that all campaigners were not of one accord – which helped no one but the antis.

To counter the perception that suffragists were complacent and passive, from 1908 onwards the NUWSS had decided to take to the road again, not in a spirit of defiance but of evangelism, and this time by caravan. There was something of a vogue for caravanning or 'land yachting' in Edwardian England, which suffrage societies of every complexion had been quick to recognize. The first suffrage tour in a caravan was undertaken by non-militant members of the Women's Freedom League. They commissioned the vehicle them-selves, covering it with massive slogans, including, of course, 'Votes for Women'. It trundled around the south of England during the summer, led by a carthorse called Asquith and with none other than Muriel Matters in charge – she who went on to find fame chained to the grille of the Ladies' Gallery and floating high above the Palace of Westminster in a dirigible. Apparently she was apt to give 'very long' speeches from the step, full of 'pungent witticisms at unfortunate man's expense.'[5]

Meanwhile, Helen Fraser of the NUWSS toured from Selkirk in Scotland to Tynemouth in north-eastern England in a caravan called *Curlew*, holding meetings as she went along, and students of Newnham College in Cambridge spent their university vacation in *Eva*, a splendid caravan in the charge of an enormous horse called Jock and a 'silent Scotchman' named Charles. Two of the students, Ray Costelloe and (Frances) Elinor Rendel, wrote a delightful arti-cle about the trip for their college magazine.[6] It opens on 2 July 1908 when Ray, Elinor and three other young women met in Beattock, a village in Dumfriesshire. The first thing they did was to explore their temporary home. It was elegant and comfortable, with three berths (one of which doubled as a linen chest) and room to stow a tent and a couple of camp beds. The walls were covered in green canvas and there were elegant art nouveau curtains at the neat little windows. It was furnished lavishly with tables and chairs, a stove, a locker, a china cupboard, a tiny bookcase, a couple of shelves and a useful row of hooks. At the back of the van was a meat safe; boxes and baskets held clothes and non-perishable food supplies, like jars of jam and tins of sardines; there was room for a box of books under one of the tables and for playing-cards, penknives 'and other useless property' on the shelves. They called the open seat at the front of the van their 'verandah', where they would take turns to sit with Charles behind big Jock.

Jock was apparently too well bred to be allowed to spend the night in a field – according to Charles he was not accustomed to gypsy ways, and if turned into a paddock might easily break his leg in the dark. This meant he disappeared each night with Charles to the nearest inn or farmhouse where he could be stabled and Charles got away from the wee lassies for a while. Using a technique that was to prove useful to the pilgrims a few years later, two of the students had bicycles with them, on which they scouted for a suitable camping ground each day. 'Near Grasmere we pitched our tent at the foot of Helvellyn, within a stone's throw of a clear hill stream, with deep sunny pools in which we bathed one happy morning.' This was idyllic. They sat on the grass every evening and ate scrambled eggs, bread and jam by moonlight, discussing the day's adventures and making plans. If it was raining, they dined inside *Eva* by candlelight.

Ray and Elinor described a typical day:

> Eight a.m., first signs of life. Someone crawls out of the tent and makes her way, half-dressed, to the back of the van where she can find soap, water and a basin. She dresses completely, shakes up her companion in the tent, who grumbles loudly, but finally gets up. Inside the caravan the sleepers wake up, and a perfect pandemonium begins in there, where three people are trying to dress at once. Meanwhile the first riser has washed the cups, put the kettle on to boil and cut the bread. Filled with demoniacal energy, she insists that those in the van shall throw their bedclothes out of the

door and windows, and she proceeds to drape them over the tent and to spread them on the ground to be aired. The effect is that of a huge rag bag. When everyone is dressed, and the patience of the earlier risers is worn to a shred, breakfast begins – tea, bread and butter, tongue, jam, and slices of melon. After breakfast Charles and the horse appear, and a wild scramble follows. One tries to sweep out and tidy up the van. A second makes the beds. A third washes the dishes and knives, and puts away the stove. The fourth and fifth fold the extra sheets and blankets, and then collect and burn the rubbish.

Charles meanwhile folds up the tent and slings it under the van, while Jock walks about and eats the grass. Whoever has finished her task first now goes to pay the farmer for the milk, eggs, butter, corn, and water, and to thank him for the kindness and hospitality which he and his family have shown. I must say here that we were always on very friendly terms with our hosts. We talked Women's Suffrage to them, and they would sympathise, perhaps inspect the van, and wish us good luck on our way. Our morning bill differed from day to day. At one delightful place in Scotland where we had ordered large quantities of milk, eggs, etc., where Charles had been given supper and a bed, and stable room had been found for the horse, when we asked how much we owed them, the farmer's wife said 'Oh, just two pence for the milk.' But her extreme generosity was an exception.

By the time all our goodbyes have been said Jock is harnessed, the bicyclists are ready, and the start is made. We drive slowly away along the high road leading south.

At Keswick, the young women were greeted by members of the suffrage society there, given beds and hot meals, and accompanied to meetings specially arranged for them to talk to locals about the need for the vote. When they left, they found *Eva* loaded with flowers, fruit and chocolates, and letters of introduction to neighbouring towns. Jock was unimpressed with the contours of the Lake District, but an extra horse was found to help him up the hills and the women made good progress. In Halifax and Huddersfield he had to contend with trams, which frightened him and made him jump, clattering *Eva*'s contents every time. Over a thousand people came to hear them speak at Derby on 23 July, mostly working men in flat caps or boaters (as was the case each time they held a meeting), with a couple of rows of children in clogs at the front and occasional women and tourists. There was always lots of background noise – carts rattling by, the church clock chiming, children giggling and whooping – but generally they were given a courteous hearing and their message got through. 'We do not want a vote for vain glory,' Ray assured her audiences, 'but so that we can help and take our share in the good government of the country.'[7]

While one of the women was speaking, the others went around with collecting boxes, selling literature, postcards and badges, answering questions and chatting. When *Eva* reached Oxford, the final destination, her occupants were sad to part with Charles, Jock and one another. The tour had been a success. The young women met with no rudeness, but much kindness, and were now convinced that the average English working man was perfectly ready to approve of Votes for Women. What's more, it had been a thoroughly liberating experience – and fun.

Four suffrage caravans went on tour during the summer of 1908: *Eva*; the equine Asquith's in Kent, Sussex and Surrey; Miss Fraser's in Scotland and the north; and another visiting Yorkshire's seaside resorts. Sadly, none of them went anywhere near Oldham, but there is no doubt that Marjory Lees will have read about them in the *Common Cause*. A socialist newspaper, the *Clarion*, ran a series of caravans in Lancashire between 1896 and 1929. Suffragette Annie Kenney, also from Oldham, remembered them travelling from village to village, spreading the word and distributing leaflets. They were staffed by women, several of whom went on to become prominent suffrage campaigners.[8]

In 1911 Ray Costelloe married into the illustrious Strachey family. Her brother-in-law was the writer Lytton; her sister-in-law,

Philippa, was Millicent Fawcett's right-hand woman at the NUWSS; her mother-in-law, Jane, signed one of the earliest suffrage petitions in 1867 and went on the Mud March; and her stepdaughter, Julia, joined the Great Pilgrimage. As chairman of the London Society for Women's Suffrage at the time, and given her gypsy experience, it can be assumed that Ray was also a pilgrim, happy to recapture the gaiety of the summer of 1908, despite the lack of Charles and Jock.

Katherine Harley, who was to propose and organize the Great Pilgrimage, was inspired by the cheerfulness of these tours, as well as by their obvious efficiency in taking the fight for women's enfranchisement to the people and explaining it to them straight from the horse's mouth, as it were. But the NUWSS could not afford to sponsor caravans for everyone. Wouldn't a walking tour be even more effective? Real pilgrimages, like the time-honoured one to Santiago de Compostela or Chaucer's to Canterbury, were undertaken on foot or horseback. Replacing the gloss of penance central to religious pilgrimages with that cheerfulness – while keeping a sense of self-sacrifice – was an inspired idea. And even though Edwardian females were popularly supposed to lack physical and moral stamina (tell that to Kate Frye), to swoon at the drop of a hat and be terrified of mixing with anyone outside their own social circle, she knew this ambitious plan had every chance of succeeding. The 'Brown Women' proved that.

These redoubtable women were given their nickname because of their uniforms: russet tweed suits and matching hats decorated with emerald green cockades. For a few weeks in the winter of 1912 they were famous. The Brown Women were gentlewomen of the road, who marched about four hundred miles from Edinburgh to London. This extraordinary enterprise was the brainchild of Florence de Fonblanque (1864–1949), a member of the Women's Freedom League, Kate Frye's New Constitutional Society for Women's Suffrage, and the Conservative and Unionist Women's Franchise Association, as well as the NUWSS and WSPU. Though not a militant herself, she admired the way the suffragettes translated their passion for justice into direct action, and hit upon the idea of a long-distance march as a demonstration of suffragist fortitude and determination.

When Mrs de Fonblanque first thought of the 'Woman's March' in September 1912, she wrote to all the suffrage societies she could identify to enlist support, with the gratifying result that some three hundred women strode out of Edinburgh on 12 October, headed by Charlotte Despard. Mrs de Fonblanque envisaged the march as a massed event publicizing not just the sturdiness of its participants, but the causes for which they wanted the vote. 'Just off,' she wrote hastily to her sister on departure. 'Pray heaven we save the sweated women and their children.'[9] Brass bands and thousands of spectators sent them on their way.

After the first few miles in awful weather the numbers dropped, and only six women went the whole distance, carrying green lanterns in the early dusk, with their luggage drawn along in a van by Mrs de Fonblanque's favourite mare, Butterfly. Others came and went along the route. They rode on the van when they were tired, with the luggage, the literature they proposed to distribute along the way and an ever-growing roll of signatures on a petition to be presented to Mr Asquith at the end: 'We, the undersigned, pray the Government to bring in a bill for Woman Suffrage this Session.' It boasted thousands of names by the time they got to London.

The six who stayed the course were mostly from the south of England. Indeed, it had been Florence de Fonblanque's original idea to do the march in reverse, from London to Scotland, until friends persuaded her of the publicity value of arranging it the other way round. She and Miss Margaret Byham were from Sussex, Mrs Jethro Robinson and Miss Sarah Bennett were Londoners and Miss White, a former missionary, came from Woking. Only Miss Nannie Brown came from Edinburgh. She had intended to turn back after a few days, but found herself enjoying the march so much that she decided to carry on. It was a matter of pride for all of them to walk as much as possible – an average of fifteen miles a day, but often twenty and on one occasion thirty, in exposed, wintry conditions – and most onlookers responded to their remarkable enthusiasm with admiration. Rare exceptions included an outraged woman from Tweedmouth who dangled a pair of gentleman's combinations out of her window in disgust as they went by; a crowd at Peterborough who refused to let them speak, and a mean-minded journalist on the *Scotsman* who caricatured them as pathetic and ineffectual. Describing their departure from Musselburgh on 14 October, he noted smugly that they were late:

> The start was timed for ten in the morning but it was nearer eleven before the demonstrators set out. In the interval the petition which is being taken to London was produced for signature, while a crowd of about 150 people watched the women arranging their banner. When at length the baggage van blazoning the purpose of the march, and driven by a brown-uniformed suffragist, moved eastward it was seen that the marchers were not strong in numbers. Only seven started. One had charge of the horse. Two held up the poles of the banner, and the other four had a cord each to steady it. A few newspapermen followed, but no one else. The wind in a frolic played tricks with the banner, and gave its bearers no end of trouble. At the eastern boundary of the town one of the marchers, who was not in uniform, surrendered her cord and parted from the company.[10]

None of these minor setbacks bothered the women much. They were perfectly capable of looking after themselves. When a number of young lads booed the beginning of her speech in Berwick, Mrs de Fonblanque soon restored order. 'I don't think that is quite cricket, do you?' she asked them with a glare. They subsided immediately.[11]

The Brown Women rested on Sundays, but on the remaining

thirty days it took to accomplish the march they held a meeting or two during the daytime and one in the evening. Just as the caravan tourists had done, they had a cycling outrider for most of the time – Isabel Cowe from St Abbs – who sped ahead to secure accommodation. Visiting speakers joined the ladies at intervals, marvelling at their resourcefulness in gathering signatures for the petition. Wherever Miss Cowe went on her bicycle, she stopped anyone she met and handed them pencil and paper. Another part-timer, Alexandra Wright of the New Constitutionals, even shinned up a telegraph pole to bag the autograph of a man working at the top of it, much to everyone's delight.

As the ladies approached London in the middle of November – appearing 'comet-like, upon the suffrage sky', according to an article in the WSPU paper the *Suffragette*[12] – news reached them that Mr Asquith had agreed to receive their petition. By now it measured nearly eight hundred yards long, each separate sheet mounted on linen and stored in a large leather case. More and more supporters began to join in as they tramped through the Home Counties. Butterfly was honourably discharged at Finchley and replaced by a more streetwise horse, and at last, on Saturday, 16 November, the Brown Women and their cohort came to a halt in Trafalgar Square. 'See the Conqu'ring Hero Comes', played the band, along with the inevitable 'March of the Women' (whose composer, noted the *Scotsman* waspishly, was a Dr Ethel Smith), and each of the six original marchers was presented with a silver medal.

Mrs de Fonblanque and Miss Byham delivered the petition box to Downing Street themselves, rapping sharply on the door of Number 10 until they were admitted. The prime minister would be pleased to give it his consideration, they were assured, as they handed over their weighty and hard-won prize. A few days later, the exhausted ladies heard his response. He had nothing to add to his previous statements. In other words, the march of the valiant Brown Women had made not a blind bit of difference.

The NUWSS gazette, the *Common Cause*, could not believe Asquith's dismissal of these women and all they had endured. Its writers vigorously championed the Brown Women and their cause, well aware that their march was about much more than the fight for the vote. 'We are not political serfs,' declared Millicent Fawcett in a leading article. 'We are working for the uplifting of women all along the line.'[13] To prove this, the *Common Cause* ran features about a day in the working life of a tea-shop girl (for instance) alongside advertisements for summer 'suffrage schools' at university colleges, or reports of sermons by women preachers in the Nonconformist Church. It included cartoons and jokes as well as serious pieces on the white slave trade or the history of the Co-operative movement. In fact, it was remarkably broad in its appeal, less like an in-house journal than a magazine for the interested general reader.

Its advertisements are irresistible, and give us a shrewd idea of the publication's scope. Busy housewives are encouraged to invest in Globe metal polish, which works 'quickly and easily with a shine that lasts', or Flako, 'the last word in soap', guaranteed not to shrink the washing. Those looking for paid employment should take advantage of Mrs Hoster's Secretarial School for Gentlewomen and buy themselves a swanky Oliver typewriter. Ladies of leisure can concentrate on cultivating an 'up-to-date shape' with JB side-sprung corsets, and learn how to look as *soignée* as the ladies in the advertisement for Cordon Rouge Turkish cigarettes.

Professional suffrage speakers tempt readers to engage them for a forthcoming meeting; Temperance Hotels announce their suitability for such women travelling alone; elocution teachers will make a speaker of *you*, then you won't need to hire anyone else. There are even remarkably personal ads for sanitary towels, false teeth, a cure for coughing up blood and a suite of Dr Jaeger's revolutionary woollen underwear.

The paper's main purpose, however, was to inform members of the NUWSS about the progress of the national and local campaign and to disseminate useful information for those involved in propaganda work. Thus we are told which newspapers around the country are sympathetic to the Cause and which less so. In advance of general or by-elections, a list of candidates is published with a note of whether they have voted in the past for women's suffrage.

The *Common Cause* came into its own during the planning stages of the Great Pilgrimage, which were rather rushed. The idea was first mentioned at an NUWSS sub-committee meeting in London on 17 April 1913 – only a few weeks before the first pilgrims set off. An awful lot of organization was required in a very short time. Much had happened since the euphoric summer days of 1911. In November that year Asquith was still making pledges to introduce a Suffrage Bill capable of amendment to include women, but instead of backing the Conciliation Bill, he announced a rival, a completely new Manhood Suffrage Bill, concentrating on those men who still did not have the vote. Fear not, he said: some eligible women might still slip through the net.

Non-militant suffragists were disappointed, but by no means in despair. Where there was life there was hope. Mrs Pankhurst and her followers, meanwhile, were furious at the latest in this sorry series of broken promises. The Conciliation Bill had progressed to its second reading in March 1912 but, in the face of this new proposal from the government about Manhood Suffrage, it was defeated. In July the terms of the new Bill were revealed. There was no provision for giving women the vote at all, though there was still a vague implication that amendments might be made further down the line.

Tucked into an innocent-looking envelope in the Suffolk Record Office is a seismic document in the history of votes for women. It is a letter, dated 25 January 1913, from Herbert Asquith to a Mr James Lowther:

I understand that you have privately intimated to some of my colleagues that the adoption of any of the Woman Suffrage amendments to the Franchise Bill would involve such a fundamental alteration as to bring it within the practice as to withdrawal.

The belief or apprehension that some such ruling may be expected tends to make the discussion which has now begun unreal. Nor is it desirable that at this stage of the Session there should be any avoidable waste of Parliamentary time.

In the circumstances although time for a direct ruling has not in strictness arrived, I propose to ask you on Monday whether you will at once favour the House with your view.[14]

James Lowther is the Speaker of the House of Commons. It is his opinion that any alteration to the Manhood Suffrage Bill to accommodate women will so change its nature that it will have to be withdrawn and completely redrafted. Asquith has heard this – with relief? – and, disingenuously explaining he wants to avoid unnecessary delays through fruitless arguments about this judgement, he asks Mr Speaker to move straight away to a direct and incontrovertible ruling, thus quashing any remaining hope of the amendment necessary to give a limited number of women the vote.

The decision was not entirely a matter of Asquith's personal antipathy to the Cause. He had had much to deal with during the last two or three years: the constitutional crisis occasioned in 1909 by Chancellor of the Exchequer Lloyd George's 'People's Budget', which the House of Lords refused to ratify, leading to highly controversial proposals to reduce the power of the Upper House; the turmoil around Irish Home Rule; and the political implications of widening the franchise. Liberals worried that most women enfranchised by property qualifications (and therefore comparatively prosperous) would vote Tory. Tories worried that if the male franchise were widened to include more of the working classes, fewer would vote for them. Both worried that, if they were distracted too much by the women's suffrage question, Irish nationalists would launch a stealth attack and catch them unawares. Muffled alarm bells were beginning to sound in the Foreign Office at Admiral Tirpitz's consolidation of the German Navy and repeated German threats to invade France. These were unquiet times. But none of this excused the government's constant prevarication, according to those fighting for women's suffrage.

The suffragists' reaction – after recovering from the shock – was to fix on two new strategies. The first was henceforth to pledge political and practical support exclusively to Labour candidates in general or by-elections. The Liberals and Tories had had their chances to change history, and had squandered them. Labour had already put on record its full support of women's suffrage, and would now benefit from money raised from a new NUWSS Election Fighting Fund. Maybe that would encourage the others to deselect anti-suffrage candidates. This pro-Labour stance was not an easy thing for many NUWSS members to accept: Millicent Fawcett was a Liberal – her husband Henry had been a minister in a Liberal government – as was Mayor Sarah Lees. Conservative Emily Davies resigned from the NUWSS in protest, but most were pragmatic enough, and by this stage desperate enough, to give anything a try.

The second strategy was the Pilgrimage. When Bertha Brewster wrote to the *Daily Telegraph* that there were only two ways to stop suffragette outrages – to kill all women or to give them the vote – she was wrong. She assumed that the only possible route to enfranchisement was militancy. Just as Mrs Pankhurst had despaired at the perceived passivity of the constitutionalists when she formed the WSPU back in 1903, so, ten years later, Mrs Fawcett and the NUWSS despaired of the suffragettes. Their hot-headed lawlessness threatened to drain the suffrage movement of any remaining dignity and credibility. They hurled the struggle into the headlines, certainly, but this was no longer helpful, especially when the number of people who could distinguish between the two wings of the movement was still negligible. They were never criticized by the NUWSS for their passion and their dedication to the Cause, but their methods were deeply worrying. There must be another way.

Mrs Katherine Harley (1855–1917) was president of the Shropshire Women's Suffrage Society and chairman of the West Midlands federation. Katherine came from stalwart stock. Her sister was Charlotte Despard, former member of the WSPU and now president of the Women's Freedom League, and her brother was Field Marshal Sir John French, commander of the British Expeditionary Force for the first two years of the Great War. Katherine's husband had been a military man too, killed during the Boer War. Perhaps it was her Christian conviction that prompted her to think of staging a crusade for the Vote (she was also a member of the Church League for Women's Suffrage). She certainly thought of the struggle towards enfranchisement in spiritual as well as political terms.

Once she had raised the idea of the Pilgrimage at that meeting in April 1913, things moved remarkably swiftly. The *Common Cause* explained to readers why this was such a brilliant concept, and what it would mean to those who took part or witnessed it. It would prove that there were thousands of law-abiding people who believed it only right and just that women should have the vote as well as men. If women were governed by the law of the land, they should have some part in the making of that law. This was an argument as old as the suffrage movement itself, put nowhere more eloquently than in an article in the *Shetland News* on 23 March 1912: 'Labour, wages, housing, education, drunkenness, immorality, and war, are all questions that concern women as deeply as men. But all the laws affecting them hath hitherto been made by men. They have not shown that they can cope with them.'

The Pilgrimage would spread the word about suffrage right across the country, so that people understood at first hand that campaigners were ordinary women working for what should be an ordinary human right. The struggle for women's enfranchisement was a people's struggle, relevant to us all, and not some elitist ideal.

There was nothing threatening about the Pilgrimage: it would be a good-natured appeal to reason, and nothing to do with force, thus differentiating the 'gists from the 'gettes. It would show how dedicated the pilgrims were to their cause, and how much faith they had in it, that they were willing to endure the hardships of life on the road – and all the political difficulties put in their way – for the sake of achieving success. Such visible dedication would be a gift to all those who had worked for the vote during the past half-century: the Pilgrimage was an act of devotion to them as well as a demonstration of determination, courage and steadfastness.

Now to more corporeal matters. In the administration of the NUWSS a robust network was already in place, extending to regional federations, with direct lines of communication cascading down from the head office in Westminster to the humblest branch member in the furthest reaches of the British Isles. This, together with weekly bulletins in the *Common Cause*, meant that arrangements could be put in place relatively quickly.

Saturday, 26 July 1913 was chosen as the date for the massed meetings in Hyde Park which would mark the climax of the Pilgrimage. Working backwards from then, timetables were calculated for the six principal routes, several of which had multiple starting points. They were named the Great North Road (which included East Anglia), the Watling Street route (with Wales), the West Country route, the Portsmouth Road, the Brighton Road, and the Kentish Pilgrims' Way. At a meeting of the hastily formed Pilgrimage Committee on 8 May, representatives from almost every federation came to London to advise the organizers on local conditions and contours; on suitable stopping places and possible overnight accommodation, including camping grounds, barns and the cheapest of cheap boarding houses. They were urged to ask their society members to consider feeding and putting up pilgrims, and, of course, to join the Pilgrimage themselves for as long or short a time as they could manage. No pressure was to be put on anyone, but the expectation of practical help and financial as well as moral support was implicit.

Costs were to be kept to a minimum. Anyone who could afford to pay their own expenses on the road was encouraged to do so. One of the aims of the Pilgrimage was to raise money as well as public awareness, so there was no policy of centrally subsidizing working women or busy wives and mothers; if local societies did what they could in terms of providing accommodation and food, and federations fundraised for the rest, it was hoped no one would be prevented from walking at least part of the way for lack of money. Lack of time was a different problem. Thirty-five pounds was set aside for the printing of posters advertising the Hyde Park meetings to be pasted on omnibuses and the walls of tube stations in London, but other publicity arrangements, and the sewing of suitable banners, were left to each route's organizing committee.

Rules for the pilgrims' 'uniform' were decided in May, with the design of the cockleshells and the green-red-and-white raffia rosettes to be worn on their hats. Two marshals were to march at the head of each contingent with pennants declaring them (to fearful onlookers) to be law-abiding and non-militant. If anyone had an available motor vehicle, could they lend it to the pilgrims for the duration? Could we have volunteer cyclists to run errands en route? Any spare horses?

An attractive map showing the major routes and timings was soon published. Those on the shortest, starting from Brighton, were to set off on 21 July, but the longest routes, from Carlisle and Newcastle, would take a full six weeks. That meant leaving on 18 June. Newspaper editors were alerted well in advance and asked not only to report on the passing of the Great Pilgrimage through their region, but to publish a letter explaining exactly what it was all about, clearly distinguishing between the 'law-abiding' suffragists and the militant suffragettes. Some editors complied with the latter request; some didn't. Once the Pilgrimage started, however, they were all eager to report on its progress. It caught the public imagination.

Anxious not to miss a trick, enterprising manufacturers started placing advertisements in the *Common Cause* and elsewhere for pilgrimage-related material. The Burberry is 'the Ideal Coat for the Pilgrimage' because of its 'rainproofness', its reliability and good ventilation, 'so that both chill and overheating are avoided.' Straw hats ready-trimmed in the NUWSS colours are available from Swan and Edgar, with elegant button-through walking skirts that won't show the dirt and matching tailored coats. 'Darn-no-More' socks are guaranteed hole-proof; wear them with a strong but elegant pair of boots from Gorringe's and some 'Atheenic underwear', and nothing will stop you. I have no idea what Atheenic underwear is. Even the local papers got in on the act, but in a rather more mischievous way. The *Thame Gazette* carried a jaunty advertisement for Parker's

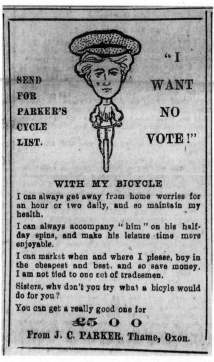

A discouraging advertisement for suffrage campaigners.

Bicycles with the picture of a slightly masculine-looking lady cyclist in a peaked cap. Mr Parker has slightly missed the point of the Pilgrimage. 'With my bicycle,' his heroine assures us, 'I can always get away from home worries . . . I can always accompany "him" on his half-day spins, and make his leisure time more enjoyable. I can market when and where I please, buy in the cheapest and best, and so save money . . . Sisters, why don't you try what a bicycle would do for you?' In large letters at the top of the advertisement runs the strapline 'I Want No Vote!'[15] An advertisement in the *Buckingham Free Press* is in appalling taste. Following a local arson attack by militants, it reads 'Advice to Government re Suffragettes. Don't Forcibly Feed, but Give Them Picton's Bacon and Eggs. They'll offer no resistance.'[16]

As the date of the Pilgrimage drew nearer, the stream of instructions from both national and local organizers swelled into a torrent. The detail included in them was remarkable. For all its spirituality, this exercise was being run by Katherine Harley like a military campaign. Every pilgrim who had signed up in advance was given a village-by-village itinerary, with all the information they could possibly need: where to stow banners in Stockport; who would be their hostesses in Cambridge; where to buy paper drinking cups at a ha'penny each in Cheshire; who was eligible to ride in a motor car and how to apply for permission to do so; and, most importantly, where the ladies' cloakrooms were.

No one was allowed to bring more than a single piece of luggage in addition to their regulation NUWSS knapsack. Doctors, nurses and members of the Red Cross League were required to wear a special badge in case of emergencies. Everyone must attend roll call each morning, when they would be given special instructions for the day, and each afternoon at teatime, when they would be told where they were staying that night. If, as was usually the case, there were no lavatories available, alternative arrangements were basic. Every so often a whistle would be blown for a ten-minute halt, presumably beside an accommodating hedge or clump of trees.

A thoughtful editorial appeared in the *Common Cause* about the death of Emily Wilding Davison in June 1913. It is worth reading in full:

> It is impossible not to put the question – who is responsible for this piteous waste of courage and devotion? The answer, as in the case of most crimes against society, must implicate many. All who believe in the enfranchisement of women and do nothing to make their belief a reality, are in some sense responsible for the desperation to which unbalanced enthusiasts have been driven; and all who, from lack of thought or more unworthy motives, refuse to face at all the problem which is crying aloud for solution. Those also who are deaf to the sufferings which have created the Suffrage movement until the militants disturb their rest, and who then seek only to suppress and not to heal, are in their measure responsible for this pitiful sacrifice. Nor are those free who led the way to it. We do not believe this act of desperation was suggested or approved by the leaders of the WSPU. They have at least been clear that they do not attack life, and it is certain that Miss Davison's attempt involved the most frightful risk to other lives than her own.[17] But we do hold that the responsibility for creating the spirit in which that attempt was conceived and carried out must rest with them. At all times there have been men and women willing to face death in the course of their work – doing the work they had in hand and taking the risk, as Mrs Josephine Butler did, or as any soldier does. This is heroism. But the spirit which goes out to seek death, which demands martyrdom, not as a risk to be faced in the course of one's work, but as an end in itself – this spirit does not deserve so fair a name, and it is one which has been deliberately fostered by the militant leaders. We appeal to them once more to hold their hands, and consider what terrible issues their leadership has already brought to some of those who follow them.[18]

Five days after this was published, the Pilgrimage began. It was the suffragists' answer to both the fanaticism of the militants and their own apparent lack of heroism: a statement of belief in the power of women and their ability, when working together, to turn the world upside down without violence or hatred. It would be dangerous, difficult, physically and emotionally challenging, and break every rule in the book about how Edwardian females of every class were supposed to behave. But it would be glorious, too. This would be their battle, a peaceful fight against low expectation, low self-esteem, constant stereotyping and the spurious comfort of the status quo. And unlike the 'gettes, the suffragists had faith that victory was assured, as long as they walked calmly and purposefully to claim it rather than charging at it in fury. They were confident that the strength of spirit embodied by the pilgrims and their supporters would prove irresistible to the government; that this time, their voices would not only be heard, but understood.

7

STEPPING OUT

The Great Pilgrimage

Women, old and young, drawn from all ranks of life, and yet bound together by a common tie of sisterhood powerful enough to break down all differences in age and social standing. Mothers and daughters as true comrades, peeresses and mill-hands as real friends, all stepping out together to convert England.[1]

IT TOOK THE officers of the NUWSS just two months to organize the Pilgrimage. Millicent Fawcett was unable to help much: she was finding work increasingly tiring now that she was in her late sixties with so many demands on her time. She was happy to delegate this complicated task to Katherine Harley and her special sub-committee. Mrs Harley had just the right combination of high efficiency and motherliness to make it a success. Millicent took a lively interest, however, and was glad to join as many meetings en route as she possibly could, especially when the pilgrims neared London in the middle of July.

We have already heard about the practical preparations for the Pilgrimage. Less obviously useful – but still very necessary – was a rapid build-up around the country of ideological support. The NUWSS had some forty-five thousand members now; all of them were urged to do their bit by holding propaganda meetings at their homes, canvassing door to door to talk about the ethos behind the

The Suffrage Atelier working to produce banners.

demonstration, wearing the colours for the duration whether they were taking part or not, and writing to the press to emphasize (for the umpteenth time) that this was a law-abiding exercise and nothing to do with smashing windows. Nor was it the latest skirmish in what was regarded by many as nothing more than a 'sex war'. Men would march as well as women, united in an amiable ambition to 'Tell All England', as the posters put it, 'Why Women Want the Vote'. All Wales and all Scotland too: in fact, all the world. The NUWSS was confident that news of this historic gesture would spread beyond the United Kingdom – and it did, being reported as far away as New York and the Antipodes.

A few mini-marches took place during the weeks leading up to the main event to help publicize the Pilgrimage and get members into

the swing of organizing and participating in a long-distance demonstration. One of these was a four-day trek to Brighton in May, led by
Florence de Fonblanque, of Brown Women fame. After the success
of the Edinburgh–London march the previous winter, Florence had
taken it upon herself to form what she called the 'Qui Vive Corps', a
body of suffragists who met on Saturday afternoons – once more in
brown uniforms – to train for emergencies by tramping around the
neighbourhood. The WSPU ran a similar corps under the leadership
of 'General' Flora Drummond, but theirs operated on bicycles. An
emergency was any occasion on which a suffrage society required
extra numbers to help with local events; if there was no emergency
available, they would simply proselytize instead.

All this preparation was like tilling the soil before setting seed
and waiting for the flowers to grow in a blaze of red, white and
green. No doubt it helped create an excited sense of anticipation in
those regions in which it was reported, and increased the numbers at
meetings along the various Pilgrimage routes. The NUWSS publicity campaign was not an unqualified success, however. When a letter
was sent to local newspaper editors in May to explain what was
about to happen, those who published it would often slip a report
about an arson attack or stone-throwing spree in the next column,
perhaps deliberately confusing the 'gettes with the 'gists. They trivi-
alized the enterprise by noting sardonically how heated was the
debate about what to wear on the road ('sumptuary wars'); what
these petticoated crusaders might use for weapons during their
massed attack on the countryside (a bunch of tiger-lilies, puzzlingly,
is the best guess); and asking what, after all, this whole thing was *for*,
before deciding that at worst it heralded a feminist apocalypse and at best
served merely 'to amuse the ladies . . . not to mention the general
public, and it certainly does nobody any harm.'[2]

For the past few weeks the NUWSS had been telling everyone what the Pilgrimage was for until it was blue in the face. One
more time: it was for explaining to the people of Britain why half

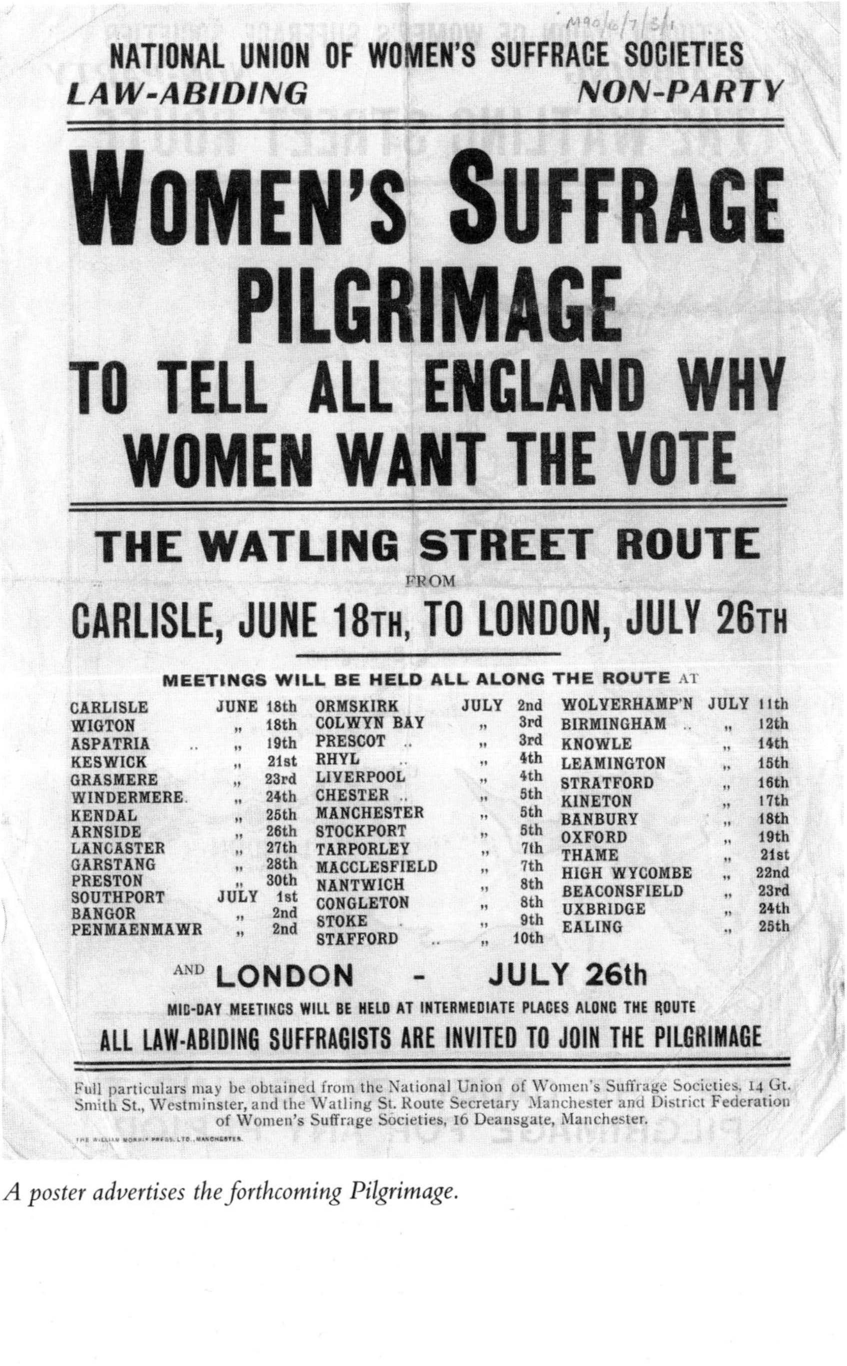

NATIONAL UNION OF WOMEN'S SUFFRAGE SOCIETIES

LAW-ABIDING *NON-PARTY*

WOMEN'S SUFFRAGE PILGRIMAGE

TO TELL ALL ENGLAND WHY WOMEN WANT THE VOTE

THE WATLING STREET ROUTE

FROM

CARLISLE, JUNE 18TH, TO LONDON, JULY 26TH

MEETINGS WILL BE HELD ALL ALONG THE ROUTE AT

CARLISLE	JUNE 18th	ORMSKIRK	JULY 2nd	WOLVERHAMP'N	JULY 11th
WIGTON	" 18th	COLWYN BAY	" 3rd	BIRMINGHAM ..	" 12th
ASPATRIA ..	" 19th	PRESCOT ..	" 3rd	KNOWLE	" 14th
KESWICK	" 21st	RHYL ..	" 4th	LEAMINGTON	" 15th
GRASMERE	" 23rd	LIVERPOOL	" 4th	STRATFORD	" 16th
WINDERMERE.	" 24th	CHESTER ..	" 5th	KINETON	" 17th
KENDAL	" 25th	MANCHESTER	" 5th	BANBURY	" 18th
ARNSIDE	" 26th	STOCKPORT	" 5th	OXFORD	" 19th
LANCASTER	" 27th	TARPORLEY	" 7th	THAME	" 21st
GARSTANG	" 28th	MACCLESFIELD	" 7th	HIGH WYCOMBE	" 22nd
PRESTON	" 30th	NANTWICH	" 8th	BEACONSFIELD	" 23rd
SOUTHPORT	JULY 1st	CONGLETON	" 8th	UXBRIDGE	" 24th
BANGOR	" 2nd	STOKE .	" 9th	EALING	" 25th
PENMAENMAWR	" 2nd	STAFFORD ..	" 10th		

AND LONDON - JULY 26th

MID-DAY MEETINGS WILL BE HELD AT INTERMEDIATE PLACES ALONG THE ROUTE

ALL LAW-ABIDING SUFFRAGISTS ARE INVITED TO JOIN THE PILGRIMAGE

Full particulars may be obtained from the National Union of Women's Suffrage Societies, 14 Gt. Smith St., Westminster, and the Watling St. Route Secretary Manchester and District Federation of Women's Suffrage Societies, 16 Deansgate, Manchester.

THE WILLIAM MORRIS PRESS, LTD., MANCHESTER.

A poster advertises the forthcoming Pilgrimage.

its inhabitants needed and deserved a vote. It was for enlisting the
public's informed support through the passing of resolutions at
countless meetings and rallies along the way, the results of which
would be presented to the government, thereby proving in black
and white how many tens of thousands of ordinary people believed
female enfranchisement to be right, just, expedient and long over-
due. It was for demonstrating that suffragists formed the peaceful
majority of campaigners, and that the 'gettes were not representative. And it was for raising money for the Cause, which would mean
bread and roses for all when women got the vote. This was a non-
denominational, apolitical, law-abiding and, above all, a non-violent
demonstration.

Millicent Fawcett's favourite word when discussing the
Pilgrimage was 'joyful'. Why, then, did the *Nottingham Evening Post*
publish an article on 10 May 1913 about an imminent invasion of
suffragists [*sic*], all 'malignant, bomb-burning feminists' intent on
destroying the city's property and peace of mind? Perhaps because
Nottingham Castle had been burned down by *male* agitators for *male*
suffrage after the disappointingly restrictive Great Reform Act was
passed in 1832. Or maybe the editor was just being malicious. He
wasn't alone. Other local newspapers obstinately insisted on describing the pilgrims as 'disciples of St Emmeline', 'suffragettes on the
warpath', a 'gigantic joke'. Mrs Fawcett responded, as she always did,
with dignity and gentle determination:

> The keynote of the pilgrimage will be the joyousness of self-
> dedication to a great cause. There will be nothing dismal about it.
> Every pilgrim will have in her heart a deep sense of reverent happiness
> that it has fallen to her lot to have the chance of dedicating herself
> to one of the greatest movements which has ever taken place in the
> history of the world.[3]

This was the spirit – mixed with trepidation – in which the first
women and men set off on their six-week journey from Newcastle,

Carlisle and Land's End in the middle of June 1913, gamely prepared
to rough it, have some fun, and finally to win the vote.

Tweed, or no tweed? Should a good suffragist do what her organizers instruct her to do, or what is sensible? It was rare for the two
not to coincide, but in the case of the Pilgrimage uniform, there
was a problem. Katherine Harley had published a request in the
Common Cause that everyone intending to march as a pilgrim, for
however short a distance, should wear a dark coat and skirt with
a white blouse. That would certainly look dashing, but was quite
impractical. Those who had been on marches before, or who had
been ambling through the British countryside in their horse-drawn
suffrage caravans during previous summers, knew that there was
nothing like dark wool or gabardine to show the dirt, and no white
blouse would remain white for long. Some pilgrims were happy to
post dirty laundry home and collect new supplies at various points
along the way, but not everyone could afford such luxury, and if you
were travelling for only a day or two, that wouldn't work.

Letters arrived at the *Common Cause* office in quick response.
Could we not wear tweed instead? It may not look as snappy as the
outfits you envisage, but by day three or four a navy or black coat
and skirt will look like tweed anyway, marled with mud and dust.
And must the blouse be white? Mrs Harley was keen to stick with
her original plan, always mindful of the fact that the press would
seize upon any opportunity they could to ridicule these tramping
women, and it was unlikely to help if they looked like a rag-tag
bunch of maiden aunts. Tweed might be serviceable and look cleaner
for longer, but it was also old-fashioned and frumpy.

In the end, in the best tradition of constitutionalists, a compromise was reached. Those who wanted to wear tweed could do so
– 'all pilgrims will be welcome whatever they wear,' conceded Mrs

The ideal coat for the Pilgrimage.

Harley eventually – but, if possible, everyone should raise the hem of her skirt to exactly four inches from the ground. Not only would this serve the practical purpose of keeping it out of the mud, it would look uniformly smart and mildly shocking: at the cutting-edge of fashion.

When she arrived in Carlisle on the morning of Wednesday, 18 June 1913, Beatrice Kemp (1871–1966) was no doubt relieved that she had not plumped for tweed. Yesterday the temperature had soared to 80° Fahrenheit (nearly 27° Celsius) and there was thunder in the air. It was disheartening to be so hot and sticky before one had even set off, but things would have been even worse if she had obeyed team orders. Beatrice was one of the Pilgrimage's celebrities, being a local heroine in Cumbria, where she and her husband had a house, and in Lancashire. There, as Lady Rochdale, she presided over the Manchester Federation of Women's Suffrage Societies. She was born Lady Beatrice Egerton, the daughter of the third Earl of Ellesmere, and in 1891 she married George Kemp, who became the first Baron Rochdale. She was a popular, down-to-earth supporter – like the Lees family – of local and national causes to do with bettering the lot of the disadvantaged, amongst whom, as a woman, she counted herself. Like Millicent Fawcett, Lady Rochdale had accompanied her husband on military service to South Africa in 1900. She was a tiny but doughty lady.

An almost palpable sense of excitement shimmered like a heat haze over the wide cobbled square in front of the town hall in Carlisle that morning. Beatrice had arrived in her own motor car from Keswick with a few others; she had no intention of riding in it during the Pilgrimage, but it would be useful for luggage and for rescuing the halt and lame. Cumbrian Caroline Marshall brought a pony-trap with her; someone else had a motorcycle; then there were a few bicycles and forty or so people on foot. Journalists described the most distinguished participants entirely in terms of their menfolk and grew quite excited at the sight of Miss Bardsley, daughter of the erstwhile Bishop of Carlisle; Mrs Chance, wife of the former MP (the fact that she was the local president of the NUWSS was not mentioned); and the assorted spouses of prominent local manufacturers and professional gentlemen.

The star of the show, however, was Lady Rochdale, and when the band struck up the National Anthem at 10.15 a.m., and the Watling Street pilgrims hoisted their many banners and set out along the road for Aspatria and Cockermouth, she strode briskly along with the rest, cheered by the crowds, who probably commented, as one does on encountering the queen, that they had no idea she was so small.

Mrs Chance turned back at Morton, just three miles from her starting point at the town hall – things to do – but Beatrice kept

Lady Rochdale strides out.

going, walking all the way. By the time they reached Keswick in the Lake District on Saturday, the 21st, she had gladly got into the rhythm of walking in the morning, stopping for lunch – a picnic or a meal at an inn – holding a meeting in the afternoon, marching some more, and then coming to rest for the night with dinner, another meeting or two, some press interviews and the usual endless explanations about how the Pilgrimage was nothing to do with the suffragettes. She soon realized that if she opened any conversation with the statement 'I am not Mrs Pankhurst', it helped things along no end.

Shoulder to shoulder with Lady Rochdale was a friend of Selina Cooper's from Lancashire, Emily Murgatroyd (1877–*c.*1970). Her circumstances were about as different from Beatrice Kemp's as one can imagine. At the time of the Pilgrimage she was in her mid-thirties.

She had worked as a weaver at a mill in Brierfield near Burnley since the age of ten and was on a wage of just over £1 a week. Out of this she supported her family and managed to save enough both to finance the Pilgrimage – walking all the way from Carlisle to London – and to leave an extra £1 at home with her mother to keep everyone going while she was away. When she returned home, there would be six weeks' worth of washing and cleaning, no doubt, and a hefty backlog of work to catch up on. Not only was Emily an active suffragist but, according to Selina Cooper, a committed trades unionist too.[4] She had many commitments. It's a mark of the Pilgrimage's credibility that she thought it worth the sacrifice, and of its inclusivity that both she and Lady Rochdale marched together in friendship. Emily had magnificent blisters, apparently, by the time she got to London, and Beatrice was filthy. They were equally exhausted and equally proud, fulfilling Millicent Fawcett's prophecy that a shared sense of sisterhood would be one of the Pilgrimage's most valuable gifts.

Beatrice and Emily each had a suffrage pedigree, having worked for the Cause within the NUWSS for several years. One of the most enthusiastic pilgrims of all, however, had been blissfully ignorant of her political handicap until the day the Pilgrimage arrived at a village just outside Keswick. She wasn't quite as bad as the mother who confessed to her daughter her amazement that women did not have the vote already, assuming her husband had been kindly voting for her all these years, but Gladys Duffield (1882–1973) had no idea that suffragists existed. She had seen suffragettes at the Christmas pantomime, where the Dame was traditionally done up like a 'Votes for Women' battleaxe, and she enjoyed the cartoons and caricatures, but it had never occurred to her to take them seriously. So when she was misinformed that the procession of women filing into the schoolroom in Braithwaite, where she was staying, were real live suffragettes (*Oh no they weren't* . . .), she was astonished. What on earth were they doing here?

Braithwaite lies at the Keswick end of the Whinlatter Pass, through which the pilgrims threaded their way after leaving Gladys's birthplace, Cockermouth, on the morning of Saturday, the 21st. It was a hard, thirteen-mile stretch and by the time they reached the village they were more than ready for tea. Gladys was enjoying a game of tennis on the lawn with her parents-in-law that afternoon. She and her five-year-old daughter, Lily, were living with them while her husband, Albert, was on a military posting to India. Curiosity got the better of her, especially when she noticed that people were also arriving from the direction of Keswick and disappearing into the school with smiles on their faces, so she bravely walked over to see what was going on, leaving the child with Granny.

Gladys got a warm welcome. Lady Rochdale was acting as hostess (also paying for the tea) and was happy to explain to the young woman all about the suffragists and their crusade. So entranced was Gladys by the spirit of the Pilgrimage and the general atmosphere of friendliness and good humour that she bought a raffia badge there and then, and signed up to membership of the NUWSS. At the mention of Mrs Fawcett she vaguely remembered something her mother used to tell her as a child about Mrs Fawcett's prodigious daughter, Philippa, who had famously beaten *everyone* in her exams at Cambridge University.

Thinking it might be a lark to walk with the pilgrims two and a half miles into Keswick, Gladys dashed home after tea to ask her mother-in-law if she would carry on minding Lily for a little while longer. It turned out that Granny had been 'a secret suffragist' for some time and was sitting at home wishing she could accompany them herself. She was only too glad to let Gladys go in her place.

One of the speakers at the meeting in Keswick that evening was an impressive-looking woman with a faintly odd accent, dressed in a voluminous mackintosh. She drew a huge crowd – there were seldom fewer than two thousand people at evening meetings on the Watling Street route and sometimes more than fifteen thousand – and she was

Gladys Duffield and her daughter Lily.

wonderful to listen to. Gladys learned her name: it was our dirigible pilot friend, Muriel Matters, mostly Australian but also partly Welsh. Gladys felt an irresistible urge to be part of it all, intoxicated by the noise and the colour, the liveliness of the audience and the speakers' heady message about women coming together to change the world.

Sunday was always a rest day for pilgrims, whatever route they were on. That meant, tantalizingly, that Gladys had a day's grace before her new friends left for Grasmere. She asked Caroline Marshall for advice: how long would the Pilgrimage last? Another five weeks. Would they be able to accommodate her if she joined them? Certainly, if she paid what she could and took pot luck. Would she be useful to them? No doubt. She could distribute literature and collect donations: the more doing that, the merrier. It was Granny who finally tipped the balance. *Her* contribution to the fight for the vote would be to look after Gladys's daughter for as long as it took.

Her mind made up, the first thing Gladys did was to write to faraway Albert to ask for his blessing, gratifyingly aware that it would take many days for the letter to get there and many more for the reply. Then she chose an outfit for the road, selecting an ancient purple costume ('rather an unwise choice', she noted afterwards) and dutifully hacking four inches off the hem. She was mortified when it was explained to her that purple was the colour of militancy, and as soon as she was able she swapped the costume for a light grey tweed, similarly cut short. In a small and disreputable-looking suitcase she crammed a raincoat, a hat and a headscarf, together with some gifts from a neighbour who was a nurse and had heard about the impending adventure. These gifts proved extremely valuable: some powdered zinc and starch to coat the soles of Gladys's feet as protection against soreness and a bottle of methylated spirits to rub into the skin should any blisters sneak through. Emily Murgatroyd could have done with that.

Gladys's favourite banner was the one telling the story of Asquith's argument that women were politically non-existent. 'Is a Woman a Person?' it read. 'The law says YES when she has to pay. The law says NO when she asks to vote how her money shall be spent. Is this fair?' It's unlikely that she ever helped carry the banner herself, however, unless it was in partnership with one of the male pilgrims: she was too tall. With her thin frame, her narrow face, long nose and pointy chin (her description) she soon earned the nickname 'Skinny Lizzie', bestowed on her by an impolite onlooker at a meeting, and she appears to have been a favourite with everyone.

Some thirty pilgrims marched out of Keswick on Monday morning. There is a glorious photograph in one of Marjory Lees's albums

taken by someone who must surely have been up a tree or a telegraph pole. It can't have been Marjory herself (although I wouldn't
put it past her), since she didn't join the Watling Street route until it
passed near Oldham in the second week of July. Probably it was an
enterprising Cumbrian journalist. It's a semi-aerial view of a column
of pilgrims swinging along the road with huge smiles on their faces.
They are marching more or less two by two, with at least half a
dozen banners. It is obviously quite warm because most of them
have abandoned their coats and are wearing blouses (still white) and
shortish skirts, with sashes over their shoulders and jaunty summer
hats. Behind them are the beautiful mountains of the Lake District,
the mist lies in the valleys and it rather looks as though rain might
be on the way.

It was. Despite the auspicious start and Gladys's infectious excitement, this turned out to be the worst day of the Watling Street
Pilgrimage so far. A fretful pilgrim from Workington had received
a letter, apparently from the chief constable, with the news that
the Pilgrimage had been forbidden by the home secretary and that
anyone who joined it would be prosecuted. They all decided, cor-
rectly, that this must be an elaborate hoax, but it left them shaken.
The rain arrived in torrents, and soon afterwards poor Mrs Marshall
sprained her ankle so badly that she was forced to go home and rest
it. About ten other people left the Pilgrimage at this point, too.

Things improved at Ambleside, where the survivors arrived that
evening. They were treated to a special concert and a hearty meal;
many also had a hot bath – particularly welcome – and a comfortable bed for the night. But their clothes were still damp the next
day. Gladys's good humour continued unabated, however. She was
almost overwhelmed when a little lad at Bowness-on-Windermere
came up and gave her half a crown after the meeting: that was *all*
his pocket money. Muriel Matters had been speaking again that
evening; according to local pilgrim Mrs Whalley, who heard her,
she was 'breezy and entertaining', even though she went on for an

hour and a quarter and somehow managed to invoke Ibsen, Florence Nightingale, Elizabeth Fry and Josephine Butler.

Like so many others, Mrs Whalley was only able to march for a portion of the way. When she arrived at her destination – Kendal – with her companions on Wednesday, the 25th, there was a slight disturbance. Rough mill girls from the tobacco factory there tried to disrupt the evening meeting and heckled Lady Rochdale when she spoke. But Muriel Matters was not to be trifled with. She was used to wearing that long mackintosh at suffrage meetings in London to shield her from the inevitable missiles of rancid eggs and rotten fish. She would hardly be put off her stride by a few choice words from some young ladies who, before the meeting at least, knew no better. Mounting the platform after Lady Rochdale, she impishly quoted Robert Burns to the simmering crowd:

> *Auld Nature swears, the lovely dears*
> *Her noblest work she classes, O:*
> *Her prentice han' she try'd on man,*
> *An' then she made the lasses, O.*[5]

That raised a cheer from the women and good-natured jeers from the men, and order was soon restored.

When the pilgrims reached Garstang on Saturday, 28 June, Gladys awarded herself a weekend off. She caught the train back to Keswick to see Lily, catch up on correspondence and wash her blouse. She also took the opportunity to change the shabby hat she had chosen in haste a week ago for a more fashionable straw toque. She would buy a new suitcase when she could. While the others continued along the road through Preston on the Monday, she jumped on the train again and joined them at Southport on Tuesday, 1 July.

Edith Eskrigge (1872–1948), who was the coordinator for this leg of the Pilgrimage and – they discovered – a distant cousin of

Gladys's, had excelled herself at Southport. 'Trust Miss Eskrigge to organise a march, or anything else for that matter,' wrote Gladys. 'She was a born organiser.'[6] Edith had not only arranged a procession through the town, but she had booked an entire floor of Rowntree's Café for them to relax in and refuel, and engaged the charismatic Miss Cicely Leadley Brown as that night's speaker. Cheshire-born Cicely was to join the Pilgrimage herself afterwards, with her own motor car to support Lady Rochdale's vehicle, and an extraordinary talent, to be revealed to stunned silence a week or two later. Everyone slept well that night, despite their aching bones. It was uniquely satisfying to be able to measure achievement in terms of miles covered and people met, particularly if you were not normally expected to accomplish anything meaningful at all.

Elsewhere, scores of pilgrims were already making their way towards London on different routes. The Great North Road contingent set off from Newcastle on the same day that Lady Rochdale and the Watling Street group left Carlisle. Northumberland was in a restive mood: Emily Wilding Davison's body had been buried in Morpeth just four days previously, ceremonially carried there by train from King's Cross. The Pilgrimage route did not go anywhere near her resting place, but suffrage was a keenly emotive topic just then, and it is perhaps unsurprising that the pilgrims encountered some hostility. At Durham, where they spent their second night, their meeting was interrupted by rowdy students. They found champions in the local miners, who had come to hear them in their hundreds, some of whom circled the speakers' platform to keep the louts away, while others caught the ringleaders and ducked them in the river.

The first serious trouble to beset any northern pilgrims happened at Spennymoor, then an overcrowded and depressed mining town between Durham and Bishop Auckland. They were stoned.

No one could bring themselves to talk about it much afterwards and luckily there were no serious injuries, but it must have been a real shock to the men and women who had set off from Newcastle a couple of days before with bands playing and flowers strewn in their path, so full of hope and goodwill. As they approached Bishop Auckland itself, they were told by their hastily arranged police escort of a rumoured riot, but still decided to go ahead and hold a meeting. As it happened, there was no unruliness that evening and the pilgrims won a good many admirers for their refusal to be cowed.

On Tuesday, 24 June the Great North Road pilgrims reached Northallerton in the North Riding of Yorkshire. The crowds there were fairly welcoming, though this was where the National League for Opposing Woman Suffrage chose to make its Pilgrimage debut by holding a blustery meeting the evening before the pilgrims arrived and hiring 'sandwich men' to distract the suffragists' audience with boards proclaiming that women did *not* want the vote. They repeated this tactic all along the route, only failing to anticipate the suffragists when the out-of-date Pilgrimage map they were carrying sent them off piste for a day or two. At Bedale, on the edge of the Dales, a local journalist described the crowd as 'flippant'; at Masham they were ominously silent; and at Ripon, which the pilgrims reached on Wednesday, the 25th, all hell broke loose.

The Pilgrimage organizers thought of most things, but what they didn't realize when they were planning itineraries was that in the north of England the most exciting event of the whole year was the local agricultural show. The show operated on two levels (and still does): as a competitive rural display of livestock, vegetables, flowers and crafts, and as an enormous party. Passions ran high among rival winners and losers, and the ale flowed freely all day. Perhaps Mrs Harley deliberately earmarked Show Day in Ripon because she imagined the extra crowds would augment support for the Cause at the pilgrims' evening meeting. She was partly right: there were undoubtedly more people than usual, but few were interested in listening to reasoned arguments about women's enfranchisement. They were roaring drunk, and looking for trouble.

They were also convinced that these women – many of whom now wore white summer dresses in pragmatic defiance of all their instructions – were devils disguised as angels. When the evening's speakers ascended their makeshift platform in the market square, they were catcalled and spat at. As they climbed down again, defeated, members of the crowd kicked and hustled them. The 'coarse brutality and rough treatment' to which they were subjected in Ripon were inexcusable, according to a local paper, especially as the pilgrims were obviously such 'refined and educated ladies'. In fact, several of them would not claim to be either refined or educated, but they were at least peaceful women and deserved a measure of courtesy and respect.

So terrified were the pilgrims by this time that they started hammering on random doors, begging for sanctuary. The Congregational minister took some of them into the manse, and when the mob refused to disperse outside his front door he threatened it with an immediate collection for the church heating fund. This seemed to do the trick, and after a little while the women ventured outside again to try to find their hostesses for the night. But they were spotted, and rushed by gangs of braying young men, forcing them to seek shelter again. It was exhausting, frightening and actually – as no one came seriously to grief – rather exciting. In retrospect, anyway. What happened at Ripon was like a baptism of fire for the suffragists: proof that the 'gettes were not the only ones to put themselves in danger for the sake of the vote.

There was an inquiry after the Pilgrimage into the behaviour of the police at various places along the routes. After speaking to local organizers, Mrs Fawcett maintained that there were simply not enough officers available in Ripon to keep the peace. Only three turned up, none of whom seemed remotely interested in arresting anyone. Meanwhile, thousands of Show Day revellers ran riot.

The Land's End party suffered similar experiences in Cornwall. A less threatening group of people it would be hard to imagine. Annie Ramsay was in her mid-fifties with a heart condition (some newspaper reports put her age as eighty, which tickled her mightily); her daughter, Mabel, was a doctor; Mrs McMillan was 'one of the smallest women I ever knew,' according to Mabel. Both Mabel and former WSPU member Helen Fraser, who travelled down from London (thus doing the Pilgrimage in reverse first), had experience of driving suffrage caravans: Mabel during summer holidays in the West Country and Helen in *Curlew*, her own caravan, in the Scottish Borders. Miss Misick, Miss Symons, Miss Fielden and Miss Baly made up the numbers, with a few children dressed in the colours and a donkey and cart. Only Mrs Ramsay, Helen Fraser, Miss Symons and a Miss Bassett Fox went all the way to London. Mabel had a surgery to run in Plymouth, and while the Pilgrimage was in striking distance she would catch a train at the end of her day's work to join her friends for the evening meeting. Then she would return to the surgery and slept on the consulting-room couch rather than going home, to save time.[7] More people came and went, of course, during the next six weeks, and when further routes fed into the main one, numbers increased.

The Land's Enders had a horse-drawn furniture van, painted red and freshly decorated with a huge calligraphic sign in red and green advertising the Pilgrimage, and driven by an amiable young lad called Jack. He and Annie Ramsay became fast friends; he taught her all about the care of horses, which she didn't really need to know, while she advised him on a future career in the police. Even the horse looked benign, festooned with gleaming brasses and a couple of tricolour flags in its collar. It is a measure of the local people's mistrust of anything to do with women's suffrage that this harmless little party was vilified right from the start. Helen Fraser's ankle was kicked and badly bruised at Penzance; thousands of mining students

Pilgrims from Land's End.

at Camborne created havoc at the evening meeting; in Falmouth they were pelted with rubbish and compost. 'You will never win!' shouted Helen, as she was forced from the platform. When they reached Fowey on Tuesday, 24 June they were deluged by a rainstorm of Biblical proportions, and in Looe poor Helen grew so frustrated at the 1,500-strong crowd obstinately insisting that they were militants that she wept. It was mortifying to be seen crying in public, but she could take no more. Annie felt more anger than anything else. She refused to faint 'as any decent old woman would have done'[8] and did her best to stamp on her assailants' feet instead.

Although some individual officers did all they could to try to protect the women – rewarded with letters of thanks from them and even, in one case, a whip-round – the Cornish police adopted a deliberate policy of non-interference at Pilgrimage meetings, perhaps wary of the publicity following Black Friday. This allowed ignorant crowds to react just as one would expect them to, in the genuine belief that the Pilgrimage was a bare-faced terrorist attack on their communities. Many of them couldn't read, so the notices describing the women as 'non-militant' meant nothing. Others didn't know what the word 'non' meant, and so disregarded it. By the time the pilgrims reached Plymouth, however, things improved. Their numbers swelled and there was better advance publicity of their arrival. Exeter, on Saturday, 5 July, was a triumph. They were met at Totnes by NUWSS members from all over Devon who marched the twenty-six miles into the city with them. After a lavish tea party they processed into the centre to hold two open-air meetings before thousands of enthusiastic listeners. Helen Fraser made a defiant speech, reported with admiration in the *Western Times*:

> Of striking personality, a ready and convincing speaker, with a thorough knowledge of her subject, she commands instant attention. She opened her short address by moving a resolution urging the Government to bring in a Bill for the enfranchisement of women. She hastened to inform her audience that the NUWSS was entirely distinct from the militant section of the Women's Suffrage movement, and with whose methods they did not agree . . . During their march through the city she had noticed, as elsewhere in the pilgrimage, the amused look and laughter of people along the route which seemed to say, 'Poor foolish women.' Those who were taking part in this campaign did not like being laughed at any more than would any of the men in that audience, and did they think they would do what they were doing, leave their homes and march behind flags and submit to the laughter [and derision] of onlookers, were it not for a cause they heartily and sincerely believed in? Well, opponents could laugh now, but the Suffragists would laugh last . . . They were going to win, let there be no mistake about that; they would get the vote as surely as the sun would rise on the morrow.[9]

That same day, four members of the Great North Road contingent –
still shaken by their experiences in Ripon – decided on an afternoon
off. They chose to visit the romantically picturesque surroundings of
Fountains Abbey, hoping to spend a few hours not as suffragists, for
once, but as tourists. The portly attendant recognized them, however; he must have been to one of their meetings and was still firmly
convinced that these were dangerous women. He took their money,
but as soon as they were through the gate he started shadowing
them. Not being fools, the pilgrims were well aware of this; they
could hear him huffing and puffing away behind them, dodging
inadequately behind a bush whenever they turned round, but – as
they steadily increased their pace – dropping further and further
behind. In the end they managed to lose him altogether. Thanks
to this gentleman and his antics, they enjoyed the afternoon even
more than they had anticipated. After presenting him with a neatly
folded suffrage pamphlet and the sweetest of smiles when they left,
they returned to Harrogate, where they were billeted that night,
with renewed spirits. The next leg of their journey, through west
and south Yorkshire to Derbyshire, went smoothly. Each day more
supporters joined them, often arriving at points along the route on
trains from outlying districts.

The pilgrims' confidence grew with every step. Journalists
reported them looking dusty but fit; a little tanned, perhaps, but
otherwise inoffensive. At Leeds they were paraded through the
streets by the Armley and Wortley Brass Band and held two huge
rallies, one at Roundhay Park and the other on Woodhouse Moor.
Wakefield welcomed them with enthusiasm, which waned only when
an aeroplane flew overhead during a meeting – much more exciting
– and when a group of lads inflamed by the antis the previous day
got over-excited, started throwing stones (which found their mark)

and had to be calmed down by the police with a hosepipe.[10]

Every week, thanks to an elaborate distribution system, itin-
erant pilgrims received the latest copy of the *Common Cause* and
caught up with the progress of other routes. The issue published
on Friday, 4 July informed them that not only were the Watling
Street, Great North Road and Land's End pilgrims about a third of
the way towards London already, but that a group had now set off
from Bangor in north Wales; on the opposite side of the country,
the north Kent pilgrims had left Margate on 1 July and their southern counterparts marched out of Sandwich two days later. Those
two bands would meet in a fortnight or so at Tonbridge and walk
the Kentish Pilgrims' Way together. The pilgrims on the final two
routes – the Portsmouth Road and the Brighton Road – had yet to
begin their journeys, and were at this moment feverishly engaged in
last-minute planning.

The Watling Street group was due to arrive at Liverpool the day
the *Common Cause* was published. A festive welcome awaited them
from a host of dignitaries and thousands of supporters. Suffragist
Councillor Eleanor Rathbone – later an MP and architect of the
Family Allowance system – would be there, as well as the Pankhursts'
old friend Keir Hardie, who recognized a good opportunity for publicity when he saw one. But so too would be hordes of working men
and women unable to march themselves, determined to show their
support just by being there.

Gladys Duffield and her companions were in good heart when
they reached Liverpool. Gladys had finally realized the point of the
Pilgrimage at Ormskirk, some fourteen miles north. There, farm
labourers were holding their first union-backed strike, supported by
local railway workers. Times were hard and the future uncertain.
As these voteless women visited them in their homes or at street-
corner meetings, a strong sense of solidarity developed between the
pilgrims, some of whom were working women themselves, and the
people they met. Emily Murgatroyd, for example, knew fine well

what it was like to manage a home, a family and a career on next to nothing, and to be disempowered to make changes. One of her sister marchers from Lancashire had brought up nineteen children.[11] The song chosen by the Watling Street pilgrims as their anthem truly meant something here:

From East to West we gather now,
But one in purpose set.
Oh! ye who need the women's vote,
We'll be victorious yet.
Men join the women of our land
And march with us today,
Come one and all, a dauntless band,
And who shall say us nay?

They shall not scorn our just demand,
Our freedom still deny;
We're marching in our thousands now
And this our reason why.[12]

A young policeman came up to Gladys at Ormskirk and confessed to her that he would much rather women had the vote than men. Women *understood*.

It would be fascinating to learn how male participants responded to the rite of passage represented by the Pilgrimage. Each route included at least a handful of male marchers at any one time, but apart from Laurence Housman's rather stylized and piecemeal account of weathering 'chickens gone wrong' in London, I have not come across any first-hand account by a man. They are mentioned in other people's diaries occasionally, coming to the rescue when scuffles turned nasty, or speaking at meetings. Several high-profile gentlemen sponsored them. But what did they think? Did they march because they believed that it was morally the right thing to do? Or to protect the ladies? How many of them had the vote themselves? Did they resent comments like the Ormskirk policeman's? None of these questions can be answered. However, the men must surely have been as surprised at the tenacity, stamina and feistiness of their female companions as the women appear to have been themselves. This march was a revelation to everyone involved, from the most timid of onlookers to fearless old campaigners like Muriel Matters, armoured in her mackintosh against all the unlovely artillery that came her way.

Following this heart-stirring episode at Ormskirk, where she felt like a woman of the people, it was confusing for Gladys to arrive at St Helens into the arms of one of the richest families in the area. She and Edith Eskrigge stayed with the Pilkingtons, famous glass manufacturers (who were no doubt enjoying a boost in fortune thanks to window-smashing suffragettes). Gladys was mortified on reaching her bedroom to find that her unprepossessing little suitcase had been meticulously unburdened of its grubby contents by the maid. The very next day she went out to buy a new one.

About three hundred Watling Street pilgrims left Liverpool on the morning of 5 July. One hundred and fifty crossed the Mersey to Birkenhead, where another fifty were waiting to greet them, including Birkenhead resident Alice New (1890–1975), her mother, her sister Hilda and her aunt, a Miss Dalby. Their travelling arrangements were complicated and demonstrate how tricky it could be to fit the Pilgrimage into busy lives. Auntie had hired a caravan, like the *Ark* and the *Sandwich*, but couldn't pick it up until she got to Chester that night. She wasn't up to walking far, so she also hired a car, in which she and a few other slightly less energetic pilgrims were driven by Alice's mother at the tail-end of the procession. Motor vehicles were always relegated to the back, to mitigate critics' taunts that this was not a Pilgrimage at all, merely a joy-ride. Gladys Duffield was with them, having found a seat in a charabanc that was also coming along to Chester for the ride. Hilda had a bicycle, which she rode from

Birkenhead to Chester before promptly turning round and riding back, as she wasn't free to join the Pilgrimage proper for another ten days. Alice and five other women also rode bikes, including the indefatigable Edith Eskrigge.

Edith was used to cycling. Like Millicent Fawcett, she embraced the independence offered to modern women by a bicycle and regularly used to disappear from her home in Wallasey on the Wirral for weekend jaunts, alone with her two wheels and a knapsack. The great thing with cycling was that, even though it encouraged women to rely on themselves, which many thought both dangerous and unseemly, it had the undeniable benefit of being good exercise. As long as one wore a skirt of some heavy material unlikely to billow about embarrassingly, or sewed lead weights into one's hem, it was perfectly possible to cycle and keep one's reputation intact. When time allowed, Edith would ride all the way from Wallasey to London and take holidays to Ireland or Wales, travelling entirely under her own steam (apart from the crossing, of course). I suspect that reputation was an irrelevance to her. If she hadn't reached anywhere suitable to stay by nightfall, she simply slept out in the open, under the stars.

It was always energizing when new people joined the ranks of pilgrims. The north Wales contingent arrived at Chester in the company of a larger-than-life American described by Gladys Duffield as 'a jolly lady voter from Denverciddy'. People thought she was permanently drunk because of her unfamiliar accent and treated her at first as a joke, but this cheerful academic from Colorado – a Mrs Breedon – soon settled into the unique rhythm of life on the road and, though at first she had intended only to march from Birkenhead to Chester, she decided to stay on and do the whole thing. The Watling Street pilgrims enjoyed her company. Several more Americans joined the Pilgrimage later on, inspiring British campaigners with tales of the wonderful things women could do when they had the vote.

For Alice New and her aunt, Chester was the first stop. They found their caravan waiting for them at an inn, with Polly the horse and a driver called Joseph. It had arrived too late for them to find a nice field for the night, so they had to stay where it was. Alice was delighted with her hammock, but Auntie announced that the 'real' bed was too hard. Gladys and the others must have envied them: as usual when they arrived at their overnight destination, the pilgrims were mustered together by Edith Eskrigge standing on a chair with a whistle, and they had to wait until everyone had been given their instructions about where they were to hold their meetings, where to eat and where to sleep before they could leave. At least Chester was a weekend stop: they would have a chance on Sunday to draw breath, wash linen, dress blisters, write letters, and perhaps go to church. Services were timetabled as closely as the rest of the Pilgrimage, with preachers carefully chosen for their bracing qualities and their sympathy to the Cause. They were not compulsory, however.

Alice and her aunt went to Chester Cathedral after preparing lunch and leaving it to cook on a state-of-the-art patent slow-cooker installed in the caravan. It poured down all day, which at least had the merit of proving the caravan watertight. At teatime they called at the house of the president of Chester Women's Suffrage Society, where Edith Eskrigge was billeted, to discuss a rather thorny topic. Auntie had not hired the caravan on her own. Her expenses were shared by the West Lancashire, West Cheshire and North-West Federation of Women's Suffrage Societies, which meant that Edith, being the official Pilgrimage organizer for these areas, had a say in who would ride in it with Alice and Auntie. Miss Herd from Liverpool would move in that night, they were told.

All that spirit of sisterhood and solidarity went out the window as soon as Alice heard this. Miss Herd was a terrible choice: she would take up far too much room, wrote Alice grumpily in her diary, as she was 'rather stout'. This was only Day Two; it was raining, Auntie was already complaining and, to top it all, they were to share their neat caravan with someone who would squash them into a corner and was probably exceedingly greedy. Alice was beginning to fall out of love with suffragism.

But not for long. The first stop on the route south from Chester was the village of Tarvin, where Cicely Leadley Brown had driven ahead in her car to arrange lunch. An old lady stood in her cottage garden and wished them all well, presenting Alice and her friend Jane Colquitt with a glorious bunch of orange-blossom. Unfortunately, while this was going on, mischievous children crept up on the caravan (and mild-mannered Miss Herd, who had been left on duty) and started tearing down a banner fixed to the back of it. Cicely was outraged – she was very quick-tempered, noted Alice with feeling – and had to be restrained from using fisticuffs. By the time the party reached Tarporley, however, on the evening of Monday, 7 July, all was comparatively well again. Cicely had calmed down, the banner was repaired, at that night's meeting nearly everyone present bought an NUWSS badge and Miss Herd, on further acquaintance, turned out to be 'the best-tempered person' Alice had ever met. This journey was full of surprises.

8

SUFFERAGE

The Pilgrimage continues

It is difficult to feel a holy pilgrim when one is called a brazen hussy.[1]

WHERE ON EARTH were those blessed keys? How stupid would it be if weeks of minute preparation and a whole day's caravan-cleaning on Saturday should come to nought, just because someone had stashed the keys to the *Ark* somewhere safe and then forgotten where? On the morning of Monday, 7 July, Marjory Lees was feeling harassed and rather cross – not at all serene like a proper pilgrim. After a frenzied last-minute search the offending keys were eventually found in a corner of the caravan itself, and she was able to set off just about on time. Scholes reported for duty at Marjory's Oldham house, Werneth Park; he then disappeared with Noah and the *Ark* towards Macclesfield – where his colleague Clapham was expected with Ham and the *Sandwich* – while Marjory bundled up some extra baggage and took the train, with her mother, to Stockport. There she met sixty-three pilgrims from the Manchester area who were planning to join the Watling Street route with her. Full of high spirits, she waved goodbye to Mrs Lees and strode out with the others, smart, neat and a little naive.

The *Ark* was a great luxury – but then, the Leeses were wealthy women. Marjory was born in the Werneth area of Oldham in 1878. She and her sister grew up there with their mother and father, both of whom were noted philanthropists. Charles Lees was the head of a family firm of cotton-mill engineers, and when he died in 1894 the little family was left extremely well off. Marjory doesn't appear to have had very much formal education, but from 1902 she was involved with the Manchester University Settlement at Ancoats Hall. The Settlement was modelled on Toynbee Hall in London, where university staff and students worked for the social welfare and education of the working-class residents of the area. She was elected a Poor Law Guardian – as so many active suffragists were – in 1904 at the age of twenty-six.

Marjory Lees.

Marjory was tiny: thin as a reed, bespectacled and, in photo-graphs at least, usually smiling. When her mother, Sarah, became mayor in 1910, Marjory was appointed her consort, her mayoress. Just before the Pilgrimage, the two of them travelled to Budapest with Millicent Fawcett and nine other British delegates to take part in the Seventh Annual Congress of the International Suffrage Alliance. Both were heavily involved with their local suffrage society as well as with the National Union for Women Workers, and, though busy women, could obviously afford the money and the time to take a proactive part in the struggle for the vote. In fact, Sarah Lees was a major donor to the Pilgrimage funds, giving £200. Marjory donated a breathtaking £500 of her fortune – in today's terms, some £40,000. This would be something of a holiday for Marjory and her friends, a bit of a lark as well as a crusade. Little did they realize the dangers ahead: they may have read about other pilgrims' problems in Cornwall or Yorkshire, but surely nothing would happen to *them*, safe in their sturdy homes-from-home with Scholes and Clapham to protect them.

While Lady Rochdale addressed a meeting at Poynton, their first stop, Marjory managed to find a small confectioner's shop and ordered what she assumed would be a crafty snack before lunch. Just as she was finishing the last crumbs of cake, she was informed that there would be no time to stop for a proper midday meal, so she quickly crammed her pockets with as many gingerbread men as they could hold to keep her going until teatime. She was excited at the thought of her first night in the sparkling caravan, with all its equipment stowed away like toys, but unfortunately the suffrage ladies at Macclesfield had assumed the *Ark* to be a motor van and arranged an indoor berth for it at a garage. Marjory didn't fancy the inevitable petrol fumes, so she and Milly Field shared a vast room at the Macclesfield Arms instead.

The next morning was sunny. Spirits were still buoyant when the *Ark* was grudgingly given leave by a local organizer to bypass the venue for the lunchtime meeting: the caravan was too wide to negotiate the winding lane. Feeling as though they were playing truant, Marjory and her friends wickedly asked Scholes to pause on the main road at an inn. She noted triumphantly in her diary that they managed two lunches that day, nicely making up for the day before. They took the opportunity to rattle an NUWSS tin while they were at the inn and collected a few pence, even though some of their donors were drunk. Maybe *because* they were drunk. A woman driving by in a motor car stopped when she saw them and donated a whole shilling, despite being a member of the WSPU, and Noah the horse had a wonderful time prancing about to the sound of the jangling coins in the tin. (The novelty soon wore off. For the rest of the Pilgrimage he was inclined to be sluggish, unimpressed by the flicking handkerchief Scholes used in place of the whip he had carelessly left behind in Oldham.)

The next stop was Congleton. Then the pilgrims marched on through the Potteries towards Stoke by way of Burslem, where they met up with the Carlisle marchers on 9 July. So far, Marjory's Manchester contingent had been treated well. A few ineffectual clods of earth had been thrown at them in Macclesfield and a crotchety old woman they met in the mining village of Golden Hill had wished them dead, but there had been nothing to cause them serious concern. In fact, a potential lack of food seems to have been Marjory's greatest worry.

Alice New from Birkenhead, on the other hand, had never felt as frightened in her life as she did in the Potteries. She and Jane Colquitt were cycling that day while Auntie and Miss Herd stayed in the caravan with the driver, Joseph. Edith Eskrigge did not accompany the young women because one of her tyres had a puncture and she had gone off to get it mended. As Alice and Jane rode through Newcastle under Lyme, somehow separated from the rest of their party, they were pelted with coal and stones thrown not by disaffected men or youths but by mothers and children. Another woman came at them brandishing a spade and tried to knock them off their bicycles. In their panic, the two pilgrims became lost as they cycled up a steep hill, lungs bursting, literally in fear of their lives. They were forced to ask the way from 'a group of horrid men', who sent them in entirely the wrong direction.

Eventually they caught up with some of their companions motoring along in a bus, having been warned that things might turn nasty, and were rescued. Jane Colquitt declared that she never wanted to cycle anywhere again. Things did not improve as they neared Stoke. With good reason, Alice was terrified that their caravan might have been attacked in her absence. Later, she wrote down what happened:

> After some difficulty, we found out the field where the caravan was, and arrived to find the gate into the field surrounded by a hooting mob of children. A sorry sight met our eyes when we reached the van. All the posters and the federation banner had been torn off, and when we got inside the van, it was to find the whole place wrecked; broken crockery, squashed tomatoes, banana skins, rotten potatoes, stones and dirt all over everywhere, and the whole van smelled abominable.
>
> We found poor Miss Herd almost exhausted; she had had no tea, and she and Joseph had borne the brunt of the battle, which had been raging round the van for the last four miles of the journey. We heard all about it by degrees; how the van had been followed by about 500 children, who had amused themselves by tearing off our posters and throwing dirt and things at Miss Herd. They went over two miles before they saw any sign of a policeman, and then a plain-clothes man came up and walked along by the van. The women in the streets encouraged the children, and ran along by the van trying to lift small children on to the front, while Miss Herd, though terrified of hurting them, simply protected herself by knocking them off with a board. Miss Herd and Joseph were covered with dirt, and got dirt in their mouths and ears . . . The children followed right up to the gate of the field, and Miss Herd then informed them that if they wanted to come inside they must pay 1/-, which wonderful to relate, they believed![2]

The violence offered to these demonstrably peaceful women (temporarily excepting Miss Herd) must have been extremely shocking. We know little of Alice New's background except that she came from a liberal, artistic family; her father was an export manager for a soap company and her uncle was the well-known illustrator Edmund Hort New. Jane Colquitt was a cheerful and energetic campaigner for the Catholic League for Women's Suffrage in Liverpool.[3] Both were presumably bright, comparatively independent individuals, idealistic and unused to personal animosity of the kind they faced in Newcastle under Lyme and Stoke. But worse than this was the fact that those who wished them most harm were the very people for whose sake they marched. That must have been difficult to accept, and even more difficult to comprehend.

It was heartening that help came occasionally from unexpected quarters. A young suffragette who had been intending to come along and heckle the evening meeting at Stoke witnessed the attack on the caravan. She quickly ran to help Miss Herd and Auntie, staying with them until Alice and Jane arrived. And that night Mr Bark, a 'kind anti-suffrage gentleman', invited them to his home close by the caravan pitch for a meal and a hot bath. They had only one cup left intact in the caravan, and had not had a chance to clean up yet. Unfortunately, the gate between the field and Mr Bark's garden was permanently locked, so they had to clamber over it in the dark (it was 11 p.m. now), which was no joke for the well-upholstered Miss Herd. A policeman detailed to guard the caravan overnight expedited matters by fetching the caravan steps, propping them up by the gate, encouraging poor, spent Miss Herd up them and then shoving her from behind at the summit. 'Tired as I was,' remembered Alice, 'I could hardly keep from laughing at seeing Mr Bark and the policeman hauling her over.'

They enjoyed a hearty breakfast at Mr Bark's the next morning, too. Polly the horse recovered her poise after the upsetting events of the previous day, and on they went – the three caravans from Birkenhead and Oldham in convoy now, for safety – until they reached Birmingham on Saturday, 12 July. Or until most of them

Noah the horse pulls the Ark. *Marjory Lees is on the left.*

did: Marjory Lees went home to Lancashire for a few days at this point, for what she referred to coyly as 'an important occasion'. She and her mother, the former mayor, were to be presented to King George V and Queen Mary on their visit to the industrial north-west. Lady Rochdale was also on royal duty. As soon as they decently could, these Very Important Pilgrims rejoined their party.

The *Staffordshire Weekly Sentinel* was loath to publicize the fracas on the way to Stoke. Instead, in a short article surrounded by bland notices about the Uttoxeter Baby Show, Sweet Pea Growing and Promising Foals, it debated the fatuous question of whether these bizarre visitors should be allowed to call themselves Watling Street pilgrims if they didn't stick to the original Roman route all the way to London. It also pointed out how grateful they should be to local heroes Messrs Telford and McAdam for providing them with such magnificent roads. Perhaps it was in reaction to ubiquitous reports like this that Edith Eskrigge stopped everyone in their tracks on Friday afternoon so that she could get some letters of complaint written. She even promised to pay sixpence to the Pilgrimage funds if Jane Colquitt, who had recovered her usual chirpiness, could manage to keep quiet for half an hour while Edith worked.

Birmingham was the perfect place to recover. In fact, the closer the pilgrims got to the great city, the more cheerful they became. Stafford was an exception. The band sent to march them into the town consisted of a fife, a side-drum and a cornet, two of the players in bowler hats and the other in a straw one. They looked and sounded pathetic. Margaret Ashton[4] was badly kicked at the meeting – her ankle was still sore more than a week later – and the wheels of Alice New's bicycle were tied together and the tyres let down, neither of which she noticed at first on collecting it in the dark at the end of the evening. This was when she learned the salutary lesson that if you want to keep yourself and your equipment intact when you're on your own, don't display your suffrage colours. At Shrewsbury some young women with infants and babes-in-arms joined the march as far as Wolverhampton, the little ones done up adorably in red, green and white. It is tempting to imagine that Emily Sproson was there, robustly cheering them on. It is she, incidentally, who used to spell 'suffrage' with an 'e' in the middle; whether deliberately or not, I'm unsure.

The pilgrims were distracted from their own troubles at West Bromwich, where they met striking metalworkers, some of whom had not eaten for two or three days. Gladys Duffield was glad to give a family her own packed lunch; many of her companions did the same. Over a hundred suffragists from the Birmingham area walked out to Hockley to meet the pilgrims, and when they arrived in the city centre everyone was presented with a glamorous little souvenir box of chocolates in a cream-and-gilt box. These were provided by Miss Ethel Naish, an NUWSS member unable to take part in the Pilgrimage herself, and were not even local (i.e. Cadbury's): they came from the House of Lombart in Paris. Luxury was not something the pilgrims were accustomed to on the march, and this imaginative gesture was life-enhancing in a way that only very expensive plain chocolate can be.

Ethel Kenway was a suffragist from Edgbaston, an enthusiastic member of the local Pilgrimage committee. She wrote a breathless letter to relatives in Cornwall after helping to host the pilgrims in Birmingham, reproduced here just as it was written. It gives us a refreshing flavour of the excitement that met these campaigners along the way: there were plenty of bouquets among the brickbats. It is now Tuesday, 15 July and Ethel has been longing to sit down to write and tell Aunt Sophie all about it, 'but yesterday after all was over I felt too tired . . .'

> Well for some time we had been looking forward to the arrival here of the pilgrims Mrs Hughes Miss Weiss and I had undertaken to provide the tea when the poor dusty things arrived at Queens College[5] & had begged eggs fried &c. & got the different departments at stores to give us cost price & Miss Drum cooked salmon for their Sunday lunch. There were heaps of preparations & lots of committees to see all went off well. Then we heard they would arrive near Farm St at 5.30 so at five we all went down to our [NUWSS] office & bearing in front a huge banner Law Abiding headed by [a] large brass band & carrying flags we all set out thro' the town collecting money & giving literature – of course we excited great interest & many well known people & a good long procession of us followed by carriages . . .
>
> At first we all felt it a horrible duty but the police protected us well & the crowd were pleasant & Annette & I laughed & laughed . . . then as we got near Farm St there were all the pilgrims looking so weary but being bright & they told us after when they heard our band & saw all of us they were beyond words comforted. There was Lady Rochdale (looking so dirty she was refused a bed at [the] Grand Hotel), Councillor Margaret Ashton Mrs Lees & daughter Mayor of Oldham factory hands everyone all one together for the Cause . . . all so enthusiastic and happy – all the smaller luggage in a motor and followed with two dear elderly ladies who couldn't walk [Miss Herd and Auntie?] in caravans. They had had rough treatment but on the whole a good reception it is to show that militants

are not the body of suffrage workers. One woman a fine Lancashire worker had had 19 children mostly now grown up[6] and she had left all tidy at home and 28 pairs of darned socks – another had washed her hair brushes [and] all her clothes and ironed them while resting here. Such a fine dignified set of women . . . I am so glad it has been so successful and is over.[7]

The Watling Street pilgrims were not the only ones in need of a little rest and recuperation. The gentle West Country group had a terrible time in Wiltshire, where they were regularly mobbed and suffered physical assaults ranging from a tomato in the face for Annie Ramsay to – if we are to read between the lines – attempted rape. Annie reckoned half the trouble was due to Emily Davison having wrecked the Derby, thus losing thousands of punters the money they laid on as bets. It is noticeable that different regions of the country reacted to these campaigners in strangely coordinated ways. With certain exceptions, people in northern towns and villages along both the Watling Street and the Great North Road routes were reported as being generally interested in what the pilgrims had to say (unless it was the local Show Day); in the Midlands, except for Birmingham itself, they were suspicious and defensive; parts of Oxfordshire and Buckinghamshire were lethal.

Southern pilgrims on the Essex, Kentish, Sussex and Hampshire routes did not experience the same levels of aggression as the others, but reported more ignorance and apathy, despite their own passionate commitment to the Cause. That might seem surprising, given these areas' comparative proximity to London. Perhaps places closer to the capital fell between two stools, not being near enough to be influenced by activities there, nor far enough away to have strong suffrage identities of their own. Or maybe women in the south and south-east were simply not engaged by the campaign and, generally having enough work to do and food to eat, did not recognize a need to fight for the vote. Certainly, Kent did not appear to be a fertile hunting ground for Margaret Nevinson when she toured there in a suffrage caravan in 1908. Parked up during a rainstorm in Canterbury one day, she was surprised to hear a desperate little voice outside the door. 'Please let me in,' it said. 'I am the only suffragette in Canterbury!'[8]

At Bristol on 14 July, the Land's Enders were joined by a Welsh contingent from Pontypridd and Blaenavon; four days later a group from Gloucester met them at Marlborough. This latter company was somewhat battered and bruised, having suffered at the hands of audiences incited by the usual band of antis holding a rally just before the pilgrims arrived at successive destinations. The press had also been unkind. 'What do those hieroglyphics stand for?' sneered a journalist confronted with the initials of the National Union of Women's Suffrage Societies, before warning his readers to steer well clear of these pseudo-pilgrims. They are parasites, he insisted, demanding hospitality from male heads of households and shamelessly begging for motor cars, carts, beds for the night and money. Real pilgrims only need a staff to walk with, not all this paraphernalia. They expect comfortable quarters where they can unwrap their luggage, sent on ahead, 'deck themselves out in their finery, and if they are permitted, stand out in the market place and criticise men, some of whom have perhaps contributed to their enjoyable little holiday.'[9]

Cheltenham is a nice place for a holiday. There, the pilgrims' banners were snatched by a crowd of several hundred men and women and the poles supporting them snapped and flung away. Troublemakers constantly rang hand-bells during the speeches so no one could hear, and when the meeting was eventually abandoned the local Unitarian minister, who had been attempting to keep order, was hit in the eye by a missile. Two Gloucester pilgrims, Miss Bode and Miss Hutton, tried to escape on their bicycles but were chased down Regent Street, pushed to the ground and then pinned against some railings while their hats 'and other articles of clothing' were torn from them. Luckily, Police Constable Turner turned up with a group of what were described in the local paper as respectable working men to rescue them, before 'the threat of even further indignities had been carried out.'[10] This atavistic behaviour was chillingly reminiscent of Black Friday.

A little further down the road, in Cirencester, they were put through the mill again when students from the Royal Agricultural College rushed the lorry they were using as a platform. Rushing was a popular form of Edwardian protest – we have seen how the suffragettes kept trying to rush Parliament – and involved people linking arms in a long line and lurching backwards and forwards, an increasing number of steps at a time, until an irresistible momentum was built up, destroying almost everything in its path. Annie Ramsay said she thought she was going to die when the breath was squeezed out of her with each surge of the crowd. Some of the students dressed offensively in drag for the occasion. They tried to upturn the lorry and pummel the speakers, again tugging at their clothes before besieging them in the house to which they had managed to escape, bruised and utterly terrified.

A similar fate befell the Great North Road travellers at Mansfield in Nottinghamshire. Millicent Fawcett counted it a mark of honour that she was present, having been invited to join the Pilgrimage for a while at that point. She witnessed the throwing of dead rats, plump with maggots, at her suffragist sisters; a male sympathizer being crushed against the platform; the filthiest obscenities flying through the air like hailstones. As well as appalling her, it made her feel proud that, at last, the NUWSS had an opportunity to show its mettle.

If truth be told, Mrs Fawcett preferred the eastern route, especially when it passed through Cambridge where she had helped to establish the local Women's Suffrage Society in 1884. The *Cambridge Daily News* was as generous in its coverage of women's suffrage activities as the *Manchester Guardian* and the *Daily News*, sometimes listing every single person in a parade or at a meeting. Cantabrigian pilgrims

Pilgrims from Newnham and Girton Colleges, Cambridge.

tended towards quiet confidence, were used to a measure of intellectual authority, yet their unofficial motto was 'the Power of Love'.[11] Their arguments appealed to the heart *and* to the mind – following the Fawcett creed – and audiences responded with attentiveness. It would be interesting to know how many converts they made.

Pilgrimage policy dictated that whenever possible a follow-up meeting should be held the morning after a riot. This served several purposes. It gave the pilgrims a chance to show that they were neither cowed (even if privately they quaked in their boots) nor ready to give up (although a few did, unable to stomach the stress). A calmer atmosphere meant that they were more likely to get their message across and it was important that, like lovers after a tiff, they should leave with a conciliatory kiss rather than a sullen scowl. It was also an opportunity to discuss publicly what had gone wrong the night before. It soon became apparent that the problem of the suffragettes was more complex than originally thought. It wasn't just that the pilgrims were being confused with militants; even if audiences appreciated what the law-abiding campaigners stood for, they were still attacked for refusing to condemn suffragette outrages from the platform. Pilgrimage speakers were always encouraged to point out the difference between the 'gettes and the 'gists, particularly for those in the audience who couldn't read, but the NUWSS refused to turn the campaign for women's suffrage into an internecine war. This mission was not principally about self-publicity, nor about discrediting the WSPU: it was about the vote. That was the common prize, the Holy Grail.

It was awkward, therefore, that the timing of the Pilgrimage coincided with some of the most vigorous militant activity of the whole campaign. WSPU members were reacting to what they considered to be the government's ultimate act of barbarism: the 'Cat and Mouse' Act, designed to prevent a rapidly increasing number of hunger strikers from becoming martyrs to the Cause. More properly called the 1913 Prisoners (Temporary Discharge for Ill-Health) Act, it legislated for the release of suffragettes so weakened by hunger or damaged by forcible feeding that they were in danger of death, on condition that they returned to jail at the end of an agreed term. The idea was that by then they should have recovered sufficiently to serve out the rest of their sentence. If they failed to present themselves to the authorities at the appointed time, the police had powers to seek them out and re-arrest them. No warrant was required to enter a house where prisoners were suspected of hiding, and failure to comply with the terms of the Act would result in extended sentences.

Occasionally, and up to a point, it worked. Discharged suffragettes might report back to Holloway, Winson Green, Strangeways or wherever they had been incarcerated on the expiry of their temporary reprieve and obediently disappear inside – but with predictable results. They promptly resumed their hunger strike, and so the grisly cycle began all over again. However, there is no such thing as a meek suffragette and it was more common for prisoners, including Emmeline and Sylvia Pankhurst, to try their utmost, weak as they were, to evade re-arrest.

If they were seriously ill on release, which most by definition were, they were immediately taken somewhere to recuperate under medical supervision. Suffragette nurse Catherine Pine ran a private nursing home in London's Notting Hill, where she and her staff worked day and night to help prisoners convalesce. Her mission was to build them up enough to go into hiding elsewhere. There was usually a gaggle of 'cats', or policemen, outside the nursing home, waiting to pounce on patients kept in beyond the specified date of their re-arrest; it was crucial that Nurse Pine should send her charges on their way within the period allowed, and equally important that the police should not see where they went next.

Members of the WSPU from all over the British Isles offered their own houses as 'mouse havens' where stealthy prisoners could stay until the opportunity arose to move on, and on again after that, perhaps changing appearance and identity each time until the police lost track of them. Militant members of the Actresses' Franchise League provided costumes for disguise and tips on how to change one's voice and gait. For those of an adventurous or perhaps a reckless disposition, these were exciting times. There was an unofficial corps of volunteers on hand to join in the espionage. One day Una Duval was asked to help 'spring' the notorious activist Lilian Lenton, temporarily released to a house in Leeds. Mrs Duval (who was in her mid-thirties) dressed up as an errand boy. Carelessly munching an apple, she sauntered in front of the policeman guarding the house in question to deliver a small hamper. She offered to carry it inside. Perhaps the policeman was fooled by the hamper's size: no chance of hiding a suffragette in there. Lilian was waiting for Una and, as soon as the front door closed behind them, the two women swapped outfits. Out came the errand boy a few moments later, chewing on the self-same apple. Lilian got away.

In a corner of the Museum of London there is a haunting display of images taken by police photographers in 1913 and 1914. Their subjects are women wearing prison dress or numbered labels, many with shadowed eyes and hollow cheeks; some with loose and greasy hair, a few smiling unguardedly but most looking jaded and tired. These are the first surveillance photographs of a terrorist organization ever taken, snapped covertly while the women were out in the exercise yard of their jail and later used by enforcers of the Act to identify fugitive 'mice'. That's why disguises were so important.

Faces like the Pankhursts' were already too well known to require verification, or − one would have thought − to attempt disguise. (Nevertheless, on the Pilgrimage an onlooker once managed to mistake stout little Annie Ramsay for the soignée Mrs Pankhurst until someone put him right: 'You're a fool. Mrs Pankhurst is a thin 'un and this one is a thick 'un.'[12]) But Emmeline still managed to dodge police officers with the help of a decoy, aided by the veil she sometimes wore. It was doubly difficult for her: not only were the police more than interested in her every move, but members of the press constantly pursued her for pictures, stories, breaking news about escapes and outrages. One of the most sensational 'Cat and Mouse' episodes was Mrs Pankhurst's re-arrest when on her way to join Emily Wilding Davison's funeral procession. She had been released from Holloway on 30 May and failed to report back as instructed a week later.

Her daughter Christabel was by this time living in Paris, where she had fled in 1912 in an attempt to control the WSPU remotely, free from the personal attentions of the police. While Emmeline was still the figurehead of the militant campaign, Christabel was its increasingly despotic chief executive. WSPU staff used regularly to cross the Channel for briefings, and Christabel did not return to England until the autumn of 1914, after war was declared.

Meanwhile, Sylvia found herself alienated from her mother and sister, whose leadership style and political ideology frustrated her. Her socialist principles led her to form an East London Federation of Suffragettes in May 1913. She ran this as a separate outfit with its own organizers, branches and activities. It was Sylvia's belief that the working population of the East End represented the suffrage campaign's most potent weapon: a massed body of activists united by class, location, life experience and political conviction. Meanwhile, she continued her militant activities while lobbying for the repeal of the 'Cat and Mouse' Act. On 7 July, the day Marjory Lees set off from Oldham, Sylvia spoke at a public meeting in London and was subsequently arrested. She immediately refused both food and drink and was temporarily released under the Act a few days later. She managed to evade the police until 27 July, occasionally appearing in public to address meetings before escaping at the last possible moment. For the rest of the year she was in and out of prison, on and off hunger strike, more or less in control of herself and her mission: suffrage indeed.

The WSPU stepped up its campaign of violent protest in response to the Act. 'Londoners are beginning to be afraid that fear of the suffragettes will have a bad effect on the social season,'[13] fretted someone in *The Times* in February 1913, before the Act was passed; come July, the papers were reporting bombings, arson, assaults on Cabinet ministers, tens of thousands of pounds' worth of damage to public and private property. The public were very afraid, not only in the capital.

One response was humour. What should be done with these unwomanly women? How about deporting them, like convicts, to some already unsavoury part of the world? One Member of Parliament nominated St Helena; a waggish writer in the *Surrey Comet* had other ideas:

> *Oh let the militants be cast*
> *At once in durance vile*
> *To think about their mis-spent past*
> *Upon some lonely isle.*
>
> *Alas! The nut is hard to crack;*
> *T'would surely not be right*
> *To put them, as their sins are black,*
> *Upon the Isle of Wight.*

And there would be exciting times
If we devised a plan
To exile women for their crimes
Upon the Isle of Man.

You could not find a better spot
Altho' you searched for miles,
To which to ship the blessed lot,
I mean, the Scilly Isles.[14]

An alternative response was to fight back, which is what the police felt they were doing under the terms of the 'Cat and Mouse' Act, what rioters were doing when they attacked pilgrims, and what the pilgrims themselves were doing, passively, with every step they took.

Harriet Blessley (1873–1964) from Portsmouth knew only too well what militancy could lead to: her brother Frederick had been arrested in June 1913, just before she set off on the Pilgrimage, for deliberately breaking a window in the town hall. When the magistrate asked him why he had done it, he explained rather vaguely, 'Well, you see, for some time I have been very much interested in the question of women's votes, and . . . the warfare and militancy that women are going in for is very largely a question of breaking windows. It is rather a piffling, idiotic way of going about it, I admit.'[15] Frederick sounds like one of Bertie Wooster's chums, caught out in some foolish jape for which he realizes he must pay the price. He did pay the price, preferring to settle a fine than go to jail.

Harriet, I'm sure, gave him short shrift. His gesture hardly bathed him or the Cause in glory. To be a pilgrim was a far grander thing than chucking a stone at a municipal pane of glass. There is

Setting off from Portsmouth, 17 July 1913.

something of Kate Frye about Harriet Blessley. Both were energetic, self-confident women who did not suffer fools gladly and knew how to enjoy themselves. Harriet's diary of the Pilgrimage is wonderfully candid. Perhaps that's a characteristic shared generally by Portsmouth people: when a local vicar addressed the crowds on Thursday, 17 July, the day the pilgrims left, he didn't mince his words. There was too much barracking going on: *pipe down*. He told the crowd that personally he didn't care tuppence for votes for women, but he did want them to have justice and fairness. He asked his 'brother sports of Pompey' to be 'courteous and kind and civil to those ladies who came there at great inconvenience and trouble to speak to them.'[16]

It wasn't the noise that bothered Harriet, it was everything else. A young lad bawled 'Down with Women!' at her as soon as she left the house, feeling horribly conspicuous in her suffragist colours. By the time she reached the send-off meeting by the town hall she was already 'hot and smelly'. The band played marches at too fast a tempo – 'to suit masculine strides' – and she had a job keeping up. Then someone threw a tomato at her hat.

The next day, a gentleman called Dick who had walked with her yesterday pathetically pleaded a chill and took to his bed. One of the contingent's main speakers, Miss O'Shea, couldn't project her voice enough to be heard. They ran out of NUWSS pamphlets on their third day, at Petersfield, where the meeting did not go well.

> Chair taken by Vicar, who it appears is very unpopular. Crowd won't listen. Cannot convince them we are not militants . . . Labour man tries his hand . . . No avail. Miss O'Shea asks for literature. Not having enough 'Protests against Militancy' I go to wagonette in stable at end of High Street to get some more. Come back and find meeting dispersing. Cannot find my party or hostess. Run into a hooligan crowd, who try to snatch my collecting box and leaflets. Policeman comes to my rescue, and escorts me through crowd to the Hotel . . . Crowd follows and waits outside. My hostess joins me, and we wait inside, till crowd disperses, and sneak out with colours down [i.e. in mufti]. I feel a coward.[17]

Appropriately enough for one who insisted she was 'like a real pilgrim going to a Holy Shrine', at Petersfield Harriet had a moment of epiphany: militancy was the work of the devil. She avowed to be 'more firmly non-militant' from now on, as violence could only breed violence. How frustrating it was that the crowds refused to respect or even to accept the suffragists' pacifism. 'When we are not militant they accuse us of being wealthy and leisured women who want to get power.' Or they taunt them as suffragettes in disguise. 'It is difficult to feel a holy pilgrim when one is called a brazen hussy.'

Harriet's diary was obviously never designed – as Marjory's and Alice's were – to be read by family and friends. It is not polite. Though most of the meetings were attended by a majority of men, she explains that she always tries to buttonhole working women because

they are patently more intelligent than their husbands and brothers. More indisputable truisms emerge as the diary progresses. Most
suffragists are vegetarians (the lowest of the culinary low). Having
a title does not confer superiority in any way: Lady Selborne, for
example, who joins them at Liphook, is an unimpressive speaker. A
pilgrim who turns up at Waterlooville is unbelievably morose, wearing funereal garb with black kid gloves, a black hat perched stupidly
on the side of her head, and a deeply dismal expression. Someone else
is summarily dismissed as 'a little oddity with short legs'; another,
who is a lady gardener, is lanky and untidy. In Godalming Harriet is
billeted with 'the most melancholy suffragist I have met', who makes
her feel as though guests are a trial to be endured. Apparently her
hostess has a weak digestion and, if over-excited, is apt to collapse.
What fun. 'I am enjoying myself immensely,' writes Harriet – and
actually, she means it.

Meanwhile, further north, the Watling Street pilgrims were
also enjoying themselves. At Stratford-upon-Avon Marjory Lees
was allowed to lay a special wreath on Shakespeare's grave (though
the meeting there was unruly). Gladys Duffield went with Mrs
'Denverciddy' Breedon to see Anne Hathaway's cottage, and Alice
New was glad of a chance to relax for a while in the cleaned-up
caravan and reflect on the past few days. At Birmingham, she and
a delighted Auntie had been presented with a beautiful new set of
crockery by Major Cecil Wedgwood (of Wedgwood china), who
had heard of their trouble at Stoke and wanted to show his support
for the Pilgrimage. Shortly afterwards, Alice was joined on the road
by a young woman who had nipped out to buy some sugar, come
across the pilgrims and spent the rest of the day with them. Poor
Jane Colquitt fainted at teatime, which caused some excitement. Her
foot had been injured by the crowds a few days previously, but she
had not told anyone and now it was infected and hurting badly. That
evening, to cheer everyone up, Gladys played the piano for singing practice in a village tea room and then gave a little impromptu

concert, which is when Cicely Leadley Brown's extraordinary talent was discovered. She was a virtuoso whistler. Her whistling was so beautiful it brought tears to the eyes. You could have heard a pin drop when she finished, remembered Alice, so lost was everyone in dreamy admiration.

Some interesting new personnel joined the Pilgrimage at Stratford: an amiable man called Mr Valentine from Manchester, who was giving up his summer holiday to walk with them to London, and a group of Oxford and Cambridge undergraduates on holiday there, who marched them out of the town playing rousing tunes with combs and brown paper. Lancashire suffragist Selina Cooper was the proud owner of a group photograph taken on the lawns outside a girls' school at Stratford, featuring her friend Emily Murgatroyd together with about fifty more women and a handful of men, apparently including the student from Balliol College, Oxford – referred to by several of the women – who stayed with them all the way to London and was six foot seven inches tall. He is sensibly standing at the back. Some new banners have arrived. One says 'A Fair Fight and No Favour', another 'The Vote. The Keystone of Liberty'.

When the pilgrims reached the village of Kineton, ten miles south of Stratford, they were invited by Lord and Lady Willoughby de Broke to camp in the splendid grounds of their family seat, Compton Verney. The Willoughby de Brokes were keen suffragists and did all they could to make their many guests comfortable, providing tents (courtesy of the Red Cross), extra mattresses, lots of blankets, boiled water and unlimited bread, milk and eggs. Cicely the whistler cooked scrambled eggs, much to Alice New's delight: 'Really, I believe that girl could turn her hand to anything, and she was the life of the party, too!' Unfortunately it rained heavily all night – so heavily that people put umbrellas up inside their tents – but everyone seems to have treated the Compton Verney stop like a holiday, except Gladys. She was invited to stay in the Big House with Lady Rochdale and Pilgrimage organizer Katherine Harley, who, along with her daughter, had joined the Watling Street route for a spell. Gladys was still embarrassed about her luggage: granted, the suitcase was new, but her striped flannelette nightdress had definitely seen better days and she feared the maids would snigger at it. She soon recovered her spirits, however, cheered by a tea party with Marjory Lees and her Oldham friends aboard the *Ark*. By the time they all reached Oxford on Saturday, 19 July, she was complimented by an onlooker who said it seemed as though she was having the time of her life. Oh, I am, replied Gladys, I am.

Someone else who relished this adventure was Vera Chute Collum (1883–1957), who joined the Watling Street pilgrims at the village of Drayton, just north of Banbury. Vera was a strong character, born in India of Irish–Australian parentage, who had travelled independently in Japan and the Far East and was currently working in the press department of the NUWSS and as a freelance journalist. She had been commissioned by the *Daily News* to be their special Pilgrimage correspondent, a post I suspect she invented for herself. She was also an experienced horsewoman. She placed a curious advertisement in the *Common Cause* on 27 June 1913: 'Wanted: a horse.' Vera explained her mission, and asked whether anyone could furnish her with a reliable mount. She planned to complete the last ten days of the Pilgrimage on horseback to give her a good vantage point for taking notes and photographs; she would be able to get to telegraph and post offices easily to file reports and collect instructions – and anyway, she liked horses. They were much more rewarding than cars or bicycles.

Vera promised that she would look after the animal with the utmost care: 'I have never yet let a horse down.' She hoped to accommodate it en route in suffragist supporters' stables or respectable inns with clean and airy equestrian quarters. She also needed a bridle and a saddle, by the way – not a side-saddle – and perhaps a roomy knapsack left over from some military campaign.

Her request must have been successful, for there she was in

Drayton, beaming in her knickerbocker suit and a hat curiously reminiscent of a sola topi, sitting astride a calm and comfortable-looking
steed with three white socks and a neat white blaze on its forehead.
The pilgrims were deeply impressed. The reports Vera sent to both
the *Common Cause* and the *Daily News* are beautifully written, with
just the right balance of good humour, respect and understated heroism. Here is how she opens her first dispatch:

> They call it a peaceful pilgrimage, but in this long thin line of one
> hundred tan-faced women swinging along in easy comradeship
> there is more of the spirit of conquering pioneers trekking into some
> new country of which they have quietly determined their right to
> take possession than of the meek spirit of old-time pilgrims laying
> unction to their souls for an arduous task painfully accomplished.
>
> Your correspondent picked them up a few miles outside
> Banbury on Friday night. They were camped by the roadside taking
> their afternoon rest, and had just held a meeting for the cottag-
> ers and been entertained to tea themselves in the rectory garden.
> A shrill whistle sounded, and the pilgrims scuttled to their places;
> the roll was called, the banners grounded ready to hoist aloft, and
> another whistle blown to stand to attention. Then a sharp word of
> command from the marshal [Mrs Harley] – a sister, by the way, of
> our most famous cavalry commander – and the pilgrims moved off,
> the leaders carrying a big blue banner with the words 'Law Abiding'
> blazoned on it.
>
> In the middle of the procession was the 'Carlisle to London'
> banner, and marching just behind it, a slight figure in the regulation
> Pilgrim kit – a (once) white haversack with 'Watling-street route'
> printed on it, a red, white and green shoulder sash, and a straw
> cockade in the colours on the hat. This was Lady Rochdale, who
> had set out with the Carlisle contingent just a month before, and
> had tramped nearly all the way.[18]

Vera goes on to mention Marjory Lees, Alice New's caravan and
Gladys Duffield, 'a lady who has marched all the way from Lakeland

and who is such a light traveller and ideal campaigner that the rumour goes round that her luggage consists of two pocket handkerchiefs!' She describes a terrifying game she witnessed in Banbury when the crowd pretended to be hunters after a fox, shouting 'Vote! Vote! Vote!' as they rushed the speakers' platform:

> One pilgrim was rather badly crushed at Banbury against the iron gate of the house she was billeted on, and was only released from her tormentors – a crowd of about 30 boys, ranging in age from 11 to 19 – by her friends making a sortie armed with umbrellas and driving off the assailants who, no doubt, thoroughly enjoyed the whole affair and bore no malice for the shrewd knocks they got from the umbrella brigade.[19]

Unsuspecting 'sandwich men' about to be overwhelmed by women who do want votes.

With Vera riding magisterially as vanguard, the pilgrims arrived early at Oxford, and had to wait on the outskirts for the local contingent of supporters to accompany them into the city. As they approached St Giles' in the centre, they almost overtook an aimless group of six sandwich-board men hired by the antis. A photograph in one of the local papers captured the moment. The men, looking slightly bemused, are standing in the foreground with their posters confidently proclaiming that women do not want the vote. Behind them, apparently unnoticed, an endless procession of smiling suffragists approaches, banners held high, threatening to overwhelm them completely.

Oxford was a weekend stop, which gave the pilgrims time to catch up again with letters, sewing and news of the other routes. Many went sightseeing, taking off their suffrage colours just in case of trouble. After several weeks on the road, the pilgrims were getting canny. Marjory recorded a whimsical coincidence just as she and her friends were coming out of Balliol College: '[A] benevolent old gentleman and a girl got out of a taxi; there seemed something oddly familiar about him and we all looked at each other and exclaimed "Asquith!"' It was indeed their arch-enemy. Despite a college boat-house having recently been torched by the suffragettes, a meeting at the town hall went spectacularly well. People clamoured at the door and the place was packed. The organist rousingly played Wagner's *Tannhäuser* Overture as the speakers strode in, and Margaret Ashton's speech 'treating the question on broad human grounds and free from bitterness' (according to Marjory) went down a storm.

Marjory stayed at a hotel in Oxford, as the police had forbidden anyone to sleep in a caravan in case they were attacked in revenge for the boathouse episode. Gladys was put up in Corpus Christi College courtesy of the Classics scholar Arthur Sidgwick and his wife, and Alice went to stay with her Uncle Edmund, the artist. Edmund Hort New's banner for the Oxford Women Students' Society for Women's Suffrage is often described as one of the most beautiful designs of the whole campaign.[20]

On Monday morning everyone met outside St John's College, where a spontaneous collection was made for the boatyard men and their families put out of work by the suffragettes' fire. Then the pilgrims marched over Magdalen Bridge towards Headington, where they called to see the suffragist veteran Florence Davenport Hill, one of the signatories to John Stuart Mill's 1866 petition, and to present her with a bouquet of red and white roses. One by one their Oxford supporters began to turn back – apart from a couple more male undergraduates who stayed with them for the rest of the Pilgrimage – until a core of about seventy people remained. The antis were still in attendance: one lot arrived in a motor car and stopped to harangue them. Embarrassingly, once they had run out of insults, their car wouldn't start. Predictably, it was Cicely Leadley Brown who came to their rescue, cheerfully fiddling about in the car's innards until it was mended. No doubt they all parted the best of friends.

Marjory Lees enjoyed Oxford. There was something spiritual about the place that chimed well with the Pilgrimage. From Boar's Hill, she watched a particularly beautiful sunset, the city's domes and spires 'piercing the twilight', and must have felt as Harriet Blessley did as the final week of their journey began: that now, they were indeed true pilgrims.

9

WE ARE PEOPLE, TOO

The Pilgrimage concludes

The 'half-angel, half-idiot' era is over for women.[1]

NEITHER GLADYS DUFFIELD nor Alice New accompanied the pilgrims on their march from Oxford to Thame on Monday, 21 July. Lucky Gladys was allowed to stay in Oxford for an extra night; she planned to catch a train straight to High Wycombe on the 22nd and wait for the others there. This was a good opportunity to get her boots mended. There's a lovely cameo in her diary of a kindly old cobbler who lends her his slippers while he does his work. In return, Gladys quietly shuffles around his kitchen, tidying up for him. Alice and her sister cyclists were sent on a mission from Oxford to outlying villages to hold a few meetings along a different route. When they reached Thame, just in time for the evening event, Alice was informed that she was billeted in a guest room that night, not in the Birkenhead caravan at the recreation ground. So neither woman knew about Marjory Lees's terrifying ordeal until the next morning.

The meeting opened at 8 p.m. in the town centre. Organizers had decided to set up two platforms on wagons at either end of the market place as there were so many people around. Good news: twice the amount of literature sold, with any luck; twice the amount of money collected, of supporters enrolled and converts to the Cause.

Lady Rochdale clambered on to one of the platforms while Mrs Harley mounted the other.

Straight away there was trouble. As usual, the majority of the crowd consisted of young men, who immediately started shouting and singing at the tops of their voices (that's what Marjory and her friends could hear from their campsite, drifting over the evening air). Then the men devised a game of British bulldog, rushing en masse from one platform to the other until each wagon in turn was hit by a tsunami of people. This was extraordinarily dangerous. After some time the police managed to break up the meeting, extract the shocked platform speakers and order all suffragists to their rooms around the town without delay, but they couldn't control the crowd, some of whom were now making for the caravans.

From the frail sanctuary of the *Ark*, Marjory, Milly Field and Eda Sharples were all too aware of their arrival. When they heard matches being struck outside, they must have feared their hour had come. They had never thought of themselves as martyrs for women's suffrage. Marjory was a wealthy young(ish) woman with a well-developed social conscience and a strong-minded mother, who just wanted to do what was right. Her friends from Oldham were hardly a bunch of Emily Wilding Davisons: they included a brush-manufacturer's wife with five children and a council-school headmistress.[2] Were they really prepared to die for the vote?

Thanks to a local doctor, the ultimate question was never asked. He arrived with more policemen in the nick of time to persuade the crowd – one with natural authority, the others with the force of law – that mass murder was not a sensible idea from any point of view. The would-be arsonists reluctantly put away their lights and began to disperse. 'Good night, you suffragettes,' they called, beerily, as they went.[3]

It was a while before the shocked pilgrims could be induced out of the *Ark*. When they did emerge, it was to find the heroic doctor and policemen sifting through the damage by lamplight. The tent's guy ropes had been cut and its contents strewn about; there were great slits in the canvas and the horses' corn was scattered all over. Miraculously, however, a full collecting box of money was intact, and the caravans had come to no serious harm. Troupers that they were, the pilgrims' first thought was to make their saviours a hot drink and hand round the biscuits. Then, under police guard, they settled down once again to sleep, which did not come easily.

It was not until a day or two after the attack on the *Ark* that Marjory learned why it had been so vicious. Apparently there had been a meeting in the market place two days before, on Saturday, 19 July, organized by one of several groups opposed to women's suffrage. They had incited the crowd, warning them not only of the perils of giving women the vote, but of the outrageous behaviour of the approaching pilgrims, who (they said) were completely deranged and a danger to life and limb.

The next morning was market day. With remarkable courage, the war-torn pilgrims mustered outside the Spread Eagle hotel, right in the middle of town, and addressed the crowds again. While most of them sped off towards High Wycombe afterwards, led by Vera Chute Collum on her horse, a few stayed behind to hold yet another meeting, including the doughty Edith Eskrigge and Mrs Harley. This time all went well: they signed up a hundred new 'Friends of Women's Suffrage' and exorcised the demons of the previous night. But everyone knew, because the police had told them so, that worse was in store. The closer the pilgrims came to London, the more retribution they should expect, because that's where the militants did their dirtiest work.

The village of West Wycombe lies three miles outside Wycombe town. The pilgrims were given a warm welcome there from the local schoolmaster and his pupils, who were allowed out of class to listen to what these strange visitors had to say. They all had a tea party and another group photograph was taken in the school grounds before they rested for a while in the lee of the Chiltern Hills. Alice New's

The Pilgrimage reaches West Wycombe in Buckinghamshire.

copy of the photo shows men, women, children and babes-in-arms, most grinning broadly. Perhaps the doom-mongers were wrong: this appeared to be a very pleasant place indeed. Marjory tells us what happened next:

> At 7 p.m. we formed up and marched into High Wycombe behind the Town Band. As we got nearer the town the character of the crowd quite changed. I never before saw so many evil faces gathered together. Eda Sharples and I with some others were sent before the band to set the pace, the police did not go in front to keep the way clear as they had done in other places and the crowd pressed right upon us. We had been told High Wycombe would be rough and had sent the caravans on . . . to pitch in the drive of the Preparatory School. When our procession arrived at the Fountain where the open air meeting was to be held the pressure was tremendous and we didn't know where to halt. We went to the end of the Square and then some of the banner bearers began to furl their banners and the crowd surrounded them so we thought it best to disperse

and followed Miss Collum and her horse who was being personally conducted. We fell in with a lady who was returning from her
shopping and she shewed us the way. We climbed a steep hill by a
cemetery; every step we took away from the town gave us a greater
feeling of security.

Gladys Duffield did not escape so easily. She recalled High
Wycombe afterwards as 'a nightmare from which we did not waken
up.'[4] She happened to be standing right by the speakers' platform as
the crowds closed in; when Mrs Harley was knocked off it (injuring
herself) Gladys managed to get her to the safety of a nearby shop,
leaving her there to recover. There must have been a temporary lull
after that, because Gladys ventured outside again, but the crowd was
instantly inflamed by anyone seen in the suffrage colours, and at
five foot ten inches Gladys's height was hard to miss. Some pilgrims
said they recognized those 'evil faces' from Thame, and there were
suggestions that the antis, who had been holding their customary
rallies to forestall the pilgrims, had hired large groups of mercenary
ruffians to follow the suffragists from place to place.

Gladys attempted to take shelter at a couple of inns, but the
landlords threw her out as soon as she was spotted. *We don't want
troublemakers like you in here.* There was nothing for it but to tear off
everything red and green about her person – no doubt feeling like
St Peter as she did so – and try to fade into the background as a
mere onlooker. But she was too easily recognizable. Eventually she
retreated to a motor garage in a side street, where she hid trembling
amidst the dirt and fumes, with stones shattering the windows, until
it was dark.

Despite the travails of the Watling Street marchers, when people
discussed the Pilgrimage afterwards and compared the fortunes of
the various routes, the general consensus was that the Great North
Road contingent had the worst of things. They suffered horribly at
towns in the East Midlands. 'Mansfield throbbed with excitement

on Tuesday evening as it has not throbbed for years!' ran a memorable local newspaper report, describing what amounted to a riot involving thousands of people in terms of a group of locals 'intent on having a lark.'[5] The pilgrims did not always help themselves in this regard. In St Neots, a Miss St John tried speaking from an upturned box after the motor car – her usual platform – had been threatened with destruction by 'a yelling mob of roughs'[6] and driven away to safety. She was knocked off this box a dozen times – thrown, even 'hurled' to the ground – and each time picked herself up and climbed on it again, once gasping 'they are only being playful' as she did so. Five more women stood around the box to guard her; almost all of them were eventually pushed down and trampled upon. A lady from the crowd came forward to help them until she too collapsed. Two more pilgrims – the Miss Westwoods, nicknamed Tweedledum and Tweedledee – sat themselves on the box to weigh it down but were soon forced away. Ida Beaver, who had walked all the way from Newcastle, rushed to their aid, fell, and was kicked and beaten 'for several minutes'.[7] At last the police managed to get them all to a hotel, where they stayed under guard, bloodied but relatively unbowed.

The women's bravery was generally applauded once the excitement had died down, but this image of the plucky young (or not-so-young) lady did occasionally militate against the pilgrims being taken seriously. They were described as being good sports and endlessly photographed marching along with breezy smiles and a sort of girl-next-door wholesomeness; people were therefore apt to miss the point that their courage was born of passion and the fiercest sort of political idealism. Perhaps if there had been a few pictures of them being kicked, stoned, assailed and assaulted, they might have been viewed differently. But they couldn't have it both ways: that sort of publicity belonged to the suffragettes.

The impression they preferred to project was one of conviction tempered by tolerance, conciliation and good humour. It is typical of

The NUWSS logo, suggesting the Tree of Life – or perhaps the Tree of Knowledge.

A WOMAN'S MIND MAGNIFIED

The frippery of the female mind as depicted in an early-twentieth-century anti-suffrage postcard.

THE NEW MRS PARTINGTON (OF THE ANTI SUFFRAGE SOCIETY)
'SOMEHOW THE TIDE KEEPS RISING'!

PUBLISHED BY ERNESTINE MILLS, 19 HOLLAND PARK ROAD, W.—COPYRIGHT.

Above: *A riposte published by suffrage campaigners, showing the inexorability of political change.*

Left: *'A woman's place is in the home.' When she leaves for the polling booth, domestic ruin will ensue.*

Bertha Newcombe's unlikely painting of Emily Davies and Elizabeth Garrett delivering the 1866 petition to John Stuart Mill.

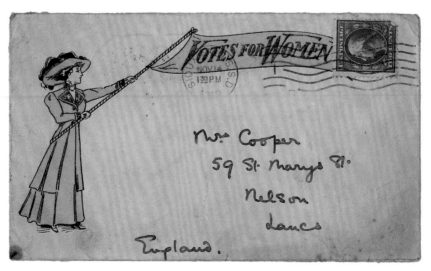

This American envelope was kept by Selina Cooper as a reminder of her days as a grassroots suffrage campaigner.

NATIONAL UNION OF WOMEN'S SUFFRAGE SOCIETIES
LAW-ABIDING   *NON-PARTY*
THE WATLING STREET ROUTE

The NUWSS issued maps detailing each route of the Great Pilgrimage. The Watling Street route was one of the longest.

Above: *An enamelled badge in 'the colours', worn by members of the NUWSS.*

Right: *Medals were awarded to those members of the WSPU who were imprisoned, with bars and a medallion for hunger strikers.*

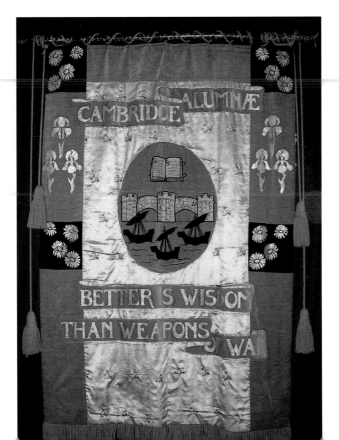

Left: *This magnificently embroidered banner is the one shown in the photograph on page 198, proudly carried by Cambridge alumnae on the Pilgrimage.*

Vera Chute Collum leads the pilgrims from Oxford towards Thame. Note the elderly couple in the fourth row.

Eda Sharples (left) and Marjory Lees (right) are helped with the washing-up outside the Ark.

THE WOMEN'S SUFFRAGE PILGRIMAGE FROM CARLISLE TO LONDON. 1913

A local newspaper published this photograph of smiling pilgrims marching through the Lake District with heads held high.

Suffragists – including men – from the north-west of England and their banners. This photograph is in the collection of Birkenhead pilgrim Alice New.

their approach to this demonstration that at one stage of the journey, for example, the Watling Street group included three harmless babies in prams with the words 'Non-Militant' stitched into their hats; that other pilgrims used to debate cheerfully whether the village ponds they passed were deep enough for them to be ducked as witches; that they laughed in genuine delight when an appreciative onlooker exclaimed that he had been expecting a load of 'bandy-legged old beanos' to turn up, assuming all suffragists to be deeply unattractive women.[8] Annie Ramsay, on the Land's End route, was baldly informed by a purple-faced Cornishman that he wanted to kill her. 'I desire to tar and feather you and to tie you up in a sack and roll you into the pond and I desire to shut you up in a lunatic asylum and to burn you,' he roared.[9] She pretended to be amused, but imagine the shock to an unexceptional middle-class woman of meeting someone shouting unprovoked death threats in your face, spit flying, when all you are doing – have ever done – is your best by your community and your beliefs.

Harriet Blessley was fortunate enough to escape such invective as she walked from Portsmouth. Contrary to received wisdom, she was confident that the closer she got to the glamorous metropolis the more intelligent and tolerant audiences would be. By the time she reached Guildford on 22 July (the day of the High Wycombe riot) she was undeniably tired, a little bored by her particular and very repetitive job of handbill-folding, but still enjoying herself immensely. She chuckled when the men in her party were joshed by onlookers as 'Suffering Gents'; she relished the beef tea and poached eggs they often had for supper, with freshly picked whortleberries for dessert. Now she had rid herself of her bicycle, which she had never quite got the hang of, she was happy to stride along the open road, occasionally hitching a ride in a motor car. 'I feel the Pilgrimage is a grand thing. I am glad to be out doing my tiny bit,' she wrote proudly.[10] Her friend Dick – the one who had given up on Day Two – reappeared to keep her company, and when she got near Richmond upon Thames, where the Land's End marchers joined them, she was taken for an outing on the river by another young man and treated to buns and lemonade: what could be nicer, especially for a single woman of forty summers?

The Brighton pilgrims did not leave home until 21 July. They spent the shortest time on the road of any route – just four days – which meant that they could afford to be rather more theatrical than the others. One hundred of them set off at ten o'clock in the morning in a parade festooned with posters and banners, with a corps of cyclists and drummers at the front, and three venerable old ladies in bath-chairs bringing up the rear with a van carrying so much luggage that it took half an hour to unload at the end of the day. There were plenty of celebrities present, among them the famous African explorer Sir Harry Johnston, who spoke at Angmering; philosopher Bertrand Russell's first wife, the American Alys Pearsall Smith, who spoke at Burgess Hill; and Lady Maud Parry, wife of the composer Sir Hubert (a fellow pilgrim).

Also closing in on the capital city right on schedule were the marchers from East Anglia and Essex, who appear to have been the only ones to fight back against their attackers. When people picking peas on the way from Witham to Chelmsford started flinging clods of earth at them as they passed, a hot-headed pilgrim ran into the field and gave the biggest of the bullies 'such a sound smack on his ears that he tumbled down and fled in tears, promising to tell his mother.'[11] Once they arrived at Chelmsford they were given a grudging welcome by a local journalist. 'I was struck by one feature of the wayfarers,' he noted. 'There did not appear to be any giddy girls among them. Most of them were of a certain – or rather, uncertain age, and therefore know what they want, if it really can be said that women do know what they want.'[12]

Harriet Blessley was right: despite the organizers' worries, once the Pilgrimage as a whole approached journey's end, there was relatively little trouble. The Kentish contingent's greatest concern along the way had been apathy rather than enmity. As they reached Bermondsey, however, they were thrilled to be greeted by massed railway workers who cheered and clapped as they passed. When the Land's End group arrived at their holding station in Warwick Gardens, West London, Annie Ramsay, the 'mother of the Pilgrimage', was presented with a congratulatory bouquet of red and white carnations by the other women in the group, who affectionately styled themselves her honorary daughters. Everyone helped to spruce up the furniture van with its rather jaded Devonian horse and to reassure its driver, Annie's friend Jack Hussey of Ottery St Mary, that he need not worry and all would be well. This was his first ever trip to London.

It was Gladys Duffield's first visit, too. Glad to put the horrors of High Wycombe firmly behind her, she looked forward to the celebrations ahead. She collected a letter from her husband on 23 July giving his completely superfluous permission to take part in the Pilgrimage, which was nevertheless encouraging. He added that he feared she might be sent to jail, but was quite confident she would never go on hunger strike. She was then told by a man calling from the upper deck of a passing omnibus that he was proud of the women of England, and, to cap it all, she was asked to carry the Keswick banner to Hyde Park on Sunday. The only thing that clouded her joy was the inescapable fact that soon this adventure would be over.

For family and friends at home, the end of the Pilgrimage could not come soon enough. However sanguine Vera Chute Collum tried to be in her reports for the *Daily News*, it was obvious that the pilgrims frequently put themselves in harm's way. The *Manchester Guardian* printed a hair-raising account of the Thame meeting the day after it happened, which terrified Sarah Lees.[13] Ever proactive, she decided not just to sit at home fretting, but to *do* something. Thus it was that on the evening of 23 July, while Marjory and the others were getting ready for bed in the *Ark* (now safely parked on a farm outside Beaconsfield), they heard a male voice outside. Their hearts must have leapt in terror: was this Thame all over again? But the voice had a familiar Lancashire burr; it turned out to belong to the Lees's gardener, Mr Mottram, who had been dispatched by Sarah, with his colleague Mr Fairbrother, to rescue her poor, beleaguered daughter.

Marjory declined to be rescued, so the bemused Mottram and Fairbrother returned to Oldham. The following day, Sarah Lees herself arrived, overtaking the Watling Street marchers in her motor car and meeting them at Gerrards Cross, where she addressed a meeting. She stayed for the rest of the Pilgrimage.

At Uxbridge the Watling Street pilgrims enjoyed their first sunny day since Banbury. The groom Scholes worked in his shirtsleeves, which was a remarkable enough event to be recorded in Marjory's diary, and all but the fussiest of pilgrims discarded their coats. This laxity scandalized an old lady, who shook her fist at them as they walked by, declaring that they'd be wanting to wear trousers next. They were pleased to see a little company of New Constitutional Society suffragists at Uxbridge, who lined the road and saluted them. Organizer Kate Frye was, sadly, not there: so exhausted was she after her evangelistic efforts in Norfolk and Kent that the doctor had signed her off work for three weeks.

On Friday, 25 July – thirty-seven days and some 350 miles after the first pilgrims had left Carlisle – the Watling Street marchers reached London. There was no let-up in their punishing suffrage schedule. They held a meeting at Ealing in the morning, then marched via Acton to Bayswater for another meeting that evening. It was fortuitous timing: the overworked Birkenhead caravan had just lost a tyre and, rather than trying to repair it, driver Joseph, Alice New and Auntie decided to discharge it honourably, with brave Polly, and send them home by train. Alice sent her bicycle back at this point, too. She and Auntie hurriedly packed a suitcase each and caught a tram to their hotel near Paddington.

Dealing with the *Ark* and the *Sandwich* was not as straightforward. In her diary Marjory describes the various arrangements of Byzantine complexity involved in getting the caravans, with Noah, Ham, Scholes and Clapham, to St Pancras Station, finding the right porter to put them in the right wagon on the right train, and making sure that the horses would be comfortable. Noah was reluctant to go. Though he didn't think much of the paved streets of London – hard on the hooves – he did enjoy the sights. Nothing would induce the star-struck animal to hurry, despite Scholes flicking his white hanky for all he was worth; he took a great interest in all he saw, remarked Marjory, and had to be sternly reminded of his duty.

The banner from Falmouth on the Land's End route was one of the most poetic of the whole campaign. It read 'Weaving Far and Weaving Free, England's Web of Destiny'. And that's what it must have felt like now, as all the separate threads of the Great Pilgrimage came together at last. The pattern it had woven so carefully across the British Isles intensified as each strand neared the centre. Soon that pattern would be complete, and though its design might not have been easily discernible in progress, once it was finished and viewed as a whole, it was bound to be impressive. As everyone went gratefully to their beds that Friday night, they felt proud as well as exhausted. Excited, too: tomorrow was the most important day of all.

It began rather shakily for Alice New and Auntie, now rejoined by Alice's sister, Hilda. In all the excitement about the broken-down caravan yesterday, Auntie had managed to leave her suitcase on the tram. As soon as they finished breakfast at their hotel, they went to the lost-property office at Scotland Yard to see if anyone had handed it in. They had: it was ten miles away at Hanwell police station. Somebody would be sent to collect it without delay, and if the ladies cared to come back in an hour, it would be ready for them. To pass

the time, they went to visit the NUWSS headquarters just around
the corner. Alice was thrilled to see the very place to which she had
written countless requests for suffrage literature over the years, and
where 'this greatest of all great demonstrations' had been planned.
Predictably, the staff were terribly busy; still, they found time to
be courteous and kind. (Harriet Blessley was not so gracious about
her leaders: when she saw Millicent Fawcett for the first time at the
end of the Pilgrimage, she described her as looking like 'a superior
charwoman'.)

After they had retrieved Auntie's precious suitcase, the three
women caught a motor bus and, checking that they hadn't left anything behind again, alighted at Elgin Avenue, West London, where
the Watling Street veterans were due to meet up for the grand procession to Hyde Park. Alice says that even though they had only
been apart for a single night, it felt as though this were a reunion of
long-lost friends. There was much to be done: banners were handed
out, looking grubby and travel-worn by now; orders were given
about where, when and with whom each pilgrim was to march;
when the three brass bands allocated to Watling Street arrived, they
were carefully (and unsuccessfully) positioned so that they would
neither drown each other out nor deafen the nearest pilgrims.
Hats were straightened, ribbons re-tied, sashes adjusted, knapsacks
brushed clean and bright new rosettes bought to replace tired old
ones. Vera Chute Collum smartened up her horse and her khaki
knickerbocker suit, and was joined by two other equestriennes:
Newnham College alumna Edith Eckhard from Manchester, who
had joined the Pilgrimage for the last few days, and Miss E. B. Jayne
from Edgware on a beautiful grey. All three became temporarily
famous when pictured on the pages of several different newspapers
over the following days.

The weekend of 26–7 July 1913 was the most successful of the
whole NUWSS campaign in terms of publicity. The message did
not always get through with precision: in a clear case of Chinese

whispers, a Spanish journalist informed his readers that fifty thousand non-militant suffragists – he got that bit right – had arrived in
London by every means of transport imaginable. Some had come
on foot, others in boats, motor cars, trains; yet more came in a balloon, two by aeroplane, and several swam to the capital.[14] Regional
and national publications in Britain covered the pilgrims' arrival and
the parade on Saturday afternoon, followed by the rally at Hyde
Park at which there were indeed in excess of fifty thousand people.
The pilgrims' numbers had swelled considerably during the last day
or two, many supporters joining various routes for the last leg, or
returning to walk again having done a stint elsewhere earlier on.
The sense of camaraderie remarked upon by so many of them was
at its height on that Saturday. Their shared experiences and achievements exhilarated them; they valued the mutual support which was
a hallmark of the Pilgrimage; and it was obviously liberating to have
had so much fun together. People from either end of the social spectrum commented on the irrelevance of class and background. When
someone asked who the pilgrims were (probably assuming them to
be leisured ladies who walked for a few miles a day and then jumped
into charabancs when no one was looking), a pilgrim on the Great
North Road gave an inspired answer. They are representatives, she
said, of everywoman:

> home-makers – wives and mothers – who feel so intensely the dis-
> abilities under which they suffer from man-made laws and yet are
> unable to come out and fight for their own enfranchisement – just
> the comparative few who had the nerve and strength to leave their
> homes and endure a few weeks of hardship, in order to help their
> less fortunate sisters.[15]

With this sort of spirit abroad, there is no wonder that the pilgrims were almost beside themselves with excitement as their final
march together began shortly after lunch on the Saturday afternoon.
This part of the Pilgrimage was even more minutely choreographed

than the rest. All those who had come from north or north-east of the capital gathered in Bloomsbury and marched along Oxford Street to Marble Arch and Hyde Park, entering just by Speakers' Corner. The East Anglian, Kentish and Brighton pilgrims met in Trafalgar Square and went via Pall Mall and Piccadilly to Apsley Gate at Hyde Park Corner. Southerners went via Kensington High Street to the Alexandra Gate next to the Royal Albert Hall; and the Watling Street contingent entered the Park through the Victoria Gate by way of Edgware Road and Sussex Place, not far from Alice New's hotel.

This was reminiscent of the Coronation Procession two years earlier: a joyful spectacle of colour and music. Planes flew overhead, scattering leaflets (perhaps that's what confused the Spaniard); people sold souvenirs at street corners, including beautiful paper napkins printed with red and green flowers giving details of speakers and timings.[16] Copies of the *Anti-Suffrage Review* and the *Suffragette* were also on sale, but that was only mildly irritating. Members of the WSPU were banned from entering Hyde Park in any numbers during the summer of 1913, or from holding meetings in the Royal Albert Hall, because of unruly behaviour; they would be no threat today. Onlookers cheered and raised their hats; clapped to the beat of the bands; swarmed into Hyde Park, where photographs and a snow-speckled newsreel suggest that, close to the action, there was hardly room to move.

Alice New had the distinct impression that, unlike other occasions on which she had marched for the Cause, this time the attention they were getting had nothing of the freak show about it. She felt an almost palpable wave of support that made her wonder whether – at last – the British people were beginning to understand what the suffragists stood for. The Oldham pilgrims felt it too. They overheard someone making a comment to a friend as they marched by. 'Oh, they don't hold with burning houses,' he explained, 'but I expect they get blamed for it all the same.'[17]

Millicent Fawcett leads the rally in Hyde Park, 26 July 1913.

The rally in Hyde Park began on the dot of five o'clock. Nineteen platforms had been erected, one for each federation, from which seventy-eight of the best speakers in the NUWSS addressed the crowds. Most of them were pilgrims. They talked about the squalid living conditions witnessed on their journey; of the need for a 'mother spirit' to come into the community; and of the redemptive powers of political enfranchisement. Some used humour, others pathos; the best spoke from the heart about what had driven them to take part in the Pilgrimage and what they hoped would be its outcome. Millicent Fawcett described a turning of the tide, a conviction that today marked the start of something new. Sensibly, only an hour was allowed for all the speeches; at six o'clock bugles sounded and the same resolution was proposed at each platform: 'that this meeting demands a Government measure for the enfranchisement of women.' It was carried unanimously.

Now it was party time.

For the Watling Street pilgrims, this meant meeting at Alan's Tea Rooms in Oxford Street for a celebratory dinner at 7.30 p.m. Alan's – run by Marguerite Alan Liddle – was a popular venue, often used by suffrage societies taking advantage of the proprietor's offer not to charge them for hiring the private room upstairs.[18] Gladys was there, so were Marjory and her friends, and Alice and Hilda New. There were so many others that those who had not been on the road for more than two days at a time were regretfully asked to leave. 'Any outsider attending the dinner would hardly have held us up as an example of peaceful folk,' commented Marjory. There was a craze at the time for autograph collecting, so everyone scuttled round begging one another's signature and address, Alice in a special birthday book with suffrage quotes for each day of the year, opportunely produced by the Highgate branch of the NUWSS.

After the meal, younger pilgrims were called upon to make speeches, then the men who had accompanied them, and finally anyone else who felt the urge. 'Wee Willie' Watson, the six-foot-seven student from Balliol, was cheered for his contribution. 'I have lunched with pilgrims,' he said, 'I have tea-d with pilgrims, I have dined with pilgrims, and the whole time, I have heard more stories that I wouldn't tell to my sisters than ever before!'[19] Lady Rochdale told anecdotes about the effect of her increasingly scruffy appearance on hosts and hostesses during the march, remembering one rather snooty lady looking her up and down and complaining, 'I was expecting a nice, respectable working woman.'[20]

Vera, now nicknamed 'our mounted Collum', refused to pontificate in public, insisting that she had never made a speech in her life (unlikely) and was certainly not going to start now, especially without her horse. Katherine Harley said the best part of the whole enterprise for her was working with young people, and Edith Eskrigge pointed out that, though it had sometimes been difficult to persuade people to join the Pilgrimage, it was going to be even harder to persuade them to part.

It wasn't all over quite yet. Though many pilgrims went home on Sunday morning, a good number stayed for the special service at St Paul's Cathedral that afternoon, at which Canon Simpson preached on 'the depression of Elijah'. His sermon was disappointingly dull, ill-advised and mumbled, and an anticlimactic end to the last few weeks. Mrs Fawcett appeared on a balcony outside the cathedral afterwards, which provided a moment of excitement, and there was another service later at the Ethical Church in Bayswater. The humanist and suffragist Maude Royden was a preacher there, and what she said to the last remaining pilgrims in London was far more memorable than Canon Simpson's downbeat effort. Alice New was especially inspired. She confesses in her diary that she hadn't really wanted to join the Pilgrimage at all; she had just been away on holiday when it began and had more than enough to catch up on at home. But she was so grateful she had gone. She had loved the outdoor life, being on the road from nine in the morning to nine at night; the challenge; the company; the comradeship; and now she felt she had a deeper understanding of and connection to her country and its people than ever before. As Miss Royden put it:

> The Pilgrimage is over, but its spirit lives on. We are all Pilgrims now, whether we have been on the road or not. We have dedicated ourselves to the service of humanity, and above all to the unfortunate. Our social system, with its cruelties and its injustices, takes from them everything and gives nothing back. It takes from them beauty, and joy, and colour, and all that makes life worth living and virtue possible. We, who are inevitably part of that social system, cannot give back what has been taken away. Some day we hope to set ourselves to the task of reform, and make these horrors impossible. Some day men and women, working side by side in the full consciousness of their great responsibility, will be able to give to the citizens of the future a fairer world to live in. But we cannot then give back what we have taken from those who suffer now. They had only one life, and we took that. We also have only one life. Let us give it.[21]

The most remarkable thing about Maude Royden's address is her willingness to accept responsibility for the state of society, despite never having voted for those who governed it in her name. This marked a shift in attitude from the NUWSS – or, more likely, an evolutionary change. The suffragists were always more likely to view the ideological campaign for the vote as a joint effort with men (as opposed to the militants' apparent 'them and us' approach), but rarely before had any of them accepted the blame for the status quo while striving to change it. Perhaps this is what Millicent Fawcett meant when she spoke about a new dawn. Inspired by the passion and commitment of the suffragettes, she recognized that, for all their meetings, processions, petitions and demonstrations, the constitutionalists had lacked drama in the past. The Pilgrimage changed all that. They were fully engaged now, having made sacrifices, faced danger and learned at first hand the effects of inequality, not just on disenfranchised women, but on working people and their families across the country. It is tempting to think that this realization was the birth of the 'big society' concept: the notion, which has nothing to do with party politics, that we are indeed all in this together.

By and large, the press reviewed the Pilgrimage kindly. *The Times* had never been a friend of women's suffrage and tended to downplay the numbers in Hyde Park and the credibility of those involved, but other papers were more positive. It could not be denied that it had been a financial triumph: pilgrims collected in excess of £8,000 from audiences along their way. They enlisted hundreds of new supporters too and, in a perfect inversion of precedent, a member of the WSPU complained that suffragette activities were being under-reported, so obsessed were journalists with the suffragists.[22] There were also some less tangible results. The pilgrims had proved that it was militancy that was unpopular, not women's suffrage. More people knew the difference now.

Even politicians acknowledged how powerful the Pilgrimage was. Ramsay MacDonald, then leader of the Labour Party, thought it had done 'an immense amount of good'. Chancellor of the Exchequer David Lloyd George called it 'one of the best political moves in recent times' and Home Secretary Reginald McKenna admitted that he sincerely admired the pilgrims' courage. 'I honestly believe that your method of action has assisted your cause.' [23] These were fine sentiments, but in the aftermath of the Speaker's bombshell that had scuppered the Reform Bill in January 1913, and the recent introduction of the 'Cat and Mouse' Act, the suffragists realized that there was still a great deal of work to be done.

Three days after the Hyde Park rally Millicent Fawcett wrote to Asquith asking him to receive a deputation from Pilgrimage leaders. She wanted to discuss the impact of the Pilgrimage with him, hoping its clear success would satisfy his old demand for proof that the ordinary men and women of the country supported women's suffrage. She also planned to present the results of the Hyde Park resolutions to him. His typewritten answer was swift and – given his previous form – spectacularly enthusiastic:

10, Downing Street,
Whitehall. S.W.
31st July, 1913.

Dear Mrs Fawcett,

In reply to your letter of the 29th, I quite recognise that the request which you put forward, after the recent law-abiding demonstration of your Societies, has a special claim on my consideration and stands upon another footing from similar demands proceeding from other quarters, where a different method and spirit is predominant.

I feel bound to warn you that I do not see my way to add anything material to what I have lately said in the House of Commons as to the intentions and policy of the Government.

If, nevertheless, you are desirous of seeing me, I shall be glad to receive your Deputation (not exceeding 12 in number) on some morning in next week or the week after.[24]

'Yours very sincerely,' he added in his own hand, 'H. H. Asquith.'

The NUWSS deputation was arranged for Friday, 8 August. Eight women went to Downing Street, including Katherine Harley and, of course, Mrs Fawcett. Judging by the transcription published in the *Common Cause* afterwards, the interview was calm and constructive. The suffragists summarized their interpretation of the last two years' broken pledges and failed legislation without rancour; they also told Asquith what had been gained from the Pilgrimage – namely, that a vast number of working people around the country could now distinguish between the militants and the moderates; that pilgrims faced opposition only when it was thought they were the former; and that the support they won along the way resulted in donations amounting to thousands of pounds, mostly given in mites by the working class. Then they all discussed what difference this success might make to the future. Asquith conceded that he had been impressed by the organization and outcome of the Pilgrimage, but warned that 'people's motives in this world are very complex' and 'Governments can do strange things.'[25] It would not be easy, he told his visitors, to translate their success into legislation (as if they didn't know that already). Even though there was a majority in the House in favour of women's suffrage, there was no party line (that's what the Conciliation Committee had been trying to address) and in these turbulent times tactics and strategy were apt to get in the way of ideals.

The members of the NUWSS made some suggestions, including the oft-quoted one that a new Reform Bill should be introduced under the title 'The Representation of the People Bill'. When asked by Asquith how that would help, they looked bemused. 'Well, women are people, aren't they?' 'I suppose so,' answered the prime minister, unconvinced.

In the end, Asquith – again – promised not to stand in the way if it became clear that, within the House as well as outside it, the majority of people wanted votes for women:

> If you can convince – you say you have, and you may be right – the judgement and conscience of the people that it is a beneficent change, there is no combination in the world which can prevent your success, and no political party will attempt to do it. If I might offer one word of counsel it would be – proceed as you have been proceeding, and continue to the end.[26]

That afternoon, Mrs Fawcett went with another deputation, this time in private, to see Lloyd George and a selection of other pro-suffrage ministers, who did at least agree to invite a suffrage speaker to address MPs in the autumn. The NUWSS suggested Muriel Matters, who though mostly Australian was also partly Welsh. Lloyd George might warm to her as a kind of countrywoman. Dr Thomas Macnamara, the secretary to the Admiralty, was there. 'I think your Pilgrimage has gone a good way to rehabilitate the Suffrage movement from the disastrous ravages of militancy,' he said. 'I should not have expected it would have such a good result.' Lloyd George himself added to his former praise, complimenting the organizers on their efficiency. The Pilgrimage was a brilliant idea, he told them, and 'uncommonly well carried out.'[27]

This was heartening, but though it was not articulated in public by anyone at the NUWSS, there was by now a new obstacle to negotiate in a struggle that had been going on for almost half a century. The more the suffragists were congratulated on making a distinction between the militant and the law-abiding wings of the campaign, the less attention appeared to be directed at the joint ambition of both, which was to win the vote. Members of Parliament were quick to commend them for being reasonable and shaming the suffragette minority, but that was only a means to an end, not the end itself.

Meanwhile, the militants were stepping up their own activities. The day after the Hyde Park rally, Sylvia Pankhurst led a raid on Downing Street following a massed meeting of the East London Federation of Suffragettes in Trafalgar Square. She was a time-expired 'mouse', having failed to report back to jail after her latest release under the Act; she and twenty-five others present at the raid were promptly arrested. During the months between now and the outbreak of war in August 1914, 'outrages' were reported in the papers almost every day, including the bombing of the Houses of Parliament, slashing of paintings in national galleries, the drawing of revolvers at public meetings and attempts to assail various members of the Royal Family.

On 13 June 1914 there was enough material to fill a whole column in an ordinary, provincial English newspaper, the *Grantham Journal*, with tales of what the sub-editor called 'The Suffragette Fanatics'. Item one: a society debutante – Miss Mary Blomfield – had sensationally been arrested for accosting the king and queen about forcible feeding while being presented at court in the Throne Room at Buckingham Palace. What made things worse, her late father was Sir Arthur Blomfield, 'the famous architect', and her grandfather was a former Bishop of London. Margaret's mother was mortified, and wanted it made perfectly clear that the incident was entirely her daughter's idea and that she and the rest of the family deeply deplored her actions.

Item two: last Sunday, during Mass at the fashionable Brompton Oratory in London, about fifteen suffragettes disturbed the reading of the Gospel by shouting and shrieking 'at the top of their voices'. They were sitting in different parts of the church, like a flash mob, and each was attacked by members of the congregation, who were cheered as they struck the protesters, drawing blood. The fracas lasted ten minutes.

Next: a suffragette took to the pulpit at Westminster Cathedral during an evening service last week, calling out 'In the presence of the Blessed Sacrament I protest at the forcible feeding of women!' She was caught and ejected, arrested and imprisoned. As she left the dock she shouted, 'We have no King, but thank God we have Mrs Pankhurst.' Item four: at recent meetings in various public parks, suffragettes were hustled and in some cases assaulted by the crowds, and had to be rescued by the police. Five: a large house near High Wycombe had been gutted by fire. Items of suffragette literature were found stuck in a hedge nearby. The house was unoccupied, but held a large number of valuable paintings and much antique furniture.

Item six: here is a report from America about the British government's attitude to suffragettes. Americans have not had to deal with militancy in this regard, explains the *Grantham Journal*, and are therefore perhaps unaware of the complexities of the campaign and the difficult position of those in authority (in other words: don't shoot the messenger):

> The new performances of the Pankhurst devil dancers seem to be grating on the nerves of our much-enduring, docile, downtrodden, henpecked English brethren. The mushy sentimental weakness and mistaken chivalry with which these sisters of Satan have been treated by the English authorities, to the full as jelly-backed and futile as even we Americans could have been in like case, have brought on a constantly more dangerous, more brutal, and more mephitic manifestation on the part of the noxious creatures. The lower classes of the people would make short work of them were it not for the police. It is right that the police should protect these enemies of society from harm. Is nobody going to protect society from them?

Item seven: arrests had been made after someone was found trying to smuggle drugs into Holloway prison. Suffragettes had been making claims that they were drugged by the prison authorities in order to make forcible feeding easier; now it appeared suffragettes were procuring their own emetics to render them so ill from vomiting that they were released earlier than might otherwise have been the case. Eight: when the king and queen attended the International Horse Show at Olympia last Monday, a suffragette tried to break into the royal box, demanding as she did so, 'Your Majesty, why do you allow women to be tortured?'

And so it goes on: on Tuesday, Ivy Bond was sentenced for attacking pictures at the Doré Gallery with an axe. 'You can sentence me to death if you like,' she shouted. 'I don't mind. I shall do it again, again and again, until you give us justice.' The same day, Bertha Ryland took a hammer to a picture by George Romney in Birmingham Art Gallery. Police have raided the WSPU offices in London and seized quantities of documents and literature. The ILP has banned militants from speaking at socialist or Labour meetings, as have several other political organizations and trades unions. And Sylvia Pankhurst has been arrested again.

It is easy to agree with Millicent Fawcett that after the Pilgrimage things were bound to change. But not entirely in the way she might have wished. The tone of that newspaper editor, his choice of words and the incidents he chose to report, reveal a great deal of heartbreak in association with the campaign for women's suffrage. The fact that few still confused the moderates with the militants was good news, but that did not condone the fact that now only the suffragettes were treated with violence. Nor should it invalidate what both factions were trying to achieve, or dilute the passion and the desperation with which they fought – as Ivy Bond did with her axe – for justice.

10

PATRIOTISM IS NOT ENOUGH

1913–1915

There is not a war in the world, no, nor an injustice, but you women are answerable for it; not in that you have provoked, but in that you have not hindered. Men, by their nature, are prone to fight; they will fight for any cause, or for none. It is for you to choose their cause for them, and to forbid them when there is no cause. There is no suffering, no injustice, no misery, in the earth, but the guilt of it lies with you.[1]

THAT WAS JOHN RUSKIN writing in 1865, before women started militating for the vote. The same John Ruskin whose feminine ideal was 'the angel in the house', society's moral compass with a duty to influence without power. Quite how he imagined women were to achieve world peace is unclear, since, like children, they were hardly supposed to speak unless spoken to; nor were they to occupy their diminutive minds with anything but thoughts of home and family. The turbulent world outside was not for them. Half a century later suffrage campaigners were still blamed for their part in conflict: this time not for passively condoning it, but for actively seeking it out to effect change. The 'gettes were accused for being violent themselves, the 'gists, in certain circles, for inciting violence as the pilgrims had – however innocently – at Thame or High Wycombe. They couldn't win.

Remarkably, though they realized that influence without power is as dysfunctional for women as power without influence is for men, most suffragists were slow-burn optimists. Speaking at a meeting some forty-five years into the crusade for the vote, Dr 'Murdie' Murdoch of Hull assured her audience 'the Parliamentary Franchise may come to women tomorrow, it may come in ten or twenty years, but as surely as the sun will rise tomorrow, it <u>will</u> come.'[2]

Kate Frye of the New Constitutional Society was an exception to the rule. Perhaps unsurprisingly, optimism was not her forte. She returned to work in the autumn of 1913. Not only had she suffered ill-health but the family's fortunes had plummeted, obliging them to move from their country retreat in salubrious Buckinghamshire to a small, 'filthy' place in Worthing. 'The gay and reckless life is over indeed,' noted Kate, wanly, in her diary. Traipsing around eastern England trying to convert 'quantities of vicars' to suffragism had been trying, but it was nothing in comparison with combing the back streets of London attempting to offload unwanted possessions to boost the family's income. 'I hated the journey and felt very nervous at my office – which was the disposal of odds & ends – including false teeth cast off by Mother and Daddie, old Muffs, trinkets etc. So I spent all the morning in and out of old clothes and bric a brac shops. It was really awful and I did wonder what I was coming to.'[3]

For the first few weeks back as NCS organizer Kate helped with a campaign among Jewish workers in Whitechapel, where Sylvia Pankhurst had formed the East London Federation of Suffragettes. Then it was on the road again, first to Kent, then Oxfordshire and Berkshire. Kate was always easily exasperated, but now there is a note of desperation in her diary entries. She often finds herself tearful with worry about her family and with exhaustion after a day's fruitless canvassing. There is the odd highlight: a comely young student who follows her out of a reading room where she has sheltered from the rain and, 'blushing purple', asks her for a coffee; a trip to a Theosophical lecture on life after death ('I much enjoyed it and had a chat with the speaker afterwards – a large pale man – who said that we might possibly meet during the night on the Astral Plain');[4] but mostly she feels herself running inexorably out of steam. Her fiancé, John, is still in the picture but somehow she can't bring herself to marry him, with the consequence that, emotionally, she is as low as she has ever been.

On 9 January 1914 she notes that it's her birthday. She is thirty-six. 'What an age – quite done for – yes, a woman is done for after 35 – especially if she can't afford to dress well or look smart. I have wept a good deal during the day – everything seems so hopeless and I hate to be back at work again . . . Wrote till 8 – supper – wept again and then to bed.'[5] As she has just hinted, things are not much better on the professional front. 'I am completely fed up with [work]. It is people's own loss if they are not Suffrage, but I seem to have lost the knack of converting them. Personally I am keener than ever but I feel I loathe and detest the work of it.'[6]

Elsewhere, suffragists were busy trying to build on the success of the Pilgrimage, working so hard that they failed to notice the Great War creeping up behind them. Buoyed by newspaper reports declaring the march to have been 'one of the greatest movements which has ever taken place in the history of the world'[7] – 'a direct appeal both to the heart and the head . . . altogether fine',[8] 'a great adventure'[9], 'inspired'[10] – the pilgrims went back to their constituencies, as it were, and prepared for government. They held more meetings in people's homes, public venues and open spaces; more fetes and bazaars to raise money; made miniature local 'pilgrimages' for a week or so at a time; and attended rallies organized by sympathetic bodies such as trades unions and local councils. When the NUWSS convened at the Royal Albert Hall one evening in February 1914, the place was absolutely packed, not only with society members from around the country but also with hundreds of supportive delegates from the worlds of business, commerce and industry, many of them men.

Petitions from signed-up suffragists continued to arrive at Westminster, together with delegations of men and women

demanding electoral reform. Speakers roamed the country – perhaps trained at one of the NUWSS summer schools – to canvass
for Labour candidates in by-elections, with the help of the Election
Fighting Fund. Selina Cooper, who had dealt so adeptly with the
fishermen (and fish) of Grimsby, was sent to Haworth during a
Keighley by-election campaign a few months after returning from
the Pilgrimage. Sadly, the message about militants and moderates had
not yet reached this particular corner of West Yorkshire, and she was
given a hard time. If anyone could cope, however, it was Selina. When
the audience tried to shout her down and started pelting her with
assorted projectiles, she informed them in no uncertain terms that she
was 'stopping here' to talk to them, come what may. She invited them
to go home and fetch all the ammunition they could; they could come
back and throw it at her to their hearts' content, then, when they had
got the violence out of their systems, they could blasted well quieten
down and listen. She was furious. 'This blooming village would
never have been known about but for three women,'[11] she pointed
out, referring to local heroines the Brontë sisters.

Meanwhile the wheels of parliamentary progress continued
to grate and seize as they turned. A new Private Member's Bill to
enfranchise nationally those women eligible to vote in local council elections reached its second reading in the House of Lords in
May 1914, but was defeated by 44 votes. Anti-suffrage politicians
came up with increasingly complicated strategies for avoiding female
enfranchisement. Why not appoint a minister for women, backed
by an advisory council which would actually include a number of
ladies? That way their interests could be represented and debated
while keeping them safely out of the way of 'real' government. Or
we could build a separate chamber for ladies in Westminster where
they could (essentially) pretend to be parliamentarians and even pass
Bills among themselves. They could confine themselves to feminine
matters like the Shops Act, the white slave trade, housing and so on.
In the meantime the other two Houses would get on with important

issues involving the armed forces, foreign affairs and the budget. Naturally, anyone who had been a militant would be barred from this House for Women for at least a probationary period.

The 'Massingham Plan' was well publicized: if it could be demonstrated that a thousand people or more in any one constituency were in favour of votes for women, a local referendum would be held. Then, if the suffragists won, all women in that constituency would automatically be enfranchised, providing they satisfied the usual qualifications. According to its architect, the Liberal journalist Henry Massingham, this scheme had the benefit of being independent of party politics, and would ensure a slow but steady spread of emancipation across the country. The idea of a national referendum appealed to Winston Churchill, among others, but the regionally based Massingham Plan never progressed beyond mere speculation.

Not surprisingly, none of these titbits satisfied the militants, whose campaign of civil disobedience or terrorism – call it what you will – reached its zenith in the early summer of 1914. As well as high-profile, high-risk episodes involving the slashing of works of art, bombing politicians' houses and workplaces or accosting royalty, small-scale acts of protest were happening in unexpected places. Winifred Starbuck was a sixth-form pupil at a girls' school where Votes for Women was all the rage. The pupils decorated their desks in green, white and violet; collected photos of their heroines – Mrs Despard, the Pankhursts – and pinned up newspaper cuttings about the latest suffragette activities. One day they were astonished to see the name of one of their favourite teachers, a shy and quiet young woman, in the list of those arrested for window-smashing. Not only did the teacher lose her job, but so did the headmistress and four other members of staff.

Winifred helped organize a schoolgirl protest, lobbying parents to sign a petition for the teachers' reinstatement and, when this failed, declaring a 'term of disorder'. She and other prefects removed all the school registers on the first day of the summer term; they also stole the school bell and gong; they refused to sit down, be quiet in the assembly hall or behave themselves in class. There was chaos. The school governors were sent for and the whole of the sixth form was suspended until further notice. At the end of term, Winifred and her friends tried to return to school but the caretaker wouldn't admit them. So they broke in and wrote slogans in Indian ink all over the walls. The police were called, but no charges were brought. In general, Winifred claimed afterwards, the parents supported their rebellious daughters, for the sacked headmistress had been a fine leader.[12]

Winifred's greatest heroine was Christabel Pankhurst, still based in Paris, whom the papers had now dubbed 'that damned elusive Christabel'. From there she had embarked upon what she called a Moral Crusade, writing a series of articles in the WSPU journal the *Suffragette* explaining how votes for women could combat venereal disease, prostitution and sex trafficking. These were published collectively as *The Great Scourge, and How to End It* in 1913, accompanied by a publicity campaign urging 'pure' men to wear white ribbons. Kate Frye asked her fiancé, John, if he was pure. He declined to answer, which depressed her even more.

Sylvia Pankhurst was expelled from the WSPU in early 1914 by Emmeline and Christabel, who were bitterly opposed to the socialist principles Sylvia espoused in the East London Federation of Suffragettes. Adela Pankhurst, who also found herself increasingly out of sympathy with Emmeline and Christabel, took a passage to Australia and settled in the state of Victoria, where women already had the vote.

Emmeline, who recognized the significance of her celebrity, continued as the most prized 'mouse' of all, never forcibly fed by the authorities, but frequently either on hunger strike or on the run. The more damage done by the suffragettes – costs amounted to some £54,000 in 1913[13] – the more were sent to prison. They had rarely been treated 'inside' with respect or compassion; now they faced gratuitous brutality.

Frances 'Fanny' Parker (1875–1924) was a New Zealander educated at Newnham College in Cambridge. She joined the WSPU in
1908. That February, she was imprisoned for the Cause for taking
part in a rowdy deputation to the Palace of Westminster. Fanny
was extraordinarily enterprising. She ran what was described as a
'suffragette dairy and farming school', training women to become
agriculturalists while raising money for the WSPU. She was a keen
suffrage speaker, touring with the Scottish University Women's
Suffrage Union in 1911 in a caravan, but was no constitutionalist:
months later she was to be found hurling stones at London windows,
for which she was sent to Holloway for four months.

In 1913 Fanny was appointed a WSPU organizer in Scotland,
where, in July 1914, she was caught trying to blow up national hero
Robert Burns's cottage in Alloway. She was held on remand in Ayr
before being sentenced. Her description of what happened there is
harrowing:

> On Thursday, 6th [July], Dr. Dunlop, medical advisor to the Prison
> Commissioners came from Edinburgh to see me. He asked me if I
> was going to take food, and said it was a very serious charge, and
> that I should certainly be forcibly fed on conviction. Before his visit
> the wardresses and a warder had taken my fingerprints, but as Dr.
> Dunlop was not satisfied with the result, another attempt was made.
> I was taken from my cell to another room, and when they found
> they could not make me sit on a chair, he ordered that I should be
> flung to the ground. He himself held the arm and hand, forcing the
> fingers open for the printing and severely bruising my arms. My
> back and sides were so bruised after this that I could not lie still
> during the rest of my imprisonment . . .[14]

After her trial Fanny was transferred to Perth prison and immediately forcibly fed. First the doctors tried to prise open her jaws with
a steel gag, warning her that if a tooth broke it would be her own
fault. When this didn't work they used a nasal tube. They held her

down afterwards and whenever she began to vomit pressed a hand over her mouth to prevent her 'letting it out'. Three times a day she was treated like this; the so-called nourishment did her no good at all and soon she was so weak that she could hardly lift her head without fainting. Nasal feeding was obviously not working. Next on the list for the authorities was – bewilderingly – to insert a tube into the rectum instead:

> The manner in which it was done was so unnecessarily painful that I screamed with agony. Later three women tried to give me an enema. Because I would not submit passively to these indignities, after everything was over, one of the women lifted me by the hair [she was small and slight] and flung me into the far corner of the bed. Another knelt on my chest to prevent me from getting up. She got off again when the first sat down heavily on my knees and said she would not get up until I promised to behave!
>
> Thursday morning, 16th [July] . . . the three wardresses appeared again. One of them said that if I did not resist, she would send the others away and do what she had come to do as gently and as decently as possible. I consented. This was another attempt to feed me by the rectum, and was done in a cruel way, causing me great pain.
>
> She returned some time later and said she had 'something else' to do. I took it to be another attempt to feed me in the same way, but it proved to be a grosser and more indecent outrage, which could have been done for no other purpose than torture. It was followed by soreness, which lasted for several days.

After her release under the 'Cat and Mouse' Act into the care of a nursing home, Fanny was examined and found to have rawness and swelling around her vagina. As soon as she was physically able, she escaped and went into hiding. Before she could be tracked down and re-arrested, war was declared.

Emmeline Pankhurst was in France with Christabel on the day she heard the news. She was able to come home at the end of August, openly, because on the 10th of that month the government offered amnesty to all suffragettes currently incarcerated or out under licence. This was for several reasons. Prison overcrowding was becoming critical, and it was expensive to keep so many women inside and to provide all the Sanatogen (a proprietary tonic wine) or other fluids necessary to force-feed them when they refused to eat. The country was in crisis and had graver matters on which to expend its energy than chasing and catching suffragettes. Besides, all the suffrage societies, militant and constitutional, had called a truce on the outbreak of hostilities, promising to use their combined efforts in the service of their country. 'Women, your country needs you,' said Millicent Fawcett to the members of the NUWSS; 'we have another duty now.'[15]

A lengthy feature appeared in a pictorial magazine, the *Ladies' Field*, in November 1914 with the title 'The Woman Suffrage Movement and the War. Some of its Leaders and their Ideals'. This was a crucial period: perhaps everything would *not* be over by Christmas after all. It was important that the population appreciated how those crowds of noisy pre-war women aspiring to a vote had changed, how seriously they took their duty as responsible citizens. Charlotte Despard's organization, the Women's Freedom League, was one of the few to maintain its primary allegiance to suffragism despite the war. She considered it her duty to keep the issue of women's enfranchisement in the public eye, which she intended to do through promoting WFL members' credentials as worthy members of society. They formed a Women's Suffrage National Aid Corps to carry out voluntary work for expectant and new mothers. They also ran a register of 'unemployed, middle-class women' and set up workrooms for their working-class sisters to earn a little money making children's clothes. Mrs Despard bought herself a house in Nine Elms, a poverty-stricken area of London, and opened a club where working women could come and rest. She even cooked them occasional dinners.

In February 1914, as a direct result of the *esprit de corps* occasioned by the Pilgrimage, Mrs Despard's sister Katherine Harley had founded what she called an Active Service League to coordinate and carry out suffrage and welfare work – not unlike Florence de Fonblanque's Qui Vive Corps. 'The Pilgrimage revealed to many of us the joy of working as one of many, rather than as units,'[16] Mrs Harley pointed out; she wanted those who had taken part to come together again in groups of, say, twenty or thirty, to dedicate between a week and a month of their time each year to good causes in the name of women's suffrage. The Active Service League was thus a forerunner of the Women's Royal Voluntary Service (founded in 1938) and acted as a conduit of energy, expertise and ideology leading directly from the Pilgrimage to all the different tasks to which NUWSS members could set themselves, often evoking the spirit of that great adventure as they did so.

Active Service League members turned their hands to many things during the war. They cleared vacant houses and fitted them out as hostels for volunteers; kept a card-index of anyone who applied for help, including enemy aliens stranded in London; organized a bureau where factories bereft of male workers could engage suitable women; and coordinated refugee relief work.

Millicent Fawcett used the *Ladies' Field* article to issue a bracing message to the women of Britain, advising 'no panic; no hoarding either of foodstuffs or gold; no waste, material or moral; and as little curtailment as possible in the volume of enjoyment.' She was all for female factory workers being trained to fill more responsible posts vacated by men: 'It would be a great triumph if in this and other similar ways we were able to wrest a positive advantage out of the stress and strain of the present crisis.'

The magazine's interview with Mrs Pankhurst is accompanied by a portrait of her looking frail and wistful. She explains that Christabel has gone to the United States 'to combat German Press influence about the war' and mentions a hospital set up by suffragette Dr Flora Murray, in Claridge's in Paris, partly funded by the WSPU. She also echoes Millicent's sentiment about the future: 'One thing is certain; the position of women must be a different one when the war is ended. We cannot, after having faced the realities of life, return again to the false standards of gentility which made men confine the energies of their womenfolk entirely to the home.'

Smaller suffrage societies are mentioned too: the Free Church League was pragmatically encouraging women to emigrate, to lessen the economic strain on Britain. Women writers were engaged in journalism and propaganda (essentially the same thing at this stage). Forward Cymric, a new Welsh group, was also working on propaganda and on the welfare of its countrywomen. Mrs Herbert Cohen, the honorary treasurer of the Jewish League, was providing paid work five days a week, plus meals, to 'gentlewomen refugees'; and Kate Frye's outfit, the NCS, opened a machine-knitting workroom.

It is obvious that suffrage campaigners were aware of the need for proactivity. They acted with imagination and enormous efficiency. But perhaps 'combined efforts' is not exactly the right phrase to describe their work. The suffrage movement had never spoken with one voice; after 4 August 1914, for a while it hardly spoke at all. The fight for the vote was no longer at the front of members' minds (Mrs Despard's organization excepted). It was important now to use the skills they had learned throughout the campaign for the benefit of the country. Few disagreed with Mrs Fawcett when she maintained that women had a duty to win victory just as much as men did, but each branch of the suffrage campaign interpreted this duty in different ways, sometimes with disharmonious results. What the Ladies' Field feature did not reveal was how the WSPU and the NUWSS were fractured by their leaders' ideologies. Scores of new

suffrage organizations sprang up, not so much peopled by converts
to the Cause as by old members unhappy with various internal party
lines. Suffragettes all but went extinct. Everyone was a suffragist
now, but as Mrs Pankhurst pointed out, what was the good of a vote
without a country to vote in?

As the war progressed, Emmeline and Christabel Pankhurst
campaigned at home and abroad for men to join up (ostentatiously
awarding them white feathers if they were reluctant to do so) and for
women to play as constructive a part in the conflict as they dared.
'I'm not nursing soldiers,' Emmeline explained rather loftily to her
followers. 'There are so many others to do that . . . it is no more
to be expected that our organisers should now necessarily take to
knitting and nursing than that Mr Asquith should set his ministers
to making Army boots or uniforms.'[17] Instead she advocated women
moving into the workplace, doing jobs previously – or still – done
by men of fighting age. While this approach goaded miners in Wales
and tram drivers in Hull to take strike action, it was one the government supported.

Extraordinarily, given their past relationship, Emmeline was
asked by the minister for munitions, Lloyd George, to organize one
more procession through London in July 1915. It was to demonstrate women's right to serve on the home front, where their help
was sorely needed. Germany had already deployed hundreds of
thousands of women to work in armaments; Britain lagged behind,
wasting a valuable resource. It was also designed to appease those
fretting about an industrial takeover by women with a soul-stirring
display of British femininity or, as Lloyd George put it, to 'create an
atmosphere in which the men . . . would be obliged to give way.'[18]
And it would raise public morale. Fabulous spectacles on the streets
of London had always done that. This time, it was hoped, there
would be no opposition to spoil the show.

Given the odd heckle about maids taking men's jobs, the march
was a great success. Thirty thousand women took part from all walks

of life, not all of them WSPU members. They were encouraged to dress in white, although forced to wear raincoats in the dismal weather, with red, white and blue trimmings replacing the old suffragette colours. Kate Frye could not resist joining in, but was canny about it: she put on a short grey linen dress, a smart woollen Aquascutum coat to keep her warm, with boots, galoshes and an umbrella. She had pounded too many pavements in English summers to be caught out. They set off from the Embankment, just like the old days, and with Mrs Pankhurst in the vanguard they snaked through Trafalgar Square to Whitehall, watched by about a hundred thousand spectators. It was pouring down, but according to an eyewitness most women (save Kate) pluckily did without brollies.

The march was divided into sections, each with a brass band and with banners straining at their tethers like kites. 'For men must fight and women must work', they read; 'Shells made by a wife may save a husband's life'; 'Women's Battle Cry is Work, Work, Work'; 'Delays have Dangerous Ends'. There was an elaborately arranged Pageant of the Allies. A girl in a tattered dress, holding aloft a torn flag, was the embodiment of 'the sorely tried, but yet unconquerable soul' of Belgium. She walked barefoot through the mud. Russia, Poland, France and Italy followed. England was represented by a young woman in a simple white frock carrying an armful of roses, while Scotland, Wales and Ireland walked beside her in their national dress. At intervals along the route there were tables where women inspired by the pageant could sign on as munitions workers or in other roles. At one of these tables an elderly lady was heard to ask, 'Do you think I could fill shells? I must do something to save my last boy. He has just sailed for the Dardanelles. The other two were taken before Christmas and my little lad is all I have in the world.'[19]

The Times was completely won over by the efficiency and effectiveness of this 'Right to Serve' march. In an article on the following Monday it praised the WSPU for its readiness to leave behind the grievances of the past and help with 'the one thing that matters, the winning of the war.' It noted how Mrs Pankhurst was cheered as she strode along at the head of the procession, and how wonderful it was that, at last, men and women were working for a common cause 'which is the cause of civilization.' How things change.

The march climaxed in the choreographed presentation by Mrs Pankhurst to Lloyd George of a petition demanding certain government measures: not the vote, of course, but the inclusion of women's names on a national register of workers and the promise of equal piece-work wages. The marchers did not seek, nor were they offered, the guarantee of working on the same terms after the war when the men came home; that was a battle for another day.

Sylvia Pankhurst was appalled by the whole thing. She and Adela were pacifists, as were other former members of the WSPU, and recoiled with horror at the thought of encouraging men to fight and women to supply their arms. She concentrated her energies on practical welfare work in the East End of London, opening a cut-price restaurant for working mothers, a Montessori nursery school at a former pub originally called the Gunmaker's Arms but now rechristened the Mother's Arms, and setting up a factory in Bow, with a crèche, producing wooden figures, soft toys and wax- or porcelain-headed dolls designed by her friends in the Arts and Crafts movement. She sold the toys to Selfridges in London, neatly filling a gap left by the halt in imports of traditional German toys.

Members of the 600-odd branches of the NUWSS did not eschew 'knitting and nursing' as Emmeline Pankhurst did. That did not mean that they lost any of their political ambition; just that they were prepared to put those ambitions on hold for a while. Florence Lockwood belonged to a suffragist society in Huddersfield and kept a diary for the duration. It opens with a meeting on 14 August 1914 including all sorts of women – 'Church, Chapel, Tories, Liberals, Socialists and Suffragists' – discussing what they can do for the war effort. Whatever they decide, writes Florence, she hopes that 'when we emerge from this pit more women will be able to see that our fall is owing to the lop-sided state of the world's governments.'[20]

Commenting on an appeal from celebrity author Baroness Orczy for a hundred thousand women to join a league to influence their husbands and brothers, sweethearts and friends to join up and fight, Florence says it's a ghastly idea: 'We are sick to death, we suffragists, of being told by men what we may do, ought to do, what is "womanly." In the name of common sense let us not copy the folly and set out to tell men what they may do and ought to do – what is "manly."' She loses patience with her sister suffragists at their annual meeting in a local café in July 1915: they should be concentrating on the business in hand, but instead of listening to the visiting speaker they behave like a bunch of daft little lasses banging doors, scraping chairs, clanking spoons, chattering, coughing, sneezing and rustling their agenda papers. Florence believed that feminism and pacifism should walk hand in hand into a future when 'everything that women do (such as bringing up children) will then be considered of importance.' Women who gossiped and rattled their teacups while important business was at hand did not deserve such a future. Florence's trenchancy proves that it was not the case, as the popular myth has it, that the Great War elevated all women to paragons of self-sacrifice and resourcefulness. What it did do was help them to prioritize, to choose how best to serve their families and communities, as well as their country.

A clash of priorities is what threatened to split the NUWSS executive apart at the beginning of the war. Millicent Fawcett's patriotism was so deep-seated that she considered pacifism to be tantamount to treachery. She was no more a militarist now than she had ever been, but she could not help feeling that those suffragists in the NUWSS who denounced the war were being disloyal to Britain. She refused to attend an International Congress in The Hague in 1915, held to promote peace, because she was convinced that, ironically, it was bound to be full of empty rhetoric and bluster, of 'violent outbursts and fierce denunciations' which would achieve nothing in the long term but ill-feeling. She firmly believed that by supporting women at home, the NUWSS would help Britain win the war, and that Britain winning the war was the best thing that could happen to the world.

·This belief led to mass resignations from the executive committee in 1915 from those who felt it behoved women everywhere to oppose all forms of violence. Only by making their views known globally would they be listened to and then, perhaps, the fighting would stop: better is wisdom than weapons of war. We are back in the realms of influence and power. Millicent, in this particular battle, wanted neither – just to serve. Some of her colleagues had higher ambitions. In the end, the disagreement did not have much of an impact on the organization of the NUWSS, since what bound members together was stronger than what forced them apart, and mutual respect was always a hallmark of the suffragist movement.

On one thing everyone was agreed: it was imperative to keep alive the spirit of the Great Pilgrimage and to use its legacy constructively. Many newspapers carried women's columns or even women's pages now, where suffragist activities were reported and features run on the social and welfare problems highlighted by the pilgrims on their travels. Their coverage of wartime activities evinced a great deal of local pride. Mansfield Women's Suffrage Society in Nottingham was typical of many provincial branches of the NUWSS. Using their experience of fundraising for the Cause in the past, members were able to send quantities of money to local regiments to pay for shirt material and wool for socks (made by Nottinghamshire women, thus giving them jobs). In August 1914 alone they put in orders for 238 new garments, 163 'renovated' ones and 14 pairs of boots, again produced by local labour. They presented a motor car to the authorities to be used for war-work; they ran a 'Mothers and Babies Welcome' – presumably a cross between a social group and a clinic; and they bravely volunteered for the new 'Women's Patrols' being set up near forces' training camps.

These patrols were not, as one might imagine, to protect young ladies from the unwanted attentions of lusty young servicemen. On the contrary. This is the account of a patroller setting out on duty in November 1914 after a dance at a Forces' Club:

As we threaded our way among the crowd of men and women jostling each other on the pavement, we were followed here and there by curious glances; ragged boys with dirty faces circled round us with excited whispers of 'Look! look! the lady p'leece!' and almost tripped us up in their efforts to read the letters on our armlets. Punctually as the church clock struck the half-hour, we reached our appointed beat and settled down into the slow walk of the patrol on duty; a brisk pace compared to that of the pickets of soldiers crawling along the gutter . . .

'Be careful, lady,' a drunken man lurched past us with an amiable smile, and added confidentially, 'I'm a little intoxicated.' Two young girls, fashionably attired, wearing pearl necklaces and sparkling ear-rings, ceased their animated conversation and stared at us in contemptuous surprise. ''Ere, what's that?' I did not catch the answer, but have no doubt it was something far from complimentary. They turned and stared again, and went off into peals of discordant laughter. Their mirth was a little forced, and the surprise over-acted, for we had met before. After they had left, my partner left me and followed them at a discreet distance, and I continued my way in the direction of the rendezvous agreed upon whenever we have occasion to separate – a little 'sausage and mash' shop down a quiet street . . .

Further on, a girl about thirteen, poorly clad, stood in a recess between two shops, gazing listlessly with forlorn air at the passers-by. A sailor, rather unsteady on his feet, stopped to greet her, and caught hold of her arm. She smiled at him as he urged her to 'come along,' and while he pleaded I approached the shop window within half a yard of the couple and pretended to be interested in the advertisement of a corn cure . . . I was conscious that the girl was watching me, and presently there was a slight scuffle. She had

shaken herself free. At that moment a group of laughing girls came
along past us, and the sailor's attention was distracted. After a second
of hesitation he lurched off in pursuit of them.[21]

The ostensible purpose of these patrols was to keep soldiers
and sailors free from sexually transmitted diseases, and to safeguard
women's morality. But volunteers like this one had another agenda:
to rescue prostitutes from danger and degradation, fully in tune with
the reforming tenets of the suffrage campaign.

The variety of work done by former pilgrims during the Great
War – individually rather than as part of an organization – is hard
to appreciate, since few courted publicity. Marjory and Sarah Lees
donated a motor vehicle to the St John Ambulance, which was
named in big white letters 'The Oldham Suffragist'. Cicely Leadley
Brown, the multi-talented whistler, toured the country giving
thrifty cooking demonstrations using home-grown vegetables
and her own invention, the 'patriotic sausage . . . guiltless of
pork',[22] while NUWSS officials Grace Hadow and Helena Auerbach
helped to found the Women's Institute movement.[23] Selina Cooper
continued as a speaker, growing increasingly interested in politics. Muriel Matters married a Mr Porter and trained as a nursery
teacher, eventually running Sylvia Pankhurst's little school set up
in the Mother's Arms in Bow. Lady Rochdale travelled to Cairo,
where her husband was stationed, and worked with Syrian
refugees. Edith Eskrigge, organizer of the Watling Street route,
joined Eleanor Rathbone in running the Soldiers' and Sailors'
Families' Association in Liverpool. Another pilgrim, Amelia Scott
of Tunbridge Wells in Kent, ran a laundry for soldiers and helped
Belgian refugees.

Refugee work seems to have been of particular interest to the
suffragists. Perhaps it was something to do with being an outcast.
In Oxford, the Women Students' Society for Women's Suffrage
held a training camp for forty-four members to learn how best to

help displaced Belgians in their own country. It was an immersive experience. Most women did half an hour's 'Swedish drill' (callisthenics or keep-fit exercises used by the military) before breakfast at eight o'clock, then their tents were inspected, waste water carried away and fresh brought up. They learned how to cook economically on a fire, how to pitch and strike a tent efficiently, how to dig a good trench for latrines and how to send signals. They were also taught rudimentary Flemish, first-aid techniques by a local district nurse, and what might happen in various worst-case scenarios by someone who had worked for the Red Cross in Belgium and been taken prisoner by the Germans.

It may have been a bit of a lark, this camp in the Cotswold countryside serviced by relays of delivery boys from the neighbouring village (one of whom was heard to remark, 'I wouldn't live 'ere, not for three pound a week.').[24] Anti-suffragists – still happy to snipe – were scathing of all such work, scoffing that 'they sew and knit comforts for the soldiers but with such a perpetual running accompaniment of suffragist self-laudation that they might as well embroider the sacred name of Mrs Pankhurst or Mrs Fawcett on every sock . . .'[25] But its purpose was deadly serious. A few weeks after this camp broke up and its members went off to practise their new skills in the field, nurse Edith Cavell was executed in Belgium for helping Allied soldiers escape to freedom. 'I realise,' she said memorably, 'that patriotism is not enough.'

We last saw Vera Chute Collum riding a borrowed horse into Hyde Park on the afternoon of Saturday, 26 July 1913. After the Pilgrimage was over she returned to work in the NUWSS press office, where she first heard about the organization that was to consume the next three and a half years of her life. It was the brainchild of a Scottish doctor, Elsie Inglis, supported by a remarkable group of suffragists whose efforts not only saved lives, but helped to change the face of professional medicine.

Elsie Inglis (1864–1917) trained in Scotland and at Elizabeth Garrett Anderson's New Hospital for Women in London. In her meagre spare time she worked for the Cause, becoming a popular and highly energetic suffrage speaker. She returned to Scotland to open her own women's hospital for the poor in 1899. From then until August 1914 she worked as a surgeon and one of the Scottish suffragists' most committed evangelists, always eager to travel and spread the word whenever her medical duties allowed. Her first thought when war broke out was to help the Red Cross by opening another hospital in Edinburgh staffed entirely by her female colleagues; when no suitable premises could be found, she offered her services to the War Office instead, suggesting that similar units should be set up on the Western Front. A preposterous idea. 'My good lady,' smiled the functionary to whom she applied, 'go home and sit still.'

No doubt spurred on by this breathtaking display of condescension, she took her idea to the Scottish Federation of Suffrage Societies, who gladly agreed to sponsor one of their own, should her offer be accepted elsewhere. So she wrote to the French and Serbian ambassadors in London, both of whom welcomed the scheme, and in November 1914 the first such unit left for France, where a Scottish Women's Hospital (SWH) unit was set up in three weeks flat in an abandoned thirteenth-century abbey, Royaumont, north of Paris. It had a hundred beds, an operating theatre, an X-ray facility and a dispensary. The basic staff included seven senior doctors, ten trained nurses, an administrator, a clerk, two cooks, two maids and four drivers; they were all paid salaries, if required. A couple of junior doctors joined them, with a group of orderlies. Apart from the cooks, all of them were women, from the chief medical officer to the lowliest hand. Their first patients arrived in early January 1915.

By the end of the war, there were fourteen hospitals like the one at Royaumont – elsewhere in France, in Corsica, Malta, Romania,

Russia, Salonika and Serbia. Their staff included Pilgrimage organizer Katherine Harley; the horse-whisperer Evelina Haverfield (an ex-suffragette) and her partner, Mrs Pankhurst's erstwhile chauffeuse Vera Holme; Cicely Hamilton, who wrote the words to Ethel Smyth's suffragette anthem 'March of the Women'; Nannie Brown, who was one of the Brown Women who walked from Edinburgh to London in 1912; and Vera Chute Collum. Not only did they treat casualties with calm efficiency and conspicuous success (many never

Katherine Harley, originator of the Pilgrimage and an administrator of the Scottish Women's Hospitals.

having had male patients before), but resident bacteriologists also conducted pioneering research into the diagnosis and treatment of gas gangrene. The death rate and number of amputations carried out at Royaumont were among the lowest of any hospital in the theatre of war.

Nicknamed simply 'Collum', Vera left her post in the NUWSS office in Westminster, where she had recently been coordinating fundraising for the SWH, and sailed on 26 February 1915 for Royaumont. She had initially applied to work there as an ambulance driver, despite her distrust of motor vehicles, but was detailed instead to the *vêtements* room, where she was expected to sort, disinfect, clean and mend all the patients' uniforms, ready for their discharge. The best disinfectant available was sulphur. At the end of each impossibly busy day, she slept on a straw mattress on the floor, with a bucket for her bathroom. Following the success of Vera's advertisement for a Pilgrimage horse, the *Common Cause* began publishing requests for hospital nightshirts, hot water bottles, thread for doing mending, another horse 'too old or young to go to the Front' to draw a hospital van, even a yacht to help transport supplies across the Channel. No doubt Vera was behind many of these appeals.

Before long, Vera was promoted from clothing duties to the X-ray department, with no other qualification than that she was a keen amateur photographer. For the rest of her time with the SWH she worked as a radiographer. The equipment she used was cutting-edge, housed in a Pandora's box of an ambulance van donated by the London branch of the NUWSS and fitted out with the advice of Marie Curie herself. When she wasn't needed in that capacity – which was rare – she deputized as a theatre orderly. After a year at Royaumont, she was allowed a month's leave, which she took back home in England.

On 24 March 1916 Vera embarked on SS *Sussex* for the return voyage to Dieppe. It was a bright, calm day, and she was longing to return to her unit. She had missed the work and the camaraderie.

Not long after leaving port, the ship was torpedoed by a German U-boat. Vera was knocked out, coming to minutes later 'in a tangle of wires and death' to find her hair down, her chin plastered with blood, and her ears ringing. She was temporarily deafened. The torpedo had sheared off the forepart of the ship, a few inches in front of her. That had sunk, but her portion of the vessel was miraculously still afloat. She managed to find herself a life jacket and swarm down a rope into an overcrowded lifeboat. Other survivors were ineffectually trying to bail out water with their hats or steadily dying. It quickly became apparent that everyone would be safer back on the remnants of *Sussex* than here in a top-heavy little boat at the mercy of currents sucking around the sunken wreckage. So Vera somehow climbed aboard again to wait for rescue. A British torpedo boat eventually saved her and, suffering from hypothermia, she was taken to hospital. Only then did she realize that she had broken her back, a foot, and had internal bruising. Much to her disgust, she wasn't allowed to leave for France for another three months.

When she did reach Royaumont again, she was just in time for the 'Great Push' at the beginning of the Somme offensive in July 1916. It was hell. A long whistle blast announced the arrival of each new wave of casualties, and she found she was taking X-rays for twenty hours a day, almost insensible to the pervasive stench of gangrene. Among the bravest of her patients were young men from Senegal, Tunisia and Algeria, who feared nothing except losing a limb, especially at the hands of a white woman, which was heartbreaking for those trying to help them.

Vera occasionally sent home descriptions of her life at Royaumont, published in the *Common Cause* or *Blackwood's Magazine* and illustrated by photographs of medical staff in immaculately white aprons tending men who look as though they appreciate the comparative calm and beauty of their surroundings. They might have been crammed into the wards two to a bed, and no one could deny the horror of what happened when ambulances arrived full of newly

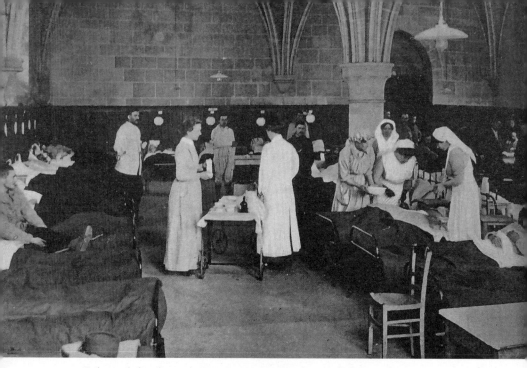

Calm and cleanliness at Royaumont Hospital on the Western Front.

injured casualties close to death, but the staff made the best of it. Although there were inevitable personality clashes, on the whole they worked with good humour (a stand-up comic was engaged on one occasion to perform in the former monks' refectory) and with great sensitivity. Vera's articles, and others, helped publicize the work of the SWH and to attract even more donations, which were already flooding in. NUWSS branches around the country adopted the Scottish Women's Hospitals as their principal wartime charity, with the result that each ward in each hospital was named after a bene-factor or a particular society, as were many of the beds within them. Two members of the Oxford Women's Suffrage Society endowed a bed at Royaumont for three months as a Christmas present to each other in December 1916; they called it after their house and even received letters from a French baker – now a soldier – who gratefully occupied it when he was wounded.

Around fifty people died on SS *Sussex*. Some of the hospital units were bombarded and their staff – including Mrs Harley – were taken prisoner. Doctors and nurses fell ill with typhus or even died. This was perilous work. Elsie Inglis herself became something of a celebrity at home and in Serbia, where she worked for most of her wartime career, for her disregard of danger. Ishobel Ross from Skye described working at the SWH with her; if Ishobel had expected to find someone aloof and authoritarian, she was mistaken. Elsie had no sense of her own importance.

> [We] went up behind the camp and through the trenches. It was so quiet with just the sound of the wind whistling through the tangles of wire. What a terrible sight it was to see the bodies half buried and all the place strewn with bullets, letter cases, gas masks, empty shells and daggers. We came across a stretch of field telephone too. It took us ages to break up the earth with our spades as the ground was so hard, but we buried as many bodies as we could. We shall have to come back to bury more as it is very tiring work.[26]

Any idea that suffragism was somehow a drawing-room pursuit – partly dispelled by the Pilgrimage – was now, surely, a distant memory. Everyone was in this pitiful war together, at home or abroad, man or woman.

11

HALF A LOAF

1916–1918

The ordinary male disbelief in our capacity cannot be argued away.
It can only be <u>worked</u> away.[1]

DR ELSIE INGLIS spent the next few years at full tilt. After oversee-
ing the organization of Royaumont hospital she stayed behind in
Scotland to raise funds for the SWH, but when the chief medical
officer of the first Serbian unit resigned in April 1915 due to ill-
health, Elsie took her place in the field. That autumn, the Germans
and Austrians re-invaded Serbia, took over Elsie's unit and put her in
charge of a prisoner-of-war hospital where she was herself interned
until February 1916. She came home to raise more money and
recover her strength, although by now she realized she was suffering
from cancer. Keeping her illness a secret, she left for southern Russia
at the beginning of September 1916 to take charge of Serbian units
there and in Romania. Her account of this mission, running field
hospitals a few miles from the front, is deceptively matter of fact.
Reading it makes one realize what remarkable personalities she and
her sister suffragists at the SWH were, and how well their pre-war
campaigning fitted them for a life of tests and challenges.

Elsie left the port of Liverpool for Archangel, via the Arctic
Circle, with seventy-five women and enough equipment to sustain a
unit with a hundred beds. This paraphernalia comprised everything

from tins of treacle to sophisticated, up-to-the-minute motor
ambulances. As had been the case at Royaumont, the majority was
donated by suffrage society members across the British Isles. From
Archangel, the travellers took a train to Odessa and then another
for what should have been a five- or six-hour journey to Reni, now
in Ukraine but then in Romania. In fact, that leg of the trip took
three days and four nights. A steamer voyage followed, with the
hospital's transport (in the charge of horsewoman and ex-suffragette
Evelina Haverfield) loaded on to separate barges. All the packing
and unpacking, checking and supervision involved in the expedition
was carried out by the women themselves, with whatever help they
could muster along the way.

When they reached their destination five miles from the front,
Elsie was allocated a barrack building and had a couple of days to
turn it into a hospital. Everyone set to, clearing it out, cleaning it,
bleaching the walls with whitewash and then installing the equipment. Astonishingly, everything arrived at more or less the same
time, except for a suspiciously missing box of golden syrup. Elsie
could see that the Serbian army officers – one of whom, surprisingly,
was an amiable young man from Belfast – had misgivings about
the women's ability to cope, but these were soon dispelled when
a complete hospital with an operating theatre, dressings room and
bathroom emerged from the chaos within hours. 'The ordinary male
disbelief in our capacity cannot be argued away,' Elsie explained in
her report home. 'It can only be *worked* away.'

The hospital received its first patients on 4 October 1916, trans-
ported by SWH ambulances from the front line. There were 102
casualties in that cohort, but two died almost immediately. All the
men were triaged, bathed, their wounds were dressed and they were
operated upon if necessary, then put to bed. More came and went
over the next forty-eight hours. It was a punishing routine for everyone. The staff were only just getting used to it when on 6 October the
Allied armies started a retreat and orders came through to evacuate

the whole place and build another hospital ten miles away. Fine, responded Dr Inglis equably; we'll pack everything up; make those patients who are accompanying us as comfortable as possible; try to find enough trains to get us there in this volatile war zone; perhaps appropriate a carriage or two to act as a temporary ward or even operating theatre; and get on with it. The SWH staff appear to have been utterly imperturbable. Just one thing caused Elsie to pause, and that was the sight of refugees at dusk one evening, fleeing the area to which she and her unit had just been sent:

> One reads of refugees, but never could one imagine such a sight. The whole road was one continuous stream of carts loaded up with luggage on which were children; men and women tramped along beside them. Every now and then there was a regular cart with boards stretched across measuring about 10 or 12 ft., piled up with household goods. They filled the whole roadway. Against the stream we tried to go, and through it barged cannon and ammunition wagons, and squadrons of cavalry; loose foals and dogs ran about everywhere; and when we turned on our headlights the whole thing became unreal, seemed like a well-staged piece at the theatre. At one point we came upon a flock of sheep, and for a minute we saw only red lights reflected from ours in their eyes – no sheep at all.[2]

The British women, walking in apparently the wrong direction, looked similarly exhausted and hungry in their travel-stained uniforms and heavy (but practical) regulation boots – so much so that a passing officer offered Elsie a precious chicken bone from his pocket and another volunteered a loaf of bread. But they kept going, diverting at one point to help in another hospital where there were eleven thousand wounded, six doctors and just one surgeon. One of Elsie's medical officers had recently broken her ankle after a kick from a horse and Elsie herself was finding it increasingly difficult to hide and cope with the cancer.

She closed her report of the three months between September

and November 1916 with a paragraph reminiscent of Millicent Fawcett's exhortation to all suffragists everywhere: that they should work for the Cause with a glad heart and good faith.

> We have made friends with many Romanian women, both in our own hospitals and others. One of them said what they loved about us was our 'simplicity.' We wondered what 'simplicity' could mean, and Dr C. suggested it must be our *boots!* There is no doubt our boots have made a great impression. We hear of them on all sides! The other thing is our cheerfulness. One of the little Russian Sisters who are to come with us said today she was so glad to come, for she had heard we were 'so joyous, and the Russians are sad.' I hope we shall be able to make her 'joyous,' too.[3]

Elsie remained in the theatre of war until the last possible moment, when she could hardly stand, in November 1917. She insisted on waiting until her Serbian patients were finally transferred out of Russia to comparative safety, sending a telegram to headquarters when that finally came to pass. It read 'On our way home, everything satisfactory and all well except me.'[4] The day after she and her staff reached England, in the unexotic setting of the Station Hotel, Newcastle upon Tyne, she ran out of life at the age of fifty-three. Her body lay in state in Edinburgh's St Giles' Cathedral before the funeral, which was attended by representatives of the British and Serbian royal families. At a memorial service in St Margaret's, Westminster, in early December, the Serbian National Anthem was played. She was the first woman to have been awarded the country's highest honour, the Order of the White Eagle. There were calls, among the tributes, for her to receive the Victoria Cross. Next to Edith Cavell, Dr Elsie Inglis was the nation's most celebrated war heroine.

Several high-profile suffragists died before the Armistice. At the back of a notebook kept by Marjory Lees on the 1913 Pilgrimage is added a tribute to Katherine Harley. Mrs Harley began her wartime

career as an administrator with the SWH in France; then she worked
with units in Macedonia and Serbia before taking charge of a flying
column of motor ambulances in the Greek mountains in July 1916.
She was hit and killed by a shell while caring for refugees – not part
of her job – at Monastir in Serbia (today's Bitola in Macedonia) on
7 March 1917; she was in her early sixties. Marjory added a quote at
the end of her handwritten obituary: 'To die for one's country is fine
. . . but to die for another country, that is superb. That is something
beyond us.'⁵ Marjory and Katherine's travelling companion, Lady
Rochdale, was equally fulsome:

> We have not sat at home while our men went out. We have gone
> out, too, and worked, some quite as hard as men. Only last week
> we heard of the death of a very keen suffragist who was killed by
> a shell as any man has been killed. We suffragists feel very proud
> of the woman who laid down her life as any man has done for her
> country. I knew her personally and walked by her side many miles
> in the suffragists' pilgrimage. We stood side by side one night when
> a great many men were hurling things at us. She stood her ground
> then as I am sure she stood it out in Serbia. We suffragists feel very
> proud of the name of Mrs Harley.⁶

Beloved Dr 'Murdie' Murdoch fell victim to influenza in March
1916. Her patients and colleagues were devastated by her sudden loss;
hundreds watched her funeral procession, led by her cherished motor
car, and laid flowers in her way.

Millicent Fawcett's sister, Dr Elizabeth Garrett Anderson, was
an old lady when she died in December 1917, around five weeks
before the Representation of the People Act, which gave women the
vote, became law. A choir consisting entirely of uniformed women
doctors sang at her funeral.

Elizabeth Wolstenholme Elmy, who had worked so hard to gather
support for John Stuart Mill's petition in 1866, passed away some
five weeks *after* the Act received Royal Assent, in her eighty-fifth

year. She was living in a Manchester nursing home at the time. I hope they told her the news, and that she understood.

Meanwhile, more and more suffragists and ex-suffragettes were coming forward to serve either their country or their communities. There is a book in the archives at Newnham College, Cambridge, opulently bound in crimson morocco with gilt edges and an exquisitely embroidered fabric dust-wrapper.[7] It is a calligraphic record of the war-work done by students and alumnae, together with a list of the honours they achieved. Dr Annette Benson was chief medical officer at one of Elsie Inglis's hospitals in Serbia; she was awarded the Royal Serbian Order of St Sava. Dr Edith Martland was an assistant surgeon with the SWH in France: *Croix de guerre avec étoile*. Elinor Rendel, who wrote that lovely account of her suffrage trip in *Eva* the caravan with Jock the Scotsman, became an X-ray assistant in Russia and Romania: the Russian Order of St George and the Royal Serbian Order of St Sava. Edith Stoney was also a radiography assistant before becoming the head radiologist and X-ray engineer at Royaumont, working with Vera Chute Collum and at another SWH hospital at Villers-Cotterêts in France; she was decorated with the Order of Chivalry of St Sava, the *Croix de guerre*, *Médaille d'honneur des Epidémies*, the Allies' Medal and a Victory Medal. Several Newnham women worked as SWH organizers, drivers, fundraisers or orderlies.

Among a myriad other occupations, we learn in this extravagant volume about agricultural researchers, metallurgists, nurses, chemists at munitions factories, women's patrollers, intelligence officers, censors, meteorologists, teachers 'as substitutes for men', private secretaries, 'replacement' surgeons, welfare workers, members of the Land Army, collectors of sphagnum moss (used for dressing wounds), tractor drivers and chicken breeders. Many of these women were members of the Girton and Newnham Suffrage Society, who collectively subsidized the second unit established by the SWH in France: a tented hospital near Troyes.

That's one college; one small group of intellectually elite and privileged people. But millions of women around the country did what they could in munitions factories – turning yellow and diseased with exposure to TNT – and in every sort of trade, industry and service, except those which required lengthy specialist training like the driving of locomotive engines. Some joined the Auxiliary Forces, flying aeroplanes or even serving on the front line in the Serbian Army.[8] Others wrote stirring propaganda, became official war artists, ran women's football clubs to raise morale or simply made vats and vats and vats of jam.

Not everyone took part. Florence Lockwood in Huddersfield despaired of the apathy of her neighbours, who while men were dying grotesquely in the trenches seemed to her to be doing nothing more strenuous than organizing whist drives and bazaars. Perhaps harshly, Florence refused to join in, preferring instead to nurture her own brand of feminism by reading about and canvassing for pacifism and the women's international suffrage movement. On one memorable occasion she hissed the jingoistic songs being performed at a public concert party, which wasn't far from treason. She believed in women challenging themselves to make a better and more peaceful world, not in patriotism at any cost. In this she was like the pacifist Sylvia Pankhurst, who, as well as supporting the working women of her East London community, was becoming increasingly engaged in a campaign for universal adult suffrage – 'human suffrage', she called it. She reported on the campaign's progress in her new magazine, *Dreadnought*, and tried (unsuccessfully) to rally the combined support of other suffrage societies at a conference in London in January 1916. No one was much interested: the stakes were too high.

Florence's slightly scathing approach to the contributions of ordinary women of all social classes was unusual. For the most part, women's achievements and readiness to do anything to help – often in the face of considerable danger – were proudly acknowledged. Their efforts represented the most convincing argument so far in favour of women's suffrage. That, and the fact that every bereaved mother was surely owed something for the life of a fallen son; every wife for her husband.

Even Asquith could see that. In March 1917, he stated that his opposition to women's suffrage had always been based 'on considerations of public expediency', whatever that means. 'I think some years ago I ventured to use the expression, "Let the women work out their own salvation." That is what they have done during this war . . . I, for my part, find it impossible, consistently with either justice or expediency, to withhold from women the power and the right of making their voices discreetly heard.'[9] At long last, this was an unqualified admission that well-behaved women deserved the vote. Perhaps the WSPU had been right after all: in the end it was deeds that mattered, not words.

That said, it is misleading to insist – as so many commentators do – that women won the vote solely because of what they did during the war; that it was a reward, in other words. Asquith was right to point out that their achievements in the workplace were deserving of it, but they might not have undertaken such a wide range of occupations, nor done them so well, were they not already seasoned by suffrage work. From mill-hands like Selina Cooper to aristocrats like Lady Rochdale, middle-class philanthropists like Marjory Lees to passionate campaigners like Emma Sproson, left-wing pacifists like Sylvia Pankhurst to right-wing imperialists like her mother: all of them had experience in organization, campaigning, accepting responsibility and working towards a more or less common cause well before the summer of 1914. Dr Elsie Inglis would not have been as effective as chief medical officer of the SWH had she not first been effective as a suffragist. The success enjoyed (if that's the right word) by women from all walks of life during the war was to some extent dependent on how the expectations of women had been slowly changing during the years – decades, even – preceding it. Their collective capability as a species had evolved quickly since Queen Victoria, that contrary monarch who according to a suffragette writer had 'never been accused of thinking *herself* undeserving of any place or any power,' came to the throne.[10] More pertinently, so had politicians' perception of that capability. The white heat of the war forged their efforts into something solid and immovable, something that could no longer be ignored.

The catalyst for change was the realization at the beginning of 1916 that a new electoral registration system was required. The current one included an occupation qualification. Also, a man had to have been resident in Britain for at least twelve months in order to vote. So where did that leave soldiers and sailors, away from home because they were fighting for their country? The rules would have to be rewritten. In May 1916, Millicent Fawcett wrote to Asquith on behalf of the NUWSS to ask him to include women in any new franchise Bill under consideration. It had been suggested that military service would be a better arbiter of the right to vote for men than occupation; why should this not apply to women too, asked Millicent, given *their* war service?

As was his habit, Asquith did not commit himself straight away, but did admit that women were doing sterling work and that when the war was over they must continue to do so to help reconstruct the country. He referred the question of a new Representation of the People Bill to a cross-party Speaker's Conference in October 1916. James Lowther was still in post. He presided over thirteen Conservatives (MPs and peers), thirteen Liberals, four Labour Party members and four supporters of Irish Home Rule. The following month Asquith was replaced as prime minister by David Lloyd George. Both wings of the women's suffrage campaign were united in Lloyd George, whose new best friend was Emmeline Pankhurst, now concerned not so much with fighting for the vote as with fighting against the twin threats of German rapaciousness and Bolshevism. The suffragists had also found a friend in Lloyd George in the past; he had been comparatively impotent then, but things were different now. And because of the wartime coalition, there was less concern about toeing party lines in tackling the previously divisive subject of women's suffrage, which boded well.

The Speaker's Conference met twenty-six times between 12 October 1916 and 27 January 1917, when Mr Lowther reported its conclusions to the prime minister. Members had voted 15 to 6 in favour of some measure of enfranchisement for women; it was not yet clear what that measure would be. They vetoed equal franchise (by a majority of just 2) but suggested instead an age qualification – perhaps thirty-five; at least thirty – so that the number of women eligible to vote did not exceed and overwhelm the number of men. At that time, given the average life expectancy of women, thirty-five was well into middle age. Two months later, Asquith, of all people, moved in the House of Commons that the report should be debated with a view to introducing a new Representation of the People Bill along the lines of the conference's findings.

The immediate reaction of the NUWSS was to organize one final deputation to Whitehall, to push home the point about women's work qualifying them to vote, and persuade members of the Houses of Commons and Lords that the age threshold should be no higher than thirty, ideally lower. However, Millicent did not want to make this latter point a deal-breaker. She would have preferred equal fran-chise, of course, 'But we wouldn't refuse half a loaf because we had asked for a whole one and were not offered it! We shall "take what we can get" and still go on asking until the sex barrier is entirely removed.'[11] The deputation on 29 March 1917 was an impressive one, including women of all ages representing a gamut of occupations. It had the august backing of the Women's Temperance Association, the National Federation of Women Workers, the National Organ-isation of Girls' Clubs, the National Union of Women Workers, the

National Women's Labour League, the Women's Liberal Federation, the Railway Women's Guild, the Women's Co-operative Guild, and twenty-four women's suffrage organizations. The scope and gravitas of all those bodies was alone an argument for being taken seriously. Remarkably, Emmeline Pankhurst was also there, together with Madge Watt, a Canadian academic responsible for establishing the Women's Institute movement in Britain.

The list of trades, professions and occupations represented by the members of the deputation is long. That was the point. In alphabetical order, there were accountants, agricultural workers, ambulance drivers, authors, bacteriologists, bakers, bookbinders, bus conductors, carpenters, chain-makers, civil servants, cutlers, dentists, dispensing chemists, doctors, dressmakers, electro-platers, headmistresses, house agents, infant welfare workers, lamplighters, midwives, munitions welfare workers, munitions workers, nannies, nurses, pit-brow women, police officers, poor law guardians, post-office workers, members of the press, railway-engine cleaners, railway women, Scottish Women's Hospital workers (and workers from other hospital units supported by the NUWSS), sanitary inspectors, shippers, silversmiths, social workers, tailors, teachers, telephonists, temperance workers, textile workers (cotton and wool), town councillors, university women, VAD workers, van drivers, weavers, oxyacetylene welders, women working in overseas dominions, and workers in 'women's services'.

Lloyd George welcomed them all, and then indulged them in some Welsh oratory about the likelihood of their success:

> I am perfectly certain that wherever the objections may come from, they will not come from the soldiers . . . who recollect that it is due very largely to the work which women have rendered that they have been able, not merely to defend themselves in the trenches, but actually to hurl back their cruel foe. But undoubtedly the main argument for women's suffrage is an argument of peace. From the

moment the Legislature began to interfere in the home, to interfere with the health of the people, with the education of their children and their upbringing, and with all the various conditions of life, it was inconceivable that half of the population which was most concerned with the home and with the health and upbringing of the children, should have absolutely no voice at all in determining what was to be done . . . There was no logic, there was no sense, there was no justice in that, and sooner or later, the whole of the opposition to women's suffrage must crumble.[12]

That rousing speech was made in 1917, but to campaigning suffragists its sentiments were half a century old. How could he still be talking about 'sooner or later'? Emmeline Pankhurst was satisfied, declaring afterwards that 'as a measure of justice to women it is admirable.'[13] Millicent Fawcett was perhaps less convinced, but prepared as always to hope for the best.

When the Bill came up for debate during the next few months, Millicent was naturally keen to be there in the House of Commons to witness what might turn out to be the most significant piece of legislation in her long lifetime. She was seventy that summer. But the Ladies' Gallery was no more accommodating than it had been in the days when Muriel Matters used to chain herself to the grille, and having to peer through the wrought-iron tracery still gave Millicent a headache. In May 1917 she drafted a letter to 'All Members of the House of Commons' to ask very politely whether they might consider improving the lot of visitors like her by at least removing the grille.[14] She pointed out how uncomfortable the Ladies' Gallery was, where little could be heard and still less seen. There were exciting times ahead in the House, of distinct and immediate interest to women; she didn't want to miss a thing. The letter was signed by scores of NUWSS members and the following August, when almost everything was over, the grille was finally and symbolically cut away.

In June 1917 the Bill passed its third reading in the House of Commons by a majority of 330. It awarded the vote to all men over the age of twenty-one (or nineteen if they were serving members of the Forces) and, in Clause 4, enfranchised women of thirty or above who were not legally or mentally incapacitated, were householders, the wives of householders, occupiers of property with an annual rent of £5 which they furnished themselves or graduates of British universities.

The battle was not quite won yet: the House of Lords must debate it first. The leader of the Upper House at that time was the reactionary Lord Curzon who had once said women should never be granted the vote because inherently they lacked the necessary calmness of temperament and balance of mind for political judgement. But even he had mellowed. Their Lordships were not quite as decisive as their colleagues in the other place: while the debate was in progress Millicent Fawcett reckoned 71 were in favour, 59 against, and the rest were either 'doubtful' or had not yet made up their minds.[15] In the end they passed the Bill in January 1918 by 134 votes to 69, and on 6 February it received Royal Assent and became enshrined in law. Millicent and a group of close friends were there to hear the result; then she flew home in a taxi to tell her daughter, Philippa, and elderly sister, Agnes, the news. It was late. As soon as the housemaid opened the door Millicent shouted 'We've won!', and when Philippa appeared in her dressing gown the women whooped with joy and fell into each other's arms.

Emmeline Pankhurst's reaction on hearing that the Bill had made its way through the House of Commons was to disband the WSPU and form the Women's Party, led by her, Christabel, 'General' Flora Drummond and Annie Kenney, veteran suffragettes all. Their platform was to fight – keep fighting – for Britain's victory in the war, with no compromises, and afterwards to secure equality in pay, employment, and in marriage and divorce laws. Their twelve-point manifesto included a call for more stringent rationing, with communal kitchens across the country to avoid waste, and a purge from the government of anyone with enemy blood or connections. They also advocated the forcible dismantling of the Habsburg Empire after the war was won. Being a political party, they expected to field candidates for the next election. A short clip from a contemporary newsreel shows the four women arriving at Queen's Hall in Langham Place, London, for their inaugural meeting on 7 November 1917. Collectively they had endured months in prison and been forcibly fed scores of times. That they were still standing – never mind campaigning on the political front line – was miraculous. They appear to be in good fettle. Flora Drummond is wearing an extraordinary hat that looks like a cross between a bishop's mitre and a Red Indian headdress. According to her, she has spent the war 'combatting the effects of pacifism' in the industrial areas of the north, and is as stalwart a figure as she ever was. Emmeline, after years of war-work involving government-sponsored propaganda tours to the United States and to Russia, looks somewhat exhausted but still elegant in a silky black coat and a sort of miniature top hat. Christabel is similarly chic, while Annie Kenney, who has also spent much of the duration working abroad, appears comfortingly ordinary. The rubric at the beginning of the newsreel tells us that the ladies were greeted with 'wild enthusiasm'; in fact there were orderly queues outside the building, mostly of thoughtful women in sober winter jackets and skirts or fur coats. Proving that old habits die hard when reporting anything to do with women's suffrage, however, the cameraman cannot resist picking out some particularly hatchet-faced characters and a few men looking amiable but slightly lost.

The party met again in March 1918, this time at the Royal Albert Hall, to celebrate the Representation of the People Act becoming law. Annie Kenney spoke about the duty of women voters to support their country and fight for their rights. When the next General Election came, she said, 'the chief cry of the Women's Party would be "down with pacifism everywhere."'[16] Sylvia Pankhurst was saddened by this bluster. All she hoped for was a kinder future, where men and women, drawn closer by the suffering and sacrifices of the war, might work together with humility and patience to build a fairer world.

Members of the NUWSS were predictably measured in their collective response to winning the vote. The secretary of a provincial women's suffrage society recorded the occasion in the minute books, writing very properly – but rather po-faced – that its members wanted to mark their

> profound satisfaction that after fifty years of ceaseless agitation the political emancipation of women has at last been achieved . . . We recognise the many and great responsibilities enfranchisement entails . . . We are conscious of the need of much education in the principles of self-government, but we believe that this measure of justice, so long denied, has liberated a new force which will increasingly tend to promote the highest and best interests of the nation.[17]

On 13 March 1918, three days before the Women's Party held its convention at the Royal Albert Hall, Millicent Fawcett and the national leaders of the NUWSS let their hair down. No doubt they would concur with the society secretary quoted above, but if ever there was a time for joy, this was it. They hired Queen's Hall, members of the Artists' Suffrage League decked it out with gorgeous banners, the programme had a radiant sunrise on the front cover and the London Symphony Orchestra was engaged to play the music. The evening opened with Beethoven's nobly energetic overture Leonore No. 3, then the choir sang Bach's 'Awake Thou Wintry Earth'. Purcell's exuberant chorus 'Soul of the World' followed, then some dances by Sir Hubert Parry. The finale was Parry's 1916 setting of William Blake's 'Jerusalem'. Everyone present was encouraged to join in. Among the speakers were Pilgrimage stalwarts Maude Royden and, of course, Millicent Fawcett herself. Selina Cooper was there, down from Lancashire; so was anyone who was anyone in the higher echelons of the constitutional campaign, men and women, trying their best not to appear undignified in their elation over this new dawn, but – one hopes – not quite succeeding. It was a happy night, and it's good to imagine the grandmotherly Millicent kicking her heels with the best.

The next issue of the *Common Cause* was a special celebratory edition with a summary of the campaign's history and messages from pioneers and supporters both within and outside Parliament. An indefatigable suffrage worker from Leeds, Isabella Ford, put it beautifully when she wrote:

> It is indeed wonderful when one wakes in the morning to remember that now, at last, one is considered to be a real, complete human being! After thirty years of endeavour to make men understand they were only half the world, and women that they were the other half, and to make both see that two halves make a whole, it is really wonderful to find they at last . . . understand it all![18]

A feature on the status of women's enfranchisement elsewhere is interesting. There were thirteen so-called Suffrage States in the US by now. New Zealand, Australia and Canada all boasted (slightly different) voting rights for women, with South Africa the only major British Dominion remaining obdurate. Russian women had been expecting the vote since the Revolution in 1917 and achieved it in June 1918. In Norway there was now full adult suffrage and even a woman MP. All the other Scandinavian countries allowed women to vote, as did Hungary (with fairly stringent qualifications) and Germany. Progress was being made in the Netherlands and Austria, but in France, Italy and Switzerland the situation still looked pretty bleak. With the sort of magnanimity only winners can achieve, the editor wished them well.

The first General Election to include women electors was also the first to be conducted on a single day: Saturday, 14 December 1918. The war had scarcely been over a month and the general opinion was that the turnout would be low. So many men were still away, and the ladies would surely need some time to get used to the idea. They might be overwhelmed by the responsibilities of democracy, or shy, or too busy doing housework or other jobs to visit the polling station. Some people thought the suffragists were fixated on victory, on the act of winning the vote, and once that had been accomplished they would lose interest in politics. After such a long struggle, surely the process of putting a cross on a ballot paper would be an anticlimax?

How wrong they were.

Three weeks before the date of the election, the Parliament (Qualification of Women) Act was passed, enabling women to stand as MPs. This was ridiculously short notice, but the Women's Party was ready, putting up Christabel Pankhurst for the Smethwick seat in the West Midlands as a Coalition candidate. Seventeen women stood for election in all, though only two for a conceivably winnable seat: Christabel and the Countess Constance Markievicz for Sinn Féin in Dublin. The countess won with a 65 per cent share of the vote but, following her party's policy, never took her seat. There are some familiar names among the other female candidates. Charlotte Despard of the Women's Freedom League stood in Battersea at the age of seventy-three; Emmeline Pethick-Lawrence in Rusholme, Manchester; and Ray Strachey of the NUWSS – who had accompanied Elinor Rendel in *Eva* in 1908 – in Brentford, Middlesex. Bizarrely, the candidate for Mansfield in Nottingham was Miss Violet Markham, who was a convert to the Cause from the fervid ranks of the Anti-Suffrage League. Selina Cooper was asked by the NUWSS if she would consider standing as a Labour candidate in Lancashire, but never did.

Emily Phipps of the WFL stood as an Independent candidate in Chelsea. She was in her early forties, described as small, apparently demure, but possessed of a 'biting tongue' and a healthy sense of humour.[19] Her account of the difficulties of starting an electoral campaign from scratch in such a short time is illuminating. She had helped with other people's campaigns before, but had never had to take sole responsibility. Emily was backed by the National Federation of Women Teachers, of which she was president; they did much of the donkey work, buying copies of the necessary legislation – including the Corrupt Practices Act – so that she didn't fall foul of the law, appointing a woman agent (there had been no such creatures before) and selecting a constituency. The next step was to find a headquarters. They settled on some committee rooms, which seemed eminently suitable until they moved in and realized there was no gas, no electric light, no water supply, no furniture. Everything there *was* was unbelievably dirty: Emily could hardly see out of the windows. This was not an auspicious start. At first she relied on candles stuck in bottles; then she hired some oil lamps and bought the oil to fuel them. For two days she and her helpers lived on the telephone, ringing up plumbers, gas fitters, coal dealers, and window cleaners. In three days the water supply was in working order; it took four days to get gas laid on. A housekeeper was engaged via the local labour exchange, but she couldn't work without tools, so Emily had to buy buckets, brushes, dustpan, kettle, fire irons, dusters, towels and cleaning materials.

Printing presented difficulties. Paper was in short supply because of the war; Emily needed a government permit to procure it, which meant arranging an appointment with a commissioner for oaths. Even when she obtained the permit, deliveries were scanty and intermittent. Getting her election literature out in the post took ages. Then there was the business of nomination, which could only be done on a certain day at a certain time in a certain place. She needed to secure the names of a proposer, a seconder and eight 'assentors', all of whom were required to be electors in the relevant borough. Like passport application forms today, any mistake in spelling a name or anything else rendered the form invalid, so as there would not be time to get another one filled in, Emily made sure she had several copies, all completed at the same time and, as far as she could see, without blemish. The reasoning was that if the authorities found an error on one paper, it wouldn't be repeated on a different copy. Risky. A deposit of £150 was payable at the time of nomination, in notes, not a cheque.

All this left Emily and the other women candidates just nine clear days to do all their canvassing and to address a host of concerns expressed by putative electors. The list of questions she received seemed endless, and answering them took an immensely long time. She was soon bewildered. 'One was asked to agree to denominational religious teaching in schools, to undenominational religious teaching, and to no religious teaching; to a reform of the divorce laws, and to leaving them as they are; to relaxing the present restrictions on the sale of liquor, and to total prohibition; to making Germany pay the whole cost of the war, and to letting Germany off scot-free.'[20]

She was promised a vote on the condition that she could guarantee a bathroom in every house after the election; another if she professed devotion to the religious prophetess Joanna Southcott, who believed herself to be the Woman of the Apocalypse spoken of in the Book of Revelation. When Emily suggested to potential constituents that working mothers should be given an allowance to pay for domestic help or childcare, she was dismayed to overhear the following response: '"Vote for her? No! She's a *dreadful* woman! She wants to turn me out of the house for a couple of hours every day, and put a strange woman in to be with my old man!"'[21]

At least the press supported her. In general, newspapers were keen to give these novel parliamentary candidates publicity, and carefully noted their share of the ballot afterwards, usually in a spirit of genuine congratulation. Christabel won 47.8 per cent of votes polled in her constituency; Charlotte Despard won 33 per cent in Battersea; and the Labour candidate Miss Mary Macarthur 32.7 per cent in Stourbridge: apart from Countess Markievicz, these were by far the most successful. Only one – Miss Eunice Murray in Glasgow – lost her deposit. According to Emily Phipps (21 per cent), she and the other women candidates would have done much better had they (a) had more time to prepare themselves and the electorate; (b) had they been allocated winnable seats instead of having to shuffle on to the edge of the political stage at the last moment; and (c) were women voters less afraid of appearing naïve and ill-informed by choosing a necessarily inexperienced candidate. Emily was confident that next time things would be different. On one thing everyone was agreed: that most women had voted with dignity and surprising self-assurance, conscious of their duty as citizens and without making a fuss.

The Representation of the People Act enfranchised a total of 8,479,156 women: about 40 per cent of the female population. It is ironic that some of the most committed champions of votes for women were not among those millions. Perhaps they were too young, like the schoolgirl suffragette Winifred Starbuck, or living overseas like hunger striker Kitty Marion, who was in America, or Adela Pankhurst in Australia. Marjory Lees satisfied the age and residential qualifications, but was unmarried and still lived at home, so had neither her own house nor her own husband. Presumably, therefore, she was not eligible to vote, although her mother, Sarah, on whom a damehood had been conferred in 1917, most definitely was. Alice New was also unmarried and, as far as I know, lived with her family. Gladys Duffield's husband was her passport to the polling station, as was Lady Rochdale's. This was 'half a loaf' indeed, and to be denied a chance to share it must have been hard to take.

No doubt the disenfranchised still turned out to support their more fortunate sisters. Contrary to popular expectation, the turnout among women was high (although the overall figure for the election was only 57.2 per cent). In many constituencies a woman was the first person to cast her vote in the morning, with some ceremony, and there were more women than men throughout the day. A *Sunday Mirror* journalist estimated that 70 per cent of electors in London were women; the figure was 75 per cent in Chelmsford and 80 per cent in Leicester.[22] Emily Phipps had the bright idea of running a crèche for those mothers forced to bring their children to the polling station; at one stage in Stourbridge, a supporter of Miss Macarthur who had rashly offered to mind voters' children ended up with sixty babies in her care. Perhaps in tribute to Dr Murdoch, dozens of women in Hull queued up before the station opened its doors in the morning. In Caernarvonshire the polling clerks (who could now be women) were forced to think laterally and commandeer some oil drums to be used as ballot boxes when the ones provided filled up; when the same problem arose in Dundee, they turned to empty shell cases from a local munitions factory.

Only the most confident of women turned up alone. Many came with their husbands or in groups of friends, giving each other courage. Those who had voted already offered to accompany anyone unsure, to show them what to do. 'Don't be frightened,' said a Battersea housewife to an obviously nervous friend she met at the polling station. 'I've just voted and it's the easiest work I've done for many a day.'[23] When a splendid motor car drew up outside the polling station in Rotherhithe, onlookers were astonished to see four venerable old ladies disembark and totter inside to cast their votes. The youngest of them was eighty-five; the others were eighty-six, ninety and ninety-four. Emily Davies voted, naturally: she was one of the few to do so who had signed John Stuart Mill's 1866 Petition. So did Annie Ramsay, the 'old lady' of the Land's End Pilgrimage: she was so delighted by the opportunity that she almost skipped to the ballot box, stout as she was. The oldest woman on the electoral register was 'Granny' Lambert of Edmonton, North London, at 105. Come 14 December, however, she claimed to be feeling 'too tired' to walk to the polling station. She had never heard of Mr Lloyd

George, she said; if she had chosen to vote (and it was gratifying to have that choice) she would have gone for anyone who promised to have 'that beast of a Kaiser shot.'[24]

Like Granny Lambert, some people declined their right to vote. One rather snooty lady was overheard telling a neighbour that she would not be going to the polling station because she wished to remain respectable. The implication was – as it had ever been – that active participation in politics was unfeminine and vulgar. One assumes that members of the Anti-Suffrage League also abstained. Someone called Margaret Willoughby, writing for the *Daily Mirror*, explained why: 'We love to be bossed,' she confessed coquettishly, 'but not by our own sex . . . You'll never get us women interested in political affairs as a live, red-hot issue. We're more interested in sleeves and hat-shapes.'[25] The last-ever issue of the *Anti-Suffrage Review*, published in April 1918, was considerably less chirpy: 'The Cause has been lost. Sentimentality won the day . . . We have drifted into Women's Suffrage as we drifted into war, because no-one had the courage to cry "Halt!"'[26] A lady in Gloucester said she had never wanted the vote: 'I didn't ask for it and I shall not use it.'[27] The suffrage societies, together with the Mothers' Union, Women's Institute and other groups, held meetings before the election to try to combat this mixture of apprehension and apathy, and were largely successful.

The press could not resist sharing with its readers some of the day's light-hearted moments. Several virgin electors, on being asked by the polling clerks to confirm their addresses, loudly announced the name of the person for whom they wished to vote. Some boasted that they were not going to vote for the same person as their husbands. At Bristol, a group of nurses arrived and refused to believe that they were not eligible. They hadn't realized that they could vote only if their names were entered on the electoral register, and theirs were unlikely to be there as they neither owned their own homes – or furniture – nor, in most cases, were they old enough. Factory workers turned up in their thousands, however, either early in the morning before their shift began or in the rainy twilight, when in parts of Lancashire they voted by candlelight because the gas workers were on strike.

A mother in Liverpool turned her back for a moment and then lost her ballot paper. She couldn't understand where it had gone, until she noticed a tell-tale corner poking out from her dribbling baby's mouth. One lady carefully filled hers in, then folded it up, popped it in her handbag and left, quite satisfied. Another posted her paper in the ballot box and then asked where she collected her fee for doing so. Others confided to husbands or clerks their choice of candidate before enquiring doubtfully whether that was the 'right' person to have gone for. It tickled journalists that most women appeared to have taken this momentous step in their capable stride, turning up in numbers, casting their votes (parking the children/dog/shopping bags somewhere while they did so) and then leaving to carry on the business of the day 'smilingly and with a subdued air or triumph.'[28]

On 3 January 1919, the Women's Freedom League held a dinner in London to celebrate the winning of the vote, and to commemorate the courage and enthusiasm of their three parliamentary candidates: Charlotte Despard, Edith How Martyn of Hendon and Emily Phipps. This was the last of the great suffrage occasions that had punctuated the long campaign, and was suitably good-humoured. No one could accuse the WFL of being profligate: the menu was interesting, but vegetarian, and no smoking was allowed. After the soup, mock duck, ravioli, potatoes, carrots, jam tarts, chocolate trifle, spice pudding and cheese – washed down with water – Mrs Despard made a speech. 'I have seen great days,' she told her audience, 'but this is the greatest . . . I never believed that equal votes would come in my lifetime. But when an impossible dream comes true, we must go on to another.'

12

THE SEQUEL

1918–1928

A vote? Well, that was nothing. It's what it led to.[1]

IN 1925 JUAN-LES-PINS was *the* place to be. The ultra-fashionable resort in the south of France was frequented by celebrities like F. Scott Fitzgerald, Pablo Picasso and Ernest Hemingway: 'fast' people, slightly louche, with recherché tastes. Its brand-new high-rise hotels reeked of glamour and the beaches were decoratively strewn with sunbathers of both sexes wearing surprisingly little. Not the sort of place, one would have thought, to open a teashop. Yet that's exactly what three English ladies decided to do that year – a mother and her spinster daughter, aged sixty-six and forty-five, and their fifty-four-year-old friend – calling it 'the English Teashop of Good Hope'. They decked it out with flowers and bright orange tablecloths; they baked cakes, arranged the crockery and waited for the customers to arrive. Within a few months, the Teashop of Good Hope had sunk without trace.

The lady who baked the cakes was Mrs Mabel Tuke, popularly known as 'Pansy' and formerly the honorary secretary of the WSPU. Her two partners were Emmeline and Christabel Pankhurst. This adventure in Juan-les-Pins was just another episode in the strange story of Emmeline's later life. Though full of political enthusiasm when she founded the Women's Party in London in 1917, she grew weary of British politics after Christabel's defeat at Smethwick in the 1918 General Election. The party petered out the following year. Next, Emmeline accepted an offer from the Canadian government to sponsor her as a resident lecturer on 'social hygiene', the subject of Christabel's book *The Great Scourge*. She moved to Toronto, supported by a small salary and the proceeds of a testimonial fund set up by ex-suffragettes at home. This raised £3,000, half of which Emmeline immediately spent on a holiday cottage in Devon which she rarely used, couldn't maintain and eventually sold at a loss.

Three of her adopted 'war babies' joined her in Canada in 1920, along with Nurse Catherine Pine, who used to run a convalescent home for hunger-striking suffragettes released under the 'Cat and Mouse' Act. Christabel joined them two years later with the fourth of Emmeline's new daughters, whom Christabel had now adopted herself. Soon after Christabel arrived, Nurse Pine left. Now there were six mouths to feed. As so often before, Emmeline and the family found themselves chronically short of funds. That's when they decided to join forces with Mrs Tuke, who had some capital, and move to the French Riviera.

By Christmas 1925 Mrs Pankhurst had returned to London. She was offered an enviable position at £400 a year with a new organization, the Six Point Group, set up to campaign for the electoral endgame, when the voting age for women would be reduced to twenty-one. Emmeline refused the offer, thinking it smacked of charity and believing anyway that this was a fight too far for her. She had done her bit and hadn't the strength to kick over the traces any more. This erstwhile pillar of the Independent Labour Party did agree to stand as the Conservative candidate, however, for a staunchly socialist seat in her estranged daughter Sylvia's neighbourhood, Whitechapel in East London. She must have known she couldn't win.

Emmeline had relinquished all her adopted children by now, unable to provide the stable life she had hoped for them. This must

Emmeline Pankhurst with her adopted 'war babies'.

have been heartbreaking. The winter of 1927–8 was long and dreary; London was repeatedly swathed in pea-souper fogs and Emmeline's health and spirits began to fail. She was in the Public Gallery on 28 March 1928 when the Representation of the People (Equal Franchise) Act passed its second reading, which was wonderful. But what finally broke her down was an announcement published in the *News of the World* a couple of weeks later that Sylvia had given birth to a 'eugenic baby', so called because his parents were 'two intelligent adults free from hereditary disease and untrammelled by social convention.'[2] In other words, he was illegitimate. For all her radicalism, Emmeline found the shame insupportable; that, and the grief of not having known anything about the baby until he was four months old. In May 1928 Emmeline caught influenza which rapidly developed into septicaemia and on 14 June she died, a month short of her seventieth birthday.

In 1929 another appeal was organized, this time for a headstone, a commemorative portrait and a memorial statue to be erected in

Emmeline's old battleground of Westminster. Former suffragettes from around the country were tasked with raising funds. Mary Hackey from Lancashire was one of them. Some of the replies she received to her requests for contributions were sobering. 'I just hate to think of the Pankhurst Campaign and all its sensational epoch,' wrote Maud Taylor from Princes Risborough. 'I think it would have done untold harm to women and their work had not the war shown what they were really made of.' Richard Holt of Liverpool agreed: 'I'm afraid I have not got sufficient regard for Mrs Pankhurst's political methods to desire to perpetuate her memory.' The suffragist and Liberal politician Nessie Stewart Brown was even more discouraging:

> I am afraid I do not entertain the high regard professed by many women and men nowadays who were in some cases 'anti' suffragists formerly, for the late Mrs Pankhurst and consider she retarded the movement for . . . years and that the Liberal Government would have enfranchised women before the war had it not been for her and her militant ladies.[3]

Despite such opposition, the necessary £2,500 was raised and at 11.45 a.m. on Thursday, 6 March 1930, Mrs Pankhurst's statue was unveiled by the prime minister, Stanley Baldwin. The ceremony was relayed by radio and featured 'General' Flora Drummond giving a speech, a piece rather alarmingly advertised as the 'Chorale of the Wreckers' by Dame Ethel Smyth and, in a spirit of supreme reconciliation (or irony), the Band of the Metropolitan Police. Baldwin said that despite his differences with Mrs Pankhurst and her methods in the past, neither he nor anyone else could deny that she was inspirational and courageous: a true British heroine.

Among the wreaths laid at Emmeline's tiny feet was one from Sylvia.

Though the WSPU was finished, and the Women's Party never really got off the ground, the new Six Point Group continued Mrs

Pankhurst's activism. Sylvia and Christabel were not involved: the former turned to communism and became an anti-fascist campaigner in Ethiopia, the country that became her much-loved home. Christabel emigrated to the United States, where she spent a considerable amount of time as a travelling evangelist for Second Adventism. Margaret Mackworth, Viscountess Rhondda (1883–1958), was a fitting leader instead. She was the only child of David Thomas, first Viscount Rhondda, a Welsh industrialist and Liberal politician, and she was one of thousands of frustrated Edwardian women who grew up in the utmost comfort yet felt restless and unfulfilled. She found purpose – and considerable excitement – in the suffrage movement:

> [F]or me and for many other young women like me,' she remembered, 'militant suffrage was the very salt of life. The knowledge of it had come like a draught of fresh air into our padded, stifled lives. It gave us release of energy, it gave us that sense of being some use in the scheme of things, without which no human being can live at peace.[4]

Margaret excelled in the WSPU as an organizer, speaker and activist, once being imprisoned (and going on hunger strike) for setting fire to a pillar box. During the war she was unconventionally employed by her father as his managing director, much to her delight. She was returning from a business trip to the United States on board the *Lusitania* when it was torpedoed off the Irish coast in May 1915 with the loss of 1,198 souls. Surviving that, she said, taught her never to be afraid of anything again: one of her greatest assets. After her beloved father's death in 1918, Margaret inherited his business interests, his wealth and his title, though not the right to sit as he had done in the House of Lords, because she was a woman and women were not granted that privilege as Hereditary Peers until 1963. She fought for that right, however, and for the rights of women in every important aspect of modern life: in politics, in the home,

the workplace, legislatively, economically and socially. That's what
the Six Point Group was all about.

In 1920 Margaret founded *Time and Tide*, a progressive journal
which remained in publication until the mid-1980s. It reflected her
feminist ideals and ambitions, with contributions by some of the
most innovative writers of the day – Virginia Woolf, Rebecca West,
Winifred Holtby, Vera Brittain – as well as old suffrage stalwarts like
Gilbert Murray and George Bernard Shaw. She did not allow Mrs
Pankhurst's refusal to join the Six Point Group to deter her from
keeping up the battle for equal franchise. In the best tradition of the
pre-war suffrage campaign, in the summer of 1926 she organized a
rally from the Embankment to Hyde Park involving three thousand
women (and the obligatory aeroplane) in the cause of equal political rights, which meant reducing the age barrier for women voters
from thirty to twenty-one. This march lacked the pageantry of
the past, although there were a few banners, including one particularly close to Lady Rhondda's heart about the right of peeresses to
sit in the Upper House. Those journalists who noticed the occasion
were quick to remind readers of the bad old days not so long ago when
suffragettes marauded through the streets of London and no one
was safe. One even commented on the notorious fickleness of
women, implying they should not be trusted to behave themselves responsibly now that they had the power of the vote in their
hands. And look: there was Mrs Pankhurst herself at the front of the
procession. Perhaps fears were somewhat allayed when Millicent
Fawcett was also spotted – she had been awarded a damehood the
previous year – and the homely figure of Mrs Margaret Wintringham,
a member of the Women's Institute who had famously been elected
an MP in 1921. Maybe this was not a latter-day ride of the Valkyries
after all. It seems inevitable that Kate Frye of the New Constitutional
Society was there to witness the fun, though not as a participant
this time. She had retired from suffrage work, and while she
thought the sight of Mrs Pankhurst 'quite delightful', she could

not resist commenting on how terribly old the veterans of the movement looked.

Although she was obviously happy to join this procession, Millicent Fawcett was wary of the approach taken by Lady Rhondda and the Six Point Group towards women's emancipation. In 1919 the NUWSS had been rebranded the National Union of Societies for Equal Citizenship (NUSEC), and Millicent retired and was succeeded as leader by Eleanor Rathbone. The focus of NUSEC members was ever conciliatory; they were not concerned so much with equality for equality's sake as with fair representation, and with working to realize all those unrequited promises they had made in the past about women using the vote to fashion a better world for everyone. The more they could demonstrate how responsible they were as voters and legislators, the more people – and the government – would trust them.

The Representation of the People (Equal Franchise) Bill finally received Royal Assent on 2 July 1928, less than three weeks after the death of Emmeline Pankhurst. According to Sylvia, ultimately awarding women the same voting rights as men came 'without effort'; once the breakthrough had been made in 1918, the rest was a matter of course, slow but sure. This is not quite true. Attempts were made to introduce a similar Bill almost every year of the decade, quashed by various inter- and intra-party agendas. It didn't help that there were so many General Elections during this period, in 1922, '23 and '24, resulting in a Conservative victory, a hung Parliament and then another Tory win. The government was understandably preoccupied with its own struggles for power and the exigencies of post-war reconstruction. The Irish Free State was born of fire in 1922. The General Strike paralysed the country in 1926; and abroad there was trouble in India and the Middle East. After the physical and emotional catastrophe of the Great War, it was feared the British public might react – as they did, to a certain extent – by relaxing too much. Restrained celebrations of victory were perfectly acceptable, but society must resist the temptation to indulge itself in frivolity. Though the Liberal and Labour Parties largely agreed with the equal franchise, back-bench Conservatives were deeply suspicious of giving modern girls the vote: it was hard to imagine anything more frivolous than a modern girl.

Stanley Baldwin broke the deadlock by setting up a cabinet committee (having pledged an all-party conference). The main question at issue was whether to lower the voting age for women to twenty-five or to twenty-one. Campaigning went on right to the very last minute and, again, it was divided on conciliatory and militant lines, raising the terrifying spectre of more suffragette outrages. The government had kept its hand in, after the prison amnesty of 1914, by meting out to convicted conscientious objectors the same sort of treatment it had given hunger-striking suffragettes, releasing them before they died, re-arresting them, and forcibly feeding them with occasionally fatal results. It wasn't exactly unknown for history to repeat itself.

One of the major arguments against extending the franchise to women of twenty-one was the unassailable fact that, if this were done, there would be more females eligible to vote than males. The *Daily Mail* was predictably sensationalist about this apocalyptic possibility: 'Men Outnumbered Everywhere,' screamed the headlines, accompanied by editorial predictions that the world would soon be ruled by a small but powerful company of 'mother-women' like queen bees, with crowds of male drones: 'They will be supported by the labour of an immense number of sterile female workers. Men will be utterly ousted.'[5] Herbert Asquith had lost his seat in the 1918 General Election, then had stood, and won, at a by-election in Scotland two years later, claiming to be a convert to suffragism. But even he experienced something of a reactionary relapse, describing the fifteen thousand women on the electoral register in his constituency of Paisley as 'a dim, impenetrable, for the most part ungettable element – of whom all one knows is that they are . . . ignorant of politics, credulous to the last degree, and flickering with gusts of sentiment like a candle in the wind.'[6]

The media were quick to pick up on the supposed fecklessness of post-war women, calling the latest suffrage campaign a sense-less quest for the 'flapper' vote. A flapper was a flibbertigibbet, a young woman so lacking in gravitas that she cut her hair off, threw away her stays (the 1920s equivalent of bra-burning), ostentatiously smoked and drank, and wore skirts down to her knees and no fur-ther, just to shock people. What would such a capricious creature do with the vote? Plunge depressed, post-war Britain into chaos; fill the Commons' benches with reactive, over-emotional air-heads; ruin us all. No doubt veterans of the anti-suffrage campaign were deliciously flushed with *Schadenfreude* on reading such gloomy pre-dictions. In many ways nothing had changed: a tendency to typecast women remained the greatest enemy of suffragists in the NUSEC. They were still having to expend considerable time and energy on combatting spurious stereotypes.

This they did with aplomb, however. There is a pamphlet by Millicent Fawcett among the possessions of Mary Ann Rawle, the young woman who was arrested at the same time as Emma Sproson and who wrote an account of her experiences alongside Emma in Holloway Prison. Published in 1926, its title is simply 'What the Vote Has Done' and it lists the most important legislation passed by Parliament since 1918, under the influence of a female electorate. It is an impressive catalogue, better than any platform argument or hast-ily gathered petition, including Acts on the registration of nurses, midwives and maternity homes; on affiliation orders for the main-tenance of illegitimate children; a Legitimacy Act to help protect single mothers and their offspring in law; Acts improving the eco-nomic and legal position of married or divorced women and those found guilty of infanticide, demanding more leniency. Public health measures were introduced; pensions for widows, orphans and the elderly; the age of consent was raised; sales of intoxicating liquor limited; and the appointment of women in the police force and the civil service approved. The Sex Disqualification (Removal) Act of 1919 was a portmanteau piece of legislation rendering it unlawful to discriminate against a woman in almost any aspect of public life on the grounds of her gender. Suddenly she was eligible to become a lawyer, a juror, a member of professional bodies – but not, as we know, to sit in the House of Lords, nor to graduate with a degree from Cambridge University, an honour which was inexplicably withheld from her until 1948.

Much of this legislation demonstrated a new compassion as well as pragmatism. And the most important Act of all was still pending at the time Millicent was writing: votes for women on the same terms as votes for men. Millicent was in the House of Commons on that summer day when the Representation of the People (Equal Franchise) Act became law. There was no triumphalism in her description of the occasion: just a quiet gratitude that she had been spared to see the campaign through to its conclusion, which she had always considered to be inevitable, even though it took over sixty years to materialize. Think what women had learned over those decades: they were better citizens now – better people – than they could ever have been had they not had to fight for their rights.

Not all of these new Acts were sponsored by female members of Parliament. They were slow to arrive at Westminster. If we don't count Constance Markievicz, who never took her seat, the first was Nancy, Lady Astor, who won a by-election in Plymouth in 1919. Her Tory husband, MP Waldorf Astor, had joined the Lords; she took his place and remained in office until retiring in 1945. Liberal Margaret Wintringham turned up in 1921, a handful more over the next few years, including suffragist Margaret Bondfield, who in 1924 became the first woman minister (Labour), and Miss (Arabella) Susan Lawrence in 1926. The latter was a rather terrifying alumna of Newnham College, Cambridge, remembered for being extremely short-sighted and peering at people menacingly through

a lorgnette, for playing the piano with a virtuosic lack of musical-
ity, and for taking her Dalmatian dog with her whenever she rode
a bicycle, which was often, to protect her from unnamed dangers.
Historically Dalmatians were used by the aristocratic English to run
alongside their carriages, looking smart and guarding their masters
from the unwelcome attentions of the hoi polloi; this seemed a logical progression.

Although forty-one women stood for Parliament between 1918
and 1928, only eleven were elected. Fourteen were returned after
the first equal franchise election in 1929, including NUSEC leader,
part-time pilgrim and full-time visionary Eleanor Rathbone. One
of her first speeches, extraordinarily, was on the subject of female
genital mutilation in India, and her crowning achievement was the
passing of the Family Allowances Act in 1945, the year before her
death. The Act encapsulated Eleanor's concerns for the dignity and
well-being of working women, of mothers and their children. In
many ways, as a suffragist she had been campaigning for that Act all
her life.

One of the most enjoyable aspects of suffrage research involves
speaking to people about their ancestors. It is exciting to be introduced to such a colourful company of women and men by those who
know them best. One of the first families I met was Millicent
Fawcett's. They proudly celebrate her intelligence, her humanism (in
the widest sense of the word), her sense of humour and her persever-
ance. Millicent never gave up. Though she resigned the leadership of
the suffragists in 1919 after more than twenty years in post, she continued to work with and for the NUSEC, campaigning not only for
equal franchise but equal opportunities for women in the professional workplace, in industry and in education. This she did in her
customary fashion, by writing letters to politicians, arranging

deputations, occasionally joining public demonstrations, and by encouraging women in all walks of life to act as she did, with cheerfulness, integrity and informed conviction. Noting her death in August 1929, *The Times* remarked on her distinction as someone who combined a hard-hitting intellect with 'mellow wisdom': 'By her death a link has been snapped with an England of another order than the present; and, if there are younger women who are inclined to take scholastic, professional, or political liberty too much for granted, they have only to think of the restrictions in place when Millicent Garrett was a girl.'[7]

Millicent Garrett Fawcett.

She was never a fuddy-duddy, claiming to envy flappers their short skirts and always pushing forward something she sought to articulate: the concept of feminism. In 1926, when she was nearly eighty, she helped found a library in London called the Women's Service Library, full of books on the past and present state of the women's movement, many of which were inherited from the NUWSS. It was renamed in her honour in the 1950s and remains at the core of the Women's Library currently at the London School of Economics. Rachel Ferguson, an ex-suffragette, once wrote that the point of the militant movement was to make women more like men: 'The suffrage campaign was our Eton, our Oxford, our regiment, our ship, our cricket-match.'[8] If asked, I think Millicent would have said that the most important achievement of the peaceful constitutionals was to give women the permission and the confidence to be themselves.

Millicent was a celebrity, of course, and it has been just as much fun learning about unknown suffrage campaigners from their descendants, perhaps breaking the news to them that, in the words of the popular song, Nana was actually more likely to have been a suffra*gist* than a suffra*gette*, yet no less adventurous or inspiring than the most purple of the militants. So many strong personalities have informed this book, and I should have liked to name them all, but I can't. None the less they are all here like a mosaic, each part of a picture that would not be complete without them. If I have not focused on those we know best, particularly the heroines of the suffragette campaign, it is only because their voices ring out elsewhere. I confess that the 'ordinary' people of the suffrage campaign fascinate me more: people like the pilgrims, local organizers like Kate Frye, well-wishers like the woman with the packed lunch, friends and neighbours doing their best for an ideal and for each other. Hearing stories like theirs reminds us that this was an intensely human campaign. Its activists and supporters belong to us all.

I mentioned the pilgrims; perhaps this would be a good point to find out what happened to some of them after they reached their Jerusalem in 1918 or 1928.

Cheerful Gladys Duffield became a professional pianist and a composer of popular songs. She was Kathleen Ferrier's accompanist when Kathleen was first 'discovered'. She had two more children after Lily, and her granddaughter Margaret remembers her as tall, fond of the limelight, *not* very fond of housework, and always surrounded by music. She spoke about the Pilgrimage often, recounting her adventures and telling Margaret how for her the struggle for the vote all began with a tennis match. Tramping the Watling Street route gave her a taste for travelling around Britain and in later life – after a little windfall – she gleefully ventured abroad. Gladys died in 1973. She was ninety-one.

Her companion on the road, Lady Rochdale, was awarded an MBE in 1920 and her name occasionally crops up in regional newspapers, hosting suffrage meetings after 1913 or being the requisite (and no doubt self-deprecatory) dignitary at local functions. She was widowed in 1945 and died at ninety-four in 1966.

Of Alice New I know nothing, except that she joined the committee of the Birkenhead Unitarian Church in 1922 and was still unmarried then, at the age of thirty-two. Her diary was bought by a private collector some years ago and now belongs to the library of Duke University in North Carolina. She died in 1975, having strolled into history during the summer of 1913 and then strolled out again.

Alice's aunt wrote a tribute to their local Pilgrimage organizer, Edith Eskrigge, praising her for her constant good humour, refusal to get 'fussed' or to worry, and her admirable ability to answer half a dozen questions at once. She was the perfect leader. Edith worked with Eleanor Rathbone in Liverpool during the war, principally with the families of servicemen. She came into a considerable sum of money when a close friend died and spent it not so much on herself – although she did take walking and cycling holidays when she could – as on members of her family. She believed passionately in the value of education and had her great-niece to stay with her when the girl was revising for exams, to give her peace and quiet. She also paid for part of her great-niece's training for a career in social work, inspired by Edith. Members of her family still talk about her forthrightness, tempered by a delightful sense of irony and humility. She died in 1948, but the spirit that carried her through the suffrage campaign is still very much alive.

Horsewoman and journalist Vera Chute Collum left the Scottish Women's Hospital in Royaumont in 1918, though the unit remained open, treating local patients, for another year. She proudly helped to run the association of SWH 'old girls', editing a chatty newsletter and staying closely in touch with surviving comrades until her death in 1957. As well as continuing her journalism, she found a new career in archaeology, working in the field and on research. Unsentimental to the last, she left her body to the Royal College of Surgeons. After the Pilgrimage, there is no record of her ever having climbed aboard a horse again.

Dr Mabel Ramsay from the Land's End route had a difficult war, working in a hospital in Antwerp which was bombarded by the Germans several times. Her mother, Annie, helped raise money for it by writing letters to local papers and giving occasional talks on the Pilgrimage. On her return to Devon, Mabel campaigned to attract more women into local government, encouraged by her friend Lady Astor, and in 1923 she visited Bermuda, her mother's birthplace, to set up a suffrage society there. It was a sadness to her that Bermudan women did not achieve the vote until 1944. The facts she chose to record in a short, unpublished autobiography (now lodged at the Royal College of Physicians in London) are endearing. After writing about her medical training and her commitment to women's suffrage, she adds that she loves animals, has received three marriage proposals in her life – none of which she has accepted – and does not fear death. Annie passed away in 1920; her daughter died suddenly during a meeting of the Women's Medical Association in 1954, still doing her duty until the very last moment.

Selina Cooper used her considerable talents as a speaker to raise public awareness in Lancashire about the campaign for Family Allowances after the war, inspired by her old friend Eleanor Rathbone. She was appointed a magistrate and continued to champion the rights of her working-class community for the rest of her life. Her daughter Mary was so proud of her. Selina died in 1946, aged nearly eighty-two.

Those newspaper reporters who commented on how healthy the Pilgrims looked as they swung along the roads during that long-ago summer before the war were right. They were made of stern stuff, undamaged by the ravages of hunger-striking and forcible feeding, and for the most part appear to have lived unusually long lives. Harriet Blessley from Portsmouth married in 1916, had a daughter at the age of forty-three and was ninety when she died. Marjory Lees was ninety-one and Muriel Matters, who spoke at Pilgrimage meetings, spoiled her Census form, chained herself to the Ladies' Gallery grille and flew an airship over Westminster, went on till she was ninety-two.

What was their legacy, these steadfast mothers of our democracy? It is said that Mahatma Gandhi was inspired by Millicent Fawcett and her campaign when he first embraced passive resistance in 1907, going on, himself, to inspire millions of others. Suffragist processions became the pattern for countless peaceful protests on the streets of our towns and cities, in this country and in the United States. The Pilgrimage foreshadowed a much more famous occasion (perhaps unjustly so) when two hundred men marched from Jarrow to London in October 1936. The women of Greenham Common enjoyed the same sort of dedicated sisterhood as the pilgrims did, any one of whom might stand as a role model today.

Ray Strachey is one of my favourites. We first met her on a caravan tour with her college friend Elinor Rendel, relishing the

Marjory Lees (centre), surrounded by her suffragist friends, 1918.

freedom and excitement of being on the road. She was a self-reliant, positive-thinking young woman, utterly caught up in the excitement of the suffrage campaign, but not so much so that she couldn't communicate meaningfully with the people she met along the way. Then she worked for the NUWSS, became Lady Astor's political secretary and stood as a parliamentary candidate herself, not once but three times. She did all this while raising small children, helping to build the family's house from scratch, and maintaining a wide and affectionate circle of friends. She wrote a highly readable history of the movement called *The Cause*, and a biography of Millicent Fawcett. For relaxation, she went swimming in the nude. She was happy, committed, creative, influential, loving, loved and useful. If that's a suffragist, I want to be a suffragist too.

I shall end this book as it began, in the company of Marjory Lees of Oldham. In many ways, nothing appears to have changed for her after the Pilgrimage. She and her mother continued to do what they could, in terms of time and money, for local causes, particularly anything connected with realizing one's potential for the good of society. They donated heavily to Ashburne Hall, a hall of residence for women at Manchester University, where a wing of the building still bears the Lees name and there's an entrance scholarship endowed by Marjory. Their house still stands on the Manchester Road, donated by Marjory with the surrounding parkland to the townspeople of Oldham in memory of Sarah. If you narrow your eyes a bit, you can still see the *Ark* drawn up at the front door, with Noah looking bored in his traces and everyone else dashing around looking for the keys.

In fact, nothing was the same for Marjory after the summer of 1913. The Pilgrimage meant so much to her that members of Oldham Women's Suffrage Society decided to present her with a souvenir album in September 1919. It is magnificent: huge and weighty, craftsman-bound in goatskin (in the suffragist colours, of course) with gilt decorations and heavily bevelled edges. Inside is the story of the Pilgrimage, told in newspaper cuttings, photographs, official NUWSS reports and programmes. There's a hand-coloured photo of the Oldham banner, a portrait of Marjory beaming through her steel-rimmed spectacles, and an exquisitely illuminated dedication from her suffragist friends.

The dedication thanks her for all her hard work throughout the campaign now that the struggle is over: 'We believe that the Great Pilgrimage which the women made through England did much to bring us to the goal, and we remember most thankfully all you did for the comfort of those who took part in it with you.'[9] It closes with a few lines of Tennyson from 'Locksley Hall Sixty Years After', about the power of evolution and a new world to come, better than 'the wildest guess of you and me.' Marjory was just one of thousands of women and men who helped to create that new world with quiet determination and a touching optimism. We can't give them and their militant sisters much in return, except a promise to use the vote they fought so hard to win and, wherever it's necessary, to keep on fighting.

Chronology

Milestones and diversions along the road to women's enfranchisement

1792

A Vindication of the Rights of Woman by Mary Wollstonecraft is published.

1819

The 'Sisters of the Earth' form Female Reform Societies in Lancashire.

Peterloo Massacre.

1832

The First Reform Act is passed.

Mary Smith of Yorkshire presents a petition to Parliament for the right to vote.

1834

The Poor Law Amendment Act is passed. Women can now vote for Poor Law Guardians.

1848

The Seneca Falls Declaration demands enfranchisement for women in America.

1851

Anne Knight and others form the Sheffield Association for Female Franchise.

Lord Carlisle presents a petition in favour of women's suffrage to the House of Lords.

Harriet Taylor Mill's article 'The Enfranchisement of Women' is published.

1857

The Matrimonial Causes Act is passed.

1865

Barbara Bodichon and other 'Langham Place Ladies' form the Kensington Society for Women's Suffrage, which in 1867 becomes the London Committee.

1866

John Stuart Mill presents a petition for women's enfranchisement to the House of Commons, bearing 1,521 signatures.

1867

Women's Suffrage Committees and Societies are formed in Manchester and Edinburgh.

The Second Reform Act is passed.

1868

Birmingham and Bristol Women's Suffrage Societies are formed; the movement quickly spreads elsewhere over the next few years.

The first public women's suffrage meeting is held, in Manchester's Free Trade Hall.

Certain women apply to vote, represented by Dr Richard Pankhurst, but lose their case.

1869

The Municipal Franchise Act empowers some spinsters to vote in town council elections and to stand as Poor Law Guardians and School Board members.

Wyoming is the first American territory to give women the vote (the rest of the United States achieve the franchise by 1920, except for Native Americans, not all of whom are given the vote until 1957).

1871

A Bill to enfranchise women nationally is lost on its second reading in the House of Commons; the matter is debated again in 1872, '75, '76, '78 and '79; in 1884, '86, '87, '91, '92, '96, '97, '98 and '99; in 1901, '04, '05 . . . and so on (and on) until 1928. Some proposed Bills exclude married women, others do not.

1872

Victoria Woodhull is nominated to stand as president of the United States.

1881

Women are given the vote on the Isle of Man.

1882

The Married Women's Property Act is passed.

1884

The Third Reform Act excludes women, yet again, from the parliamentary franchise.

Limited franchise for women in Ontario, Canada; it is not until 1940 that all Canada's women can vote.

1886

Repeal of the Contagious Diseases Act.

1888

Women can vote for, but not stand as, county councillors after the passing of the Local Government Act.

1889

The Women's Franchise League is formed to fight the putative exclusion of married women from the electoral roll.

Mrs Humphry Ward publishes 'An Appeal against Female Suffrage'.

1893

New Zealand is the first entire country to give women the Vote.

Formation of the Independent Labour Party.

1894

Women are allowed (under certain conditions) to vote for and stand as parish councillors following the Local Government Act.

1897

The National Union of Women's Suffrage Societies (NUWSS) is formed, under the leadership of Millicent Garrett Fawcett.

1900

The North of England Society for Women's Suffrage organizes a working women's petition for the right to vote.

Women are enfranchised in Western Australia. All the other states follow by 1908, though Aboriginal women do not get the vote until 1962.

1903

The Women's Social and Political Union (WSPU) is founded by Emmeline Pankhurst.

1905

Combined suffrage supporters lobby the House of Commons.

WSPU members Christabel Pankhurst and Annie Kenney are arrested in Manchester and imprisoned; the militant campaign begins.

1906

The term 'suffragette' is first used in the *Daily Mail* in a short article published on 10 January.

The first women's march to Parliament is organized: there are ten arrests.

A 257,000-signature petition signed by professional and other working women is presented to Parliament.

Finland becomes the first European country to give women the vote.

1907

The NUWSS's 'Mud March' is the first large-scale outdoor women's suffrage demonstration.

The first WSPU 'Women's Parliament' is held at Caxton Hall, followed by a march on Parliament. Fifty-four suffragettes are arrested.

The Qualification of Women Act empowers women to stand as mayors.

The Women's Freedom League is formed by disenchanted former WSPU members after Emmeline and Christabel Pankhurst deny the democratic constitution of the WSPU.

1908

A WSPU window-breaking campaign is launched.

Herbert Asquith replaces Henry Campbell-Bannerman as prime minister.

There are several high-profile processions in London involving thousands of suffragettes and suffragists, including the NUWSS 'Mud March' in February and the WSPU 'Women's Sunday' rally in June.

The Women's Anti-Suffrage League and Men's League for Opposing Women's Suffrage are formed.

1909

The NUWSS organizes a Pageant of Women's Trades and Professions.

The WSPU Women's Exhibition is held at the Prince's Skating Rink, Knightsbridge.

Marion Wallace Dunlop is the first suffrage campaigner to go on hunger strike.

Forcible feeding begins (at Winson Green Prison in Birmingham).

The Women's Tax Resistance League is founded.

1910

A 'Conciliation Bill' is introduced and in June passes its second reading before foundering.

The WSPU 'From Prison to Citizenship' parade involves 10,000 marchers.

The WSPU suspends militant tactics, except for a week in November, until November 1911.

18 November becomes Black Friday.

1911

There is a rise in WSPU militancy, involving arson and stone-throwing.

Herbert Asquith is returned after the General Election; there are hopes of a second 'Conciliation Bill'.

The anthem 'March of the Women' is launched at a WSPU meeting at the Royal Albert Hall.

Suffragists and suffragettes boycott the Census.

A joint Women's Suffrage procession celebrates the coronation of King George V.

A Manhood Suffrage Bill is announced, still supposedly capable of amendment.

1912

The new 'Conciliation Bill' is defeated; Asquith's Reform Bill is introduced with no provision for women.

The 'Brown Women' march from Edinburgh to London.

1913

A working women's deputation organized by the WSPU appears before Parliament to present the case for women's suffrage.

The Speaker of the House of Commons rules that any amendment to the new Reform Bill in favour of women's suffrage will alter it insupportably. The Bill is withdrawn.

Sylvia Pankhurst forms the East London Federation of Suffragettes.

The 'Cat and Mouse' Act is passed.

The WSPU is banned from holding meetings in the Royal Albert Hall and in the open air.

The International Woman Suffrage Alliance's meeting is held in Budapest.

Suffragette Emily Wilding

Davison is killed at the Epsom Derby.

The Great Pilgrimage begins in June and culminates in a rally at Hyde Park in July.

1914

Sylvia Pankhurst is barred from the WSPU and her sister Adela emigrates to Australia.

The *Rokeby Venus* and other works of art are damaged by suffragettes.

War is declared, and suffragette prisoners are granted an amnesty.

Women's suffrage organizations cease active campaigning.

1915

The first Scottish Women's Hospital unit opens in France.

Demand grows for the enfranchisement of servicemen.

A procession demonstrating 'Women's Right to Serve' is organized in London.

1917

The Representation of the People Bill, backed by Asquith, is debated and passed by the House of Commons. It allows qualified women to vote if they are aged thirty or over.

1918

The Act receives Royal Assent on 6 February.

The Great War ends.

The Parliament (Qualification of Women) Act, giving women the right to stand as Members of Parliament, is passed three weeks before December's General Election.

Germany and Russia give women the vote.

1919

The first woman MP in the UK, Nancy Astor, takes her seat.

The Sex Disqualification (Removal) Act is passed.

1928

The Representation of the People (Equal Franchise) Act is passed, allowing women to vote at twenty-one.

1929

At the first General Election to include women on equal terms, they constitute 52.7 per cent of the electorate.

Parliament's first woman minister, Margaret Bondfield, is appointed.

1944

Women in France win the right to vote.

1945

Italy and Japan give women the vote.

1950

Indian women are enfranchised.

1958

Women are allowed to sit in the House of Lords as Life Peers. They cannot sit as Hereditary Peers until 1963.

1971

Switzerland becomes the last entire European country to give women the vote.

1979

Margaret Thatcher becomes the first woman prime minister appointed in the UK. Assorted anti-suffragists from the past century and a half turn in their graves.

Dramatis Personae

A brief guide to some of the people featured in this book. Although grouped here as suffragists and suffragettes, the distinction between non-militants and militants was not always clear.

The suffragists

Amberley, Katherine Louisa, Viscountess (1842–74). ◆ Despite Queen Victoria's comment that she should get 'a good whipping' for her extreme views on women's emancipation, Lady Amberley was a suffragist, a high-profile signatory to **John Stuart Mill**'s 1866 petition and a steadfast ally of pioneers **Elizabeth Garrett Anderson** and **Emily Davies**.

Anderson, Elizabeth Garrett (1836–1917). ◆ Although best remembered as the first woman to be admitted – grudgingly – to the Society of Apothecaries (in 1865), the first to be entered on the Medical Register in Great Britain – essentially, the first to qualify as a doctor – and for her establishment of a women's hospital in London, Elizabeth Garrett Anderson was also a committed feminist. She presented the first mass petition for women's suffrage to **John Stuart Mill** in 1866 and went on to play a prominent part in the campaign for the vote as a suffragist with her sister **Millicent Garrett Fawcett** and briefly as a member of the WSPU. Her commitment to making the medical profession more accessible to women informed her suffrage activities. In 1908 she became the UK's first female mayor. Pilgrim **Sarah Lees** was the second.

Ashton, Margaret (1856–1937). ◆ A graduate of Manchester University, Miss Ashton became the city's first woman councillor in 1908 after chairing Withington Urban District Council for several years. She was one of the Great Pilgrimage's star orators, despite being injured en route.

Auerbach, Helena (1871–1955). ◆ After serving as an official in the NUWSS, Mrs Auerbach went on to pioneer the Women's Institute movement in the UK. She was the WI's national treasurer for many years.

Becker, Lydia (1827–90). ◆ One of fifteen children, Miss Becker was educated at home in Manchester. She was a keen amateur botanist and an enthusiast for literary and scientific pursuits. After hearing **Barbara Bodichon** speak in 1866, she transferred her considerable energies to the cause of women's suffrage, founding the Manchester Women's Suffrage Committee that same year and spending the rest of her life guiding the early movement forward.

Bennett, Sarah (*fl.*1912). ◆ One of the 'Brown Women' who marched from Edinburgh to London during the winter of 1912, named after the colour of their uniforms. Miss Bennett was a Londoner.

Blessley, Harriet (1873–1964). ◆ A music-seller's daughter from Portsmouth, Harriet wrote a diary of her Pilgrimage experience. She married in 1916, had a daughter at the age of forty-three and was ninety when she died. Her brother, Frederick Blessley, styled himself a militant and was arrested for breaking a window in Portsmouth in support of women's rights in 1913. Harriet was not amused.

Bodichon, Barbara (1827–91). ◆ A legal, political and educational reformer of great intelligence and influence, Barbara Leigh Smith Bodichon co-founded the Langham Place Group and the first ever Women's Suffrage Committee, which in 1866 organized **John Stuart Mill**'s petition to Parliament. Her talks on women's suffrage inspired many of the people in this book to join the Cause.

Breedon, Mrs (*fl.*1913). ◆ An American suffragist from Denver City, Colorado, who joined the Watling Street pilgrims in 1913. Her accent was so strange that many of her companions thought she must be permanently drunk.

Brown, Nannie (1866–1943). ◆ The only member of the 'Brown Women' to come from Edinburgh, Miss Brown walked all the way from her home city to London in 1912. She became a pioneer of the Women's Institute movement in Scotland, and worked all her life to promote opportunities and an appetite for civic awareness among women.

Byham, Margaret (1865–c.1913). ◆ Another of the 'Brown Women' who marched for women's suffrage from Edinburgh to London in 1912. This was essentially a suffragist exercise, but Margaret was also a member of the militant WSPU and the Church League for Women's Suffrage.

Collum, Vera Chute (1883–1957). ◆ Born in India of Irish-Australian parents, Miss Collum was a freelance journalist who worked in the press department of the NUWSS and in 1913 was commissioned by the *Daily News* to be their special Pilgrimage correspondent, an assignment she completed on horseback. Two years later she left the NUWSS offices to work with the SWH in France. After the war and the vote were won, she found a new career in archaeology, working in the field and on research.

Colquitt, Jane (*fl.*1902–18). ◆ An energetic member of the Catholic League for Women's Suffrage in Liverpool, Jane was a cycling pilgrim on the Watling Street route in the Great Pilgrimage. The previous year she had toured by caravan through west Cheshire and Lancashire to explain to local people what votes for women would mean to them.

Cooper, Selina (1864–1946). ◆ Having worked in a cotton mill in Barnoldswick, Lancashire, from the age of eleven, Selina Cooper later joined the Nelson Cotton Workers' Union and attended evening classes at the local Women's Co-operative Guild. She also joined the local branch of the NUWSS, where she flourished as a brilliant speaker. By now she was involved in local politics, elected on to the Burnley Board of Guardians in 1901. Mrs Cooper used her considerable talents as a speaker to raise public awareness in Lancashire about the campaign for Family Allowances after the war, inspired by her old friend **Eleanor Rathbone**. She was appointed a magistrate and continued to champion the rights of her working-class community for the rest of her life.

Costelloe, Ray *see* **Strachey, Ray**

Cowe, Isabel (1868–1931). ◆ A member of the 'Brown Women' who marched from Edinburgh to London in 1912, campaigning for women's suffrage along the way. Miss Cowe was a boarding-house keeper in the Scottish borders, renowned for her strong social conscience and fearlessness in standing up to be counted. She once refused to pay her rates in protest against the ineffectiveness of her local council, resisting the bailiffs armed with a hatchet and a fire extinguisher.

Craigen, Jessie (1834/5–99). ◆ One of the Scottish campaign's most spirited evangelists, Jessie Craigen was the daughter of a ship's captain and an Italian actress and had some experience of the theatre herself. In 1870 she started travelling around the United Kingdom with her dog as a professional suffrage speaker, a career that sadly waned as her eccentricities waxed.

Davenport Hill, Florence (1828/9–1919). ◆ It was at Miss Davenport Hill's house near Oxford that the pilgrims paused in 1913 to pay homage to one of the suffrage movement's pioneers. A member of a dynasty of reformers, her focus had always been to improve conditions for paupers, particularly poor children. She recognized that this could only be done effectively if women were empowered to make changes through Parliament.

Davies, Emily (1830–1921). ◆ One of the suffrage movement's most influential pioneers, helping to organize **John Stuart Mill**'s petition to Parliament in 1866 with her friends **Barbara Bodichon** and **Elizabeth Garrett Anderson**; founding Girton College at Cambridge – the UK's first university college for women – despite the lack of a formal education herself; and campaigning all her life for equal opportunities for women. She was the only one of the Langham Place Group to survive long enough to cast a vote in 1918.

Duffield, Gladys (1882–1973). ◆ Known as 'Skinny Lizzie' on the Watling Street route of the Great Pilgrimage, Mrs Duffield was a Cumbrian housewife and mother in 1913. After the Great War she became a professional pianist and a composer of popular songs. She was Kathleen Ferrier's accompanist when the great contralto was 'discovered'. She wrote a spirited (unpublished) account of the Pilgrimage, *On the March*.

Elmy, Elizabeth Wolstenholme (1833–1918). ◆ Her dedication to the Cause was born of a mixture of personal experience and idealism. Though highly intelligent, formal education was denied her; though politically aware, she was not allowed a voice in Parliament. So instead she became an activist for higher education and votes for women, involved in **John Stuart Mill**'s 1866 petition to Parliament and still campaigning into her eighties.

Eskrigge, Edith (1872–1948). ◆ Her family are very proud of cycling pilgrim 'Aunt Edith', who worked as a social reformer in the north-west of England. She was a local NUWSS organizer and speaker, and during the Great War worked with **Eleanor Rathbone** for the Soldiers' and Sailors' Families' Association in Liverpool. She was an evangelist of higher education and self-sufficiency for women all her life.

Fawcett, Millicent Garrett (1847–1929). ◆ It cannot have been a shock to her parents that Millicent turned out to be a firm believer in women's rights. Her eldest sister Louisa lived in London and was involved with the Langham Place Group. The next eldest Garrett girl, the future **Elizabeth Garrett Anderson**, was inspirational and Elizabeth's friend **Emily Davies** is said to have recognized Millicent's potential as a leader. Her career as a public speaker for women's suffrage began in 1867 and culminated in her appointment at the head of the newly formed NUWSS thirty years later. She led the suffragists to victory with tact, resourcefulness and an infectious sense of optimism before retiring in 1919. According to her, the Great Pilgrimage was one of the non-militant campaign's greatest achievements. She was made a Dame of the British Empire in 1925.

Field, Milly (*fl.*1913). ◆ From Oldham in Lancashire, Miss Field was one of **Marjory Lees**'s companions on the Watling Street route of the Great Pilgrimage.

Fonblanque, Florence de (1864–1949). ◆ A former actress, Mrs de Fonblanque was the originator of the 'Brown Women' march from Edinburgh to London in 1912, which inspired the Great Pilgrimage the following year. She belonged to both the NUWSS and the WSPU, as well as to several other suffrage organizations.

Fraser, Helen (1881–1979). ◆ An artist who resigned from the WSPU in 1908, as she disagreed with its policy of militancy, and instead joined the NUWSS, where she soon became known for her skills as a suffrage speaker. She took part in several caravan tours, including the Great Pilgrimage, and after the war was increasingly involved in Liberal politics. She emigrated to Australia in 1939.

Frye, Kate (1878–1959). ◆ Thanks to the suffrage historian Elizabeth Crawford, who published Kate Frye's diaries, we know her to be one of the liveliest and most hard-working of campaigners. She worked first as an actress, then as a paid travelling organizer for the New Constitutional Society for Women's Suffrage, retiring after her marriage in 1915.

Hadow, Grace (1875–1940). ◆ An accomplished academic, administrator, social reformer and pioneer of the Women's Institute movement in the UK. She was also a confirmed suffragist, with occasional militant tendencies, widely respected for her skills as a public speaker.

Harley, Katherine (1855–1917). ◆ Younger sister of **Charlotte Despard**, Mrs Harley was president of the Shropshire Women's Suffrage Society and chairman of the West Midlands federation of the NUWSS when in 1913 she came up with the idea of the Great Pilgrimage. Her family's army background lent an air of military efficiency to everything she did, including establishing the Active Service League, a voluntary organization within the NUWSS, and organizing field ambulances for the SWH unit in France during the Great War. She was killed in action in 1917.

Herd, Miss (*fl.*1913). ◆ This stout-hearted and popular lady was a companion of **Alice New** from Birkenhead. They shared a caravan on the Watling Street route of the Great Pilgrimage.

Hobhouse, Emily (1860–1926). ◆ An active philanthropist, working for the relief of Cornish miners who had emigrated from their home county (and hers) to the United States, and of Boer women and children held in British camps in South Africa during the Second Boer War (1899–1902). She was also a suffragist, whose belief in constructive, non-militant campaigning was underpinned by her pacifism.

Housman, Laurence (1865–1959). ◆ Like his brother, the poet Alfred Edward, Laurence Housman was a writer. He was also an artist and a committed suffragist, as was his sister Clemence. He was a founder member of the MLWS and of the Suffrage Atelier, a collective of artists dedicated to forwarding the Cause 'by means of pictorial publications'. He was a proud participant in the Great Pilgrimage.

Inglis, Dr Elsie (1864–1917). ◆ As chief medical officer of the SWH, Dr Inglis was a figurehead as well as a hard-working surgeon. She qualified in Scotland in 1892 and practised in Edinburgh, where she acted as honorary secretary of the local branch of the NUWSS. The Scottish Women's Hospital unit, supported by the NUWSS, was her brainchild. She inspired a generation of female doctors by her passion to reform both surgical techniques and the lot of women in medicine.

Kemp, Beatrice *see* **Rochdale, Lady**

Kenway, Ethel (*fl.*1913). ◆ A suffragist campaigner in Birmingham, who described in a breathless letter to her aunt the excitement of welcoming the Great Pilgrimage to her city.

Leadley Brown, Cicely (1882–c.1942). ◆ Pilgrim Miss Leadley Brown was something of a Renaissance woman, lending to the women's suffrage movement her talents as a motivational speaker, a musician, a mechanic and a cook. During the Second World War she toured the UK giving demonstrations on the benefits of vegetarian cuisine.

Lees, Marjory (1878–1970). ◆ Very much her mother **Sarah Lees**'s daughter, Marjory acted as 'Lady Mayoress' to Sarah and followed her as a town councillor, Poor Law Guardian, member of the National Council of Women and officer of the local branch of the NUWSS. She was also a generous philanthropist. Her diary of the Watling Street route of the Great Pilgrimage is at the heart of this book.

Lees, Sarah (1842–1935). ◆ Already a heroine in her native Oldham when she joined the Great Pilgrimage. As a wealthy widow, she supported local causes, and the national women's suffrage campaign, with spectacular generosity. She was a town councillor, became Britain's second female mayor in 1910, received an honorary doctorate from the University of Manchester in 1914 and a damehood in 1917.

Leigh Smith, Barbara *see* **Bodichon, Barbara**

Lockwood, Florence (1861–1937). ◆ A trenchant suffragist, feminist and pacifist, Mrs Lockwood embroidered a 'Votes for Women' banner for campaigners in Huddersfield, kept a diary of her suffrage (and other) activities and published an autobiography, *An Ordinary Life*, in 1932.

Lowndes, Mary (1857–1929). ◆ A trained stained-glass artist who formed the Artists' Suffrage League in 1907. She designed many of the league's banners, several of which are now housed in the collections of the Women's Library at the London School of Economics.

Lucas, Margaret Bright (1818–90). ◆ A member of a Quaker dynasty renowned for social reform. With her siblings **Priscilla Bright McLaren** and Jacob Bright, she campaigned for women's enfranchisement, believing in the potentially civilizing influence of her sex both at home and in Parliament.

McLaren, Priscilla Bright (1815–1906). ◆ The elder sister of **Margaret Lucas**, she was an inspirational campaigner against the Contagious Diseases Acts of 1864 and 1866, for the Married Women's Property Act of 1882, for access to higher education for women and for women's suffrage.

Marshall, Caroline (c.1853–1927). ◆ Joined the Great Pilgrimage in her native Cumbria, but was soon injured and had to return home. She was a member of a notable family of Quaker radicals involved in the Cause and her daughter Catherine became hon. parliamentary secretary of the NUWSS.

Matters, Muriel (1877–1969). ◆ Born in Australia (although with some Welsh blood) and trained as a musician and an actress, pilgrim Miss Matters came to the UK in 1906 and promptly joined the WSPU. She followed **Charlotte Despard** to the WFL the following year. Highlights of her suffrage career included public speaking, spoiling her Census form, chaining herself to the Ladies' Gallery grille in the House of Commons and scattering propaganda from an airship over Westminster. She married in 1914.

Mill, Harriet Taylor (1807–58). ◆ The author of the seminal essay 'The Enfranchisement of Women' married **John Stuart Mill** in 1851 after her first husband died, although the two had been close for many years. She was a major influence on Mill's work as a supporter of women's rights.

Mill, John Stuart (1806–73). ◆ One of the political economist and philosopher's first tasks on being elected to Parliament in 1865 was to present a petition of 1,521 women's signatures demanding the vote (1866). This marked the beginning of the modern suffrage campaign, which eventually culminated in the Equal Franchise Act of 1928.

Murdoch, Dr Mary (1864–1916). ◆ Scottish GP 'Murdie' Murdoch was a much-loved character in Hull, where she practised. She was devoted to and worked tirelessly for her patients, her community and votes for women. No doubt many were converted to the Cause through the sheer force of her personality.

Murgatroyd, Emily (1877–c.1970). ◆ From the age of ten, Emily worked as a weaver at a mill near Burnley in Lancashire. She walked the whole of the Watling Street route, managing to finance herself from what she had saved from her meagre wages and also leaving enough to support her family while she was away. As well as being a member of the NUWSS, Emily was a committed trades unionist.

Nevinson, Margaret (1858–1932). ◆ A graduate of St Andrews University in Scotland, Margaret married the journalist **Henry Nevinson** in 1884 and worked as a school manager and Poor Law Guardian for many years. She was a compelling speaker on women's suffrage; a founder member of the WFL and a campaigner for legal and marital rights for women. Unlike her husband, she would not have described herself as a militant.

New, Alice (1890–1975). ◆ Joining the Great Pilgrimage from Birkenhead, Alice New travelled with her aunt and sister. Like her friend **Jane Colquitt**, she was a keen cyclist. She was a niece of the artist Edmund Hort New, who designed an iconic suffrage banner for the Oxford University Women Students' Suffrage Society. Alice's diary was an important source for *Hearts and Minds*.

Parry, (Elizabeth) Maud, Lady (1851–1933). ◆ The wife of composer **Sir Hubert Parry** was a prominent suffragist in Sussex, walking the Brighton–London route of the Great Pilgrimage and happy to lend her high-profile name to the Cause.

Parry, Sir (Charles) Hubert (1848–1918). ◆ The English choral composer is best remembered now for his setting of William Blake's 'Jerusalem', which was used (with his blessing) as an anthem for the women's suffrage movement from 1918. He took part in the Great Pilgrimage with his wife.

Phipps, Emily (1865–1943). ◆ A member of the WFL who stood unsuccessfully as a Liberal candidate in the General Election of 1918 backed by the National Federation of Women Teachers. She resigned her post as a headmistress on being called to the Bar in 1925.

Ramsay, Annie (d.1920). ◆ The wife of a naval officer, Annie was born in Bermuda and eventually settled in Plymouth, Devon. She supported her suffragist daughter **Dr Mabel Ramsay** and, though she intended to march only for a day or two on the Great Pilgrimage, she ended up completing the whole route from Land's End to London, withstanding various assaults en route and relishing the experience.

Ramsay, Dr Mabel (d.1954). ◆ Trained in Edinburgh, Dr Ramsay ran a surgery in Plymouth. Though loath to abandon her patients to take part in the Pilgrimage, she did join the Land's End marchers after hours whenever it was practical. She served in Belgium during the Great War.

Rathbone, Eleanor (1872–1946). ◆ Born into a family of Liberal Liverpool merchants and philanthropists, her innate feminism was nurtured at Somerville College, Oxford, where she took part in various suffrage activities. She devoted her life to social work, promoting women's rights

– succeeding **Millicent Fawcett** as leader of the NUWSS (rebranded the NUSEC in 1919) – and to politics. She was elected an independent MP in 1929 and remained in Parliament until her death. Perhaps her greatest legacy was the Family Allowances Act of 1945.

Rendel, Frances Elinor (1885–1942). ◆ A college friend of **Ray Strachey**, the two went on the road in a suffrage caravan in 1908, writing a delightful account of the trip now held in Newnham College Archives. After working for the NUWSS Ellie joined the SWH and nursed in Russia and the Balkans during the Great War.

Robinson, Mrs Jethro (*fl.*1913). ◆ One of the 'Brown Women' who marched for women's suffrage from Edinburgh to London in 1912, led by **Florence de Fonblanque.**

Rochdale, Lady (1871–1966). ◆ Born Lady Beatrice Egerton, pilgrim Lady Rochdale was the daughter of the third Earl of Ellesmere. Her husband, George Kemp, became the first Baron Rochdale. She worked hard for local and national causes to help the disadvantaged, including women. She joined the Watling Street pilgrims from Carlisle to London.

Ross, Ishobel (1890–1965). ◆ A suffragist and a teacher from Skye, Miss Ross joined the SWH in 1916 as a volunteer cook.

Royden, (Agnes) Maude (1876–1956). ◆ A graduate of Lady Margaret Hall in Oxford, she was the most eloquent of suffragists, renowned for her heartfelt speeches on social justice from a devoutly Christian and feminist point of view. In demand as a lay preacher as well as a suffrage speaker, she later took a leading part in the campaign to ordain women in the Church of England.

Sanderson, Anne Cobden (1853–1926). ◆ Inheriting her famous father Richard Cobden's passion for campaigning and for social reform, Mrs Cobden Sanderson devoted her life to women's suffrage. Though initially a member of the NUWSS, she later joined the WSPU and was imprisoned after a violent demonstration in 1906, before helping to found the WFL.

Scott, Amelia (1860–1952). ◆ Founder of a branch of the National Union of Women Workers in Tunbridge Wells, Kent, in 1895, Miss Scott later became an officer of the local branch of the NUWSS. She was an enthusiastic pilgrim on the Kentish Pilgrims' Way in 1913. The regulation leaflet bag she carried with her is held by the Women's Library at the

London School of Economics. After the Great War she worked for local welfare associations and for the newly established National Council for the Unmarried Mother and her Child.

Sharples, Eda (*fl.*1913). ◆ One of **Marjory Lees**'s companions in their caravan, the *Ark*, on the Watling Street route of the Great Pilgrimage.

Smith, Mary (*fl.*1832). ◆ Described as 'a lady of rank', Mary was from Yorkshire. She petitioned her MP in 1832, demanding to know why she did not have a share in the election of a parliamentary representative since she paid taxes and was liable to all the punishments of the law, decided by a male judge and juror. This caused much amusement in the House of Commons.

Strachey, Ray (1887–1940). ◆ A graduate of Newnham College, Cambridge, whose account of a 1908 suffrage tour by caravan with college friends is held in the archives there. She worked for the NUWSS, became MP Lady Astor's political secretary and stood three times as a parliamentary candidate herself. She also wrote a highly readable history of the movement called *The Cause*, and a biography of **Millicent Fawcett**.

Taylor, Clementia (1810–1908). ◆ Mrs 'Mentia' Taylor seems to have been connected to all the big names in the early history of women's suffrage, including the Bright family, **Millicent Fawcett** and **John Stuart Mill**. Before her marriage she worked as a governess; afterwards her home became a meeting place for all who were interested in radically improving the lot of women.

Wedgwood, Major Cecil (1863–1916). ◆ A partner in the family pottery firm, Major Wedgwood became the first mayor of Stoke-on-Trent in 1910 after a distinguished army career, and an ally of the suffragists. He supported the Great Pilgrimage by attending rallies and supplying a delighted **Alice New** with new crockery after hers had been smashed in an attack on her caravan.

White, Miss (*fl.*1912). ◆ One of the 'Brown Women', she completed the entire march from Edinburgh to London in 1912 for the cause of women's suffrage.

Wolstenholme, Elizabeth *see* **Elmy, Elizabeth**

Wright, Alexandra (1879–1942). ◆ A graduate in chemistry from Bedford College, London, Miss Wright was an early supporter, with her sister Gladys, of the New Constitutional Society for Women's Suffrage, of which she became honorary organizing secretary. She also joined the 'Brown Women' periodically on their long march south from Edinburgh to London in 1912.

The suffragettes

Allan, Janie (1868–1968). ◆ The daughter of a wealthy – but socialist – shipping-line owner, she first joined the NUWSS but in 1907, attracted by its militant ethos, became a member of and major donor to the WSPU. She was arrested for window-smashing and, after going on hunger strike, became increasingly concerned with the physical and legal treatment of victims of forcible feeding.

Ball, William (*fl.*1911–13). ◆ A male suffragette and a working-class member of the Men's Political Union, William Ball was arrested in 1911 for window-smashing. He was sentenced to two months' hard labour in Pentonville, went on hunger strike and was forcibly fed for five weeks, at the end of which he was certified insane and committed to a public lunatic asylum. Questions were asked in the House about whether his treatment had caused his mental breakdown and several high-profile suffragettes campaigned on his behalf.

Billinghurst, (Rosa) May (1875–1953). ◆ Known as 'the cripple suffragette', Miss Billinghurst was a wheelchair-user. As a volunteer at her local workhouse, the misery she witnessed convinced her that if women had more political power, society would improve immeasurably. She founded a branch of the WSPU in Greenwich and was arrested and even imprisoned more than once for resorting to force rather than persuasion.

Billington-Greig, Teresa (1876–1964). ◆ Teacher Miss Billington (later Mrs Billington-Greig) was one of the first three suffragettes to be arrested in London, in June 1906. The following year she left the WSPU, where she worked as an organizer and speaker, to set up the WFL with **Charlotte Despard**. She styled herself a non-violent militant but was arrested several times, once using a horse-whip in political protest and on another occasion her bare fists.

Blomfield, Mary (*fl.*1914). ◆ Dubbed 'the Debutante Suffragette' by the press after using the occasion of her presentation at court in June 1914 to fall to her knees and beg the king and queen 'for God's sake' to put an end to forcible feeding. They serenely ignored her, then promptly cancelled all forthcoming garden parties at Buckingham Palace.

Davison, Emily Wilding (1872–1913). ◆ The most famous name in the campaign for women's suffrage belongs to a university graduate and former governess whose devotion to the Cause was at times too intense even for the officers of the WSPU. They did not always approve of what they considered to be maverick stunts designed to draw attention to the individual rather than the campaign – attempting suicide in prison, for example – but no one could question her courage and commitment. When she died under the hooves of the king's horse during the Epsom Derby in June 1913, she was apparently acting on her own initiative. The episode came to define the whole movement, however, and the WSPU were quick to call her a martyr. She inspired many suffragettes, alarmed many suffragists, and will never be forgotten.

Despard, Charlotte (1844–1939). ◆ A romantic novelist, a philanthropist, a social reformer and a feminist activist, Mrs Despard was closely associated with the WSPU, acting as its honorary secretary, but left **Emmeline Pankhurst**'s organization in 1907 to help form the WFL. She stood as a pacifist Labour candidate in the 1918 General Election and later transferred her energies to campaigning for the Communist Party. Pilgrimage organizer Katherine Harley was her younger sister.

Drummond, Flora (1878–1949). ◆ Mrs Drummond's first experience of prejudice – being refused a position as a postmistress, despite being qualified, because she was an inch below the regulation height – seems to have fuelled a life-long appetite for protest and natural justice. She was a paid organizer for the WSPU, nicknamed 'the General', and a loyal ally of **Christabel** and **Emmeline Pankhurst**.

Dunlop, Marion Wallace (1864–1942). ◆ After studying at the Slade School of Fine Art, Miss Wallace Dunlop was already a successful artist when she sensationally stencilled an extract from the Bill of Rights on to the wall in the Palace of Westminster in 1909. During her subsequent imprisonment, she became the first member of the WSPU to go on hunger strike.

Duval, Una (1879–1975). ◆ After hearing a speech by **Christabel Pankhurst** in 1907, she joined the WSPU and became a committed militant. She married Victor Duval, the founder of the MPU, in 1911, famously refusing to utter the requisite promise to 'obey' him during the marriage service.

Franklin, Hugh (1889–1962). ◆ A Jewish member of the MPU, Hugh Franklin was first arrested in 1910 when, as a passionate young man of twenty-one, he attempted to assault Home Secretary Winston Churchill with a dog-whip, in protest against the state's barbaric treatment of suffragettes. Two months later he found himself back in jail after throwing rocks at Mr Churchill's windows. The third time, it was for arson. On all three occasions he went on hunger strike and was forcibly fed over a hundred times. He was also a victim of the 'Cat and Mouse' Act.

Haverfield, Hon. Evelina (1867–1920). ◆ A keen horsewoman and initially a member of the NUWSS, but she turned to militancy in 1908 and was arrested several times. During the Great War she worked with the SWH in Russia, and afterwards founded an orphanage in Serbia where she was working when she died of pneumonia.

Hockin, Olive (1881–1936). ◆ An artist who designed banners for WSPU parades and took part in several high-profile arson attacks during her career as a suffragette. During the Great War she worked as a land girl.

Keller, Phyllis (1888–1977). ◆ An active suffragette, incarcerated in Holloway prison during March 1912 at the same time as **Emmeline Pankhurst** and **Ethel Smyth**. From 1912 to 1913 she became **Christabel Pankhurst**'s informal secretary and assistant in Paris. Phyllis – later Mrs Murray – was also an accomplished painter, dancer, woodworker, car mechanic, golfer, tennis player, gardener, knitter and seamstress.

Kenney, Annie (1879–1953). ◆ In many ways the poster girl of the suffragette movement, Annie Kenney started work in the local cotton mill in Lancashire on her tenth birthday. An early protégée of the Pankhursts, she was arrested in Manchester with **Christabel Pankhurst** in 1905 and operated at the heart of the WSPU (which her sister Jessie also joined) as an officer and activist, even touring America during the Great War to promote the militant ethos of the suffragettes. She married in 1920.

Leigh, Mary [Marie] (*fl.*1885–1965). ◆ Drum major of the WSPU's fife-and-drum band, and an enthusiastic militant, Mary Leigh has the unenviable distinction of being the first suffragette to be forcibly fed. Her health suffered from hunger strikes and from injuries received in the course of uncompromisingly combative protests. By 1913 she was working more closely with **Sylvia Pankhurst** in East London than with the WSPU, turning to socialism after the war but never forsaking the memory of her WSPU colleague and friend **Emily Wilding Davison**, whose grave she visited every year.

Lenton, Lilian (1891–1972). ◆ When the nasal tube through which she was being forcibly fed in prison in 1913 entered her lungs, Miss Lenton nearly died. With great courage she continued committing acts of violence and arson, resulting in further arrests, and spent many months evading the police, or 'cats', while on the run as a suffragette 'mouse'. She worked with the SWH during the Great War and as a speaker and organizer for the WFL afterwards.

Lytton, Lady Constance (1869–1923). ◆ Charmed into joining the WSPU by **Annie Kenney** and **Emmeline Pethick-Lawrence**, 'Conny' Lytton soon became one of the suffragettes' most determined activists. At first the authorities refused to imprison her, realizing her aristocratic background and unstable health; it was only when she assumed the pseudonym of 'Jane Warton' that she was incarcerated and forcibly fed. She wrote about her prison experiences afterwards, until she was partially paralysed by a series of strokes possibly catalysed by her treatment in prison.

Mackworth, Margaret see **Rhondda, Viscountess**

Marion, Kitty (1871–1944). ◆ Kitty Marion was the stage name of German-born actress Katherina Schafer, who freely confessed herself 'inclined to violence'. She wrote a vivid unpublished account of her imprisonment, hunger strikes and repeated forcible feeding, now held by the Museum of London.

Marsden, Dora (1882–1960). ◆ Feminist Rebecca West considered Dora Marsden 'one of the most marvellous personalities the nation has ever produced.' After working as a pupil-teacher she studied at the University of Manchester before becoming a paid organizer in the WSPU. She resigned, however, in 1910, disillusioned by the autocracy of **Christabel** and **Emmeline Pankhurst**. Thereafter she campaigned independently for feminism as a writer and philosopher.

Mitchell, Hannah (1871–1956). ◆ In her autobiography *The Hard Way Up* (1968), Mrs Mitchell tells a story of domestic hardship, socialism and suffragism. She was a loyal worker for the WSPU, but felt the **Pankhursts** did not support her enough when she fell ill due to overwork, and transferred her allegiance to the WFL. After the Great War she was elected a city councillor in Manchester.

Nevinson, Henry (1856–1941). ◆ A prominent journalist whose interest in social reform led him to support the suffragette movement. He was a founder member of the MLWS and of the male equivalent of the WSPU, the MPU. His wife, **Margaret Nevinson**, was a founder member of the WFL.

Ogston, Helen (1883–1973). ◆ 'The woman with the whip' achieved notoriety in December 1908 after protesting with other WSPU members at a meeting between the Women's Liberal Federation and David Lloyd George in the Royal Albert Hall. When stewards tried to remove her from the premises, she drew out a dog-whip and started to hit them with it. In 1910 she joined **Kate Frye** as an organizer for the New Constitutional Society for Women's Suffrage.

Pankhurst, Adela (1885–1961). ◆ The fourth of **Emmeline** and **Richard Pankhurst**'s five children. She worked as a pupil-teacher in Manchester before joining the WSPU on its inception in 1903. Her instincts tended towards Christian Socialism, unlike her mother's and sister Christabel's, and by 1912, in poor health, she withdrew from the suffragette campaign. In 1914 she emigrated to Australia, where she married and lived for the rest of her life, estranged from her mother and sisters.

Pankhurst, Christabel (1880–1958). ◆ Her sister **Sylvia Pankhurst** always maintained that Christabel was their mother's favourite. She was **Emmeline** and **Richard Pankhurst**'s eldest child, trained as a lawyer, and was beautiful, charismatic and astute. She ran the WSPU with her mother from 1906 onwards and was never afraid of militant activism, although in 1912 she fled to France to evade imprisonment and therefore ensure continuity in the leadership of the suffragettes. In 1918 she stood unsuccessfully as a parliamentary candidate for the newly formed Women's Party. After receiving a damehood in 1936 she moved to California, where she died. She was probably responsible for converting more militants to the Cause than anyone else, being an irresistible public speaker with an almost spiritual aura. Always fashionably dressed, she looked utterly feminine.

Pankhurst, Emmeline (1858–1928). ◆ The matriarch of the suffragettes was born into a family of Lancashire reformers and grew up restless in the knowledge that boys were assumed superior to girls, and men to women, in almost every sphere of life. She married fellow suffrage campaigner **Dr Richard Pankhurst** in 1879 and, after his death, worked as Manchester's first female Registrar of Births and Deaths. Before that she had kept a 'fancy goods' shop while campaigning for the Independent Labour Party and the women's suffrage movement. Disillusioned with the constitutionalists' approach, she founded the WSPU in Manchester in 1903, moving to London three years later. She remained the figurehead of the militant campaign for the rest of her life. She died shortly before the Equal Franchise Act was passed in 1928. Two years later a statue of her was erected outside the Houses of Parliament.

Pankhurst, Dr Richard (1834–1897). ◆ A barrister whose suffrage pedigree is unimpeachable: he was a member of the Manchester National Society for Women's Suffrage in 1867 (founded by **Lydia Becker** and **Elizabeth Wolstenholme Elmy**); drafted the first Women's Suffrage Bill in 1869 and the 1882 Married Women's Property Act; and campaigned for votes for women all his life. Perhaps his most valuable legacy, however, is the influence he brought to bear on his wife, **Emmeline Pankhurst**.

Pankhurst, (Estelle) Sylvia (1882–1960). ◆ In a family of rebels, artist Sylvia was the most rebellious. Not only did she protest against the system as a suffragette, but from 1911 she protested against her mother and sister, **Emmeline** and **Christabel Pankhurst**, by founding her own more democratic movement, the East London Federation of Suffragettes; she was subsequently expelled from the WSPU. Her new organization was no less militant than the WSPU: Sylvia was arrested eight times between February 1913 and the outbreak of war in August 1914. After the war, now virtually estranged from her family, she embraced communism, had a child out of wedlock and eventually came to rest in Ethiopia as a much-loved anti-imperialist journalist.

Parker, Frances 'Fanny' [alias Janet Arthur] (1875–1924). ◆ A New Zealander who came to the UK in 1896 to take up a place at Newnham College, Cambridge. She was first arrested in 1908 after a violent 'Votes for Women' demonstration in London and later became a WSPU organizer in Scotland, where she was arrested under the pseudonym Janet Arthur for attempting to set fire to the poet Robert Burns's cottage in Ayr in 1914.

During the Great War she joined the Women's Army Auxiliary Corps and was awarded an OBE for her efforts.

Paul, Alice (1885–1977). ◆ An American Quaker and a confirmed suffrage campaigner who was converted to militancy after a visit to England in 1907. She took home to the United States the WSPU's ideals, seasoned by several bouts in prison, and campaigned all her life for equal rights for men and women.

Pethick-Lawrence, Emmeline (1867–1954). ◆ Miss Pethick's interest in women's suffrage stemmed from her work running clubs for working girls. After her marriage to lawyer Frederick Lawrence in 1901, both became officers of the WSPU: Emmeline was its treasurer and Frederick its legal advisor. The couple broke with the **Pankhursts**, uncomfortable with their ethos of militancy, and left the WSPU in 1912. After the Great War, Emmeline worked with the Women's International League for Peace and Freedom.

Pethick-Lawrence, Frederick (1871–1961). ◆ As its legal advisor, Frederick Pethick-Lawrence was the only man closely involved with the WSPU; he was always loyal to the suffragettes and their leaders, but when he and his wife, **Emmeline Pethick-Lawrence**, questioned the **Pankhursts'** increasing commitment to violence as the campaign progressed, they were 'frozen out' and forced to resign. As a Labour parliamentary candidate Frederick – later Baron Pethick-Lawrence – defeated Winston Churchill in the General Election of 1923 and later served as a privy councillor.

Pine, Catherine (1864–1941). ◆ Trained as a nurse at St Bartholomew's Hospital in London and worked there until 1907, when she opened a clinic in Notting Hill. The clinic became a convalescent home for suffragettes released under the 'Cat and Mouse' Act. Nurse Pine also acted as a private medical advisor to members of the **Pankhurst** family. In later life she returned to mainstream nursing as one of the first practitioners to become a State Enrolled Nurse.

Rawle, Mary Ann (1878–1964). ◆ A Lancashire mill-worker who joined the WSPU in 1906. For a while she worked as an organizer in Oldham as **Hannah Mitchell**'s assistant, but after a spell in Holloway Prison she joined the WFL and by 1913 was an officer of the NUWSS. Her prison diary (1906) is held by the Women's Library at the London School of Economics.

Rhondda, Viscountess (1883–1958). ◆ Welsh heiress Margaret Mackworth, *née* Thomas, was inspired by an aunt to join the WSPU in 1908 and horrified her husband by being imprisoned for arson (they later divorced). After her father's death she ran the family's publishing and business interests and inherited his title, though was unable to take her seat – as a woman – in the House of Lords. After the partial suffragist victory of 1918 she campaigned vigorously for equal franchise, publicizing her arguments in the feminist journal *Time and Tide*, which she founded in 1920.

Richardson, Mary (1882/3–1961). ◆ Miss 'Slasher' Richardson's sensational memoirs are generally believed to be somewhat unreliable, but it is certain that she was a militant member of the WSPU and suffered sorely after hunger-striking and being forcibly fed. In 1914 she notoriously slashed Velazquez's painting *The Toilet of Venus* (*The Rokeby Venus*) in London's National Gallery, which led to a policy refusing access to single women at many of the country's galleries and museums. After the Great War Miss Richardson joined the British Union of Fascists.

Smyth, Ethel (1858–1944). ◆ This composer, writer and suffragette was a force of nature. Her strength of spirit was evident in her success as a professional musician (in a man's world) and in her ardent support for the suffrage campaign. She composed the song that became the suffragette anthem, 'March of the Women', and was a fearless activist, once imprisoned for window-smashing in company with **May Billinghurst**. She was awarded a damehood in 1922.

Sotheran, Florence (1866–1918). ◆ The daughter of London bookseller Henry Sotheran, Florence took part in the fracas that led to 'Black Friday' in 1910. She was arrested, and gave evidence of the suffragettes' treatment by the police. As a former constitutionalist she turned to militancy, she said, in despair of the law-abiding suffragists ever achieving progress.

Sproson, Emma (1867–1936). ◆ Although she had no formal education as a child, Mrs Sproson went on to enjoy a career in Wolverhampton as a public speaker, a politician and a suffrage campaigner. Like many others, she was a courageous member of the WSPU until the suffragettes' policy of increased militancy grew too hard to stomach and she defected to the WFL. Her papers are held in Wolverhampton City Archives.

Starbuck, Winifred (*fl.*1914). ◆ In 1958 Winifred Starbuck recorded an interview with the BBC, recalling the part she played in organizing a militant protest among sixth-form pupils at her school. She and her friends organized a 'term of disorder', spurred on by the dismissal of teachers known to have been involved in suffragette activities.

Tuke, Mabel (1871–1962). ◆ Honorary secretary of the WSPU from 1906 until 1914, Mrs 'Pansy' Tuke was once imprisoned for throwing a stone through the window of 10 Downing Street. In 1925 she opened a teashop with **Emmeline** and **Christabel Pankhurst** in the south of France, an enterprise doomed to failure.

Williams, Henria (1867–1911). ◆ Well known in her home town of Upminster in Essex for her 'frantic enthusiasm' for the cause of women's suffrage. She took part in the terrifying events of 'Black Friday' in 1910, and testified to the fact that she was assaulted by the police. She died of heart failure six weeks later.

Wright, Ada (c.1862–1939). ◆ There is an iconic photograph, published on the front page of the *Daily Mirror* in November 1910, showing a woman lying on the pavement, her hands to her eyes, surrounded by men. This is social worker Miss Ada Wright, knocked to the ground by a police officer, in fear of her life. Originally a member of the NUWSS, she later joined the WSPU and remained loyal to the **Pankhursts** in deed and in memory all her life.

Further biographical information will be found within the text, and by exploring the Select Bibliography.

Notes and References

For full details of sources quoted, please see the **Select Bibliography**, page 345.

Introduction

1 *Votes for Women*, October 1907.
2 Victoria Liddiard and Grace Roe were interviewed on BBC radio's *Woman's Hour* on 3 May 1983 and 6 February 1968 respectively.

1 Bread and Roses

1 Page, *Woman Suffrage*, page 11.
2 Lees, *Diary of the Great Pilgrimage*, 7 July. There are several versions of Marjory's diary: manuscripts in the collections of the Women's Library (2OWS/1 & 2); and a transcript with the added subtitle 'The Adventures of the Ark and the Sandwich' in Oldham Local Studies and Archives (M90/6/7/3/13), together with another manuscript account in the same hand as the Women's Library version, bound in a notebook with a paper label 'Pilgrimage 1913' (D. Lee/301). They all differ slightly.
3 From a letter to Sir Theodore Martin, 29 May 1870.
4 Lord Curzon, *Fifteen Good Reasons Against the Grant of Female Suffrage*. National League for Opposing Woman Suffrage (*c.*1912).
5 Ibid.
6 Dr Henry Maudsley, *Sex in Mind and in Education* (1874).
7 *The Times*, 30 March 1912.

8 Ibid.

9 H. A. Tooley, *The Militant Suffragette*. Island Archives, Guernsey (Tooley Collection, AQ 1129/08-002).

10 Low, Sidney, *Ought Women to be Abolished?* Undated pamphlet in the Philippa Foote Collection, Somerville College, Oxford.

11 Ethel Williams in *Common Cause*, 17 October 1913.

12 Charlotte Godley, *Letters from Early New Zealand* (1936); quoted in Robinson, *Parrot Pie*, page 170.

13 Deputation from Working Women Suffragists, 23 January 1913. The National Archives (TNA T172/110).

14 Beatrice Chapman was kindly brought to the author's attention by her granddaughter Diana Spence.

2 *Silence Is Requested*

1 Mitchell, *Hard Way Up*, page 149.

2 This figure was calculated by the artist Mary Branson during background research for *New Dawn*, her installation at the Houses of Parliament celebrating the women's suffrage campaign.

3 Mary Collier, 'The Woman's Labour' (1739).

4 Quoted in Jenkins, *Burning Question*, page 2.

5 Michael Herbert in the *Guardian*, 15 August 2012.

6 Mill, 'Enfranchisement of Women', pages 295 and 304.

7 Quoted in Bounds, *A Song of their Own*, page 7.

8 For bringing so many of the original petitioners to life, I am indebted to the research of Ann Dingsdale, developed from her thesis about the 1866 petition, *Generous and Lofty Sympathies*.

9 Quoted in Bradbrook, *Infidel Place*, pages 10–11.

10 Lord Cromer; quoted in Marlow, *Votes for Women*, page 82.

11 *The Times*, 21 April 1865; quoted in Crawford, *Women's Suffrage Movement*, page 409.

12 Emily Davies to H. R. Tompkinson; quoted in ibid., page 756.

13 Quoted in ibid., page 756.

14 Vote100, *Women in Parliament*, page 3.

15 This is Ann Dingsdale's point (conversation with the author).

16 Quoted in Crawford, op. cit., page 757.
17 Quoted in Dingsdale, *Generous and Lofty Sympathies*, page 101.
18 *Dunfermline Saturday Press*, 16 June 1866.
19 *Liverpool Mail*, 21 July 1866.
20 *Nottinghamshire Guardian*, 8 June 1866.
21 *Fife Herald*, 14 June 1866.
22 Lady Amberley; quoted in Fulford, *Votes for Women*, page 60.
23 April 1868; quoted in McDonald, *Florence Nightingale on Society*, pages 404–5. Columbia University, Presbyterian Hospital School of Nursing (C90).
24 Nightingale, *Suggestions for Thought*, vol. 2, page 402.
25 30 November 1858. British Museum (Add. Mss. 45, 788); quoted in Forster, *Significant Sisters*, page 94.
26 Leneman, *Guid Cause*, page 12.
27 Quoted in Fulford, op. cit., page 90.
28 Pankhurst, *Suffrage Movement*, page 47.
29 Parliamentary Archives (HL/PO/6/11A).
30 Fulford, op. cit., page 21.
31 *Northern Star*, 29 April 1843. See Sarah Richardson, www.victoriancommonswordpress.com, 18 March 2013.
32 Strachey, *Fawcett*, page 70.
33 Rev. Charles Aked in *The Times*, 22 December 1901. See www.reformationsa.org.
34 *Manchester Guardian*, 10 December 1876. Fawcett Family Papers, private collection (courtesy of Mrs M. Day).
35 Dr Garrett Anderson was elected mayor of her home town of Aldeburgh, Suffolk, in 1908.
36 See Chapter 11, 'Breeding White Elephants', in Robinson, *Bluestockings*, page 202.
37 *Common Cause*, 15 March 1918.

3 Deeds and Words

1 Billington-Greig, *Non-violent Militant*, page 114.
2 Sproson Papers, Wolverhampton City Archives (DX-686).

3   In fact Emmeline resigned the registrarship just two months later, in April 1907.

4   Partially quoted in Rosen, *Rise Up*, page 80.

5   Sproson Papers; see note 2.

6   *London Daily News*, 15 February 1907.

7   Sproson Papers; see note 2.

8   Mary Ann Rawle Papers, Women's Library (7MAR/04).

9   Ibid.

10   Sproson Papers; see note 2.

11   Ibid.

12   Museum of London Suffragette Collections (57.57/66).

13   See www.blog.oxforddictionaries.com/2013/05/woman-or-suffragette for a further discussion of the etymology.

14   Suffragist Helena Swanwick; quoted in Marlow, *Votes for Women*, page 267.

15   H. A. Tooley, *The Militant Suffragette*. Island Archives, Guernsey (Tooley Collection, AQ 1129/08-002).

16   *Morning Post*, 13 February 1907.

17   *Tribune*, 11 February 1907; quoted in Tickner, *Spectacle*, page 75.

18   *Manchester Guardian*, 11 February 1907; quoted in Tickner, op. cit., page 79.

19   Strachey, *The Cause*, page 306.

20   Mrs Pankhurst liked to pronounce the word with a hard 'g', because, as she said, she meant to 'get' the vote.

21   *Women's Franchise*, 25 May 1908, page 564; quoted in Tickner, op. cit., page 80.

22   Handbill in the Museum of London Suffragette Collections (50.82/650b).

23   Newspaper cutting in the Artists' Suffrage League scrapbook, Women's Library (10/01).

24   Quoted in Tickner, op. cit., page 83.

25   Rosen, op. cit., page 106.

26   *Votes for Women*, 4 June 1908.

27   Morris, *Rights and Wrongs of Women*, opening page.

28   Royden, *Plain Answers*, page 22.

29 Unpublished typescript autobiography, Museum of London Suffragette Collections (50.82/1124).
30 Ibid.

4 Foot Soldiers

1 Laurence Housman, 'Woman This and Woman That', in *Articles of Faith in the Freedom of Woman*, 1910.
2 Reported (perhaps surprisingly) in the *Anti-Suffrage Review*, 10 December 1910.
3 *Cambridge Daily News*, 18 February 1909. Cutting in the Cambridge Association for Women's Suffrage Papers, Cambridgeshire Archives (455/Q2).
4 Birmingham Archives and Heritage (MS 841 B/514).
5 Mansfield Women's Suffrage Society Minutes, Nottinghamshire Archives (DD1354/72/3).
6 There is just such a slip, printed in bright green, in the Women's Library (2LSW/E/02/39).
7 Hamilton, *Life Errant*, page 73.
8 This tip was provided by northern suffragist Selina Cooper. Selina Cooper Papers, Lancashire Archives (DDX 1137/1; NB the reference DDX 1137 covers the whole Cooper collection).
9 Housman, *Unexpected Years*, pages 269–70.
10 Kate Frye's 'Organiser's Report Book' for the New Constitutional Society for Women's Suffrage, 1912–14, Women's Library (uncatalogued when the author worked on it in 2016).
11 'Standard bread' was introduced in 1911 in a deliberate attempt to improve the nation's health. It was made of wholemeal flour, rather than the often heavily adulterated white flour used ubiquitously beforehand.
12 Frye, *Campaigning for the Vote*, pages 36-7.
13 Ibid., page 65.
14 Housman, op. cit.
15 Cooper Papers; see note 8.
16 Journalist Henry Nevinson was a hero of the suffrage movement as

well as a famous war correspondent. His wife and mistress were both
active suffragettes.

17 *Hull Daily Mail*, 17 February 1909.

18 Cambridgeshire Archives (455/Q52).

19 Parliamentary Statute Book, Somerville College Archives.

20 Most of these japes were reported in the *Common Cause*, 6 June 1913.

21 See Sparham, *Soldiers and Suffragettes*.

22 Quoted by Anne Sebba, *Sunday Telegraph* magazine, 26 April
   2009. There is a copy of the programme at the Women's Library
   (PC/06/396-11/04).

23 Reported in – among other places – the *Dundee Evening Telegraph*, 9
   May 1912.

24 Women's Library (2LSW/E/02/39).

25 Letter from Housman to S. Clarke, 20 August [1913]; quoted in
   Holton, *Suffrage Days*, page 190.

26 See www.guildford-dragon.com.

27 According to June Purvis, interviewed by Radhika Sanghani in the
   Daily Telegraph, 12 October 2015.

28 Recorded interview in the Women's Library (8SUF/B/126b).

29 Mitchell, *The Hard Way Up*, page 140.

30 Ibid., page 130.

5 Bad News

1 The wording of a banner displayed at the funeral of Emily Wilding
  Davison.

2 Murray and Brailsford, *Treatment*, page 44.

3 Ibid., page 30.

4 Ibid., page 33.

5 Ibid., pages 23-4.

6 Ibid., page 29.

7 Ibid., page 20.

8 Parliamentary Debates, House of Commons, Official Report, 5th
  series, 1910, vol. 20, page 389; quoted in Morrell, *Black Friday*, page 37.

9 Ibid. (1911, vol. 22), page 836.

10 Kenney, *Memories of a Militant*, pages 156–7.

11 Frye, *Campaigning for the Vote*, page 54.

12 Hertha Ayrton; quoted in *Suffrage Meetings at the Royal Albert Hall*, RAH Archives team, August 2014.

13 Pankhurst, *Suffragette Movement*, page 415.

14 The *Suffragette* was the WSPU's successor to *Votes for Women* and was first published in 1912.

15 *Brighton Herald and Hove Chronicle*, 26 July 1913.

16 Lytton, *Prisons and Prisoners*, page 164.

17 Ibid., page 275.

18 I am indebted to Phyllis Keller's grandson Dr Simon Murray for telling me about her and allowing me to have a copy of her wonderful letter home.

19 You might remember from Chapter 2 that not everyone was as fulsome about Dr Garrett Anderson's bedside manner.

20 Pethick-Lawrence, *Fate has been Kind*, page 69.

21 *Daily Telegraph*, 26 February 1913.

22 *The Times*, 20 June 1913.

23 This comment was made during a speech at the Connaught Rooms, London, on 16 February 1912.

24 The scrapbook is with the New Family Papers, David M. Rubenstein Rare Book and Manuscript Library, Duke University (RL.11080). It is most unlikely, however, to have belonged to Alice Margery New herself, who was a suffragist.

25 For Dora Marsden's story, read Garner, *A Brave and Beautiful Spirit*.

26 The date of the photograph is 8 October 1908 and the 'rush' happened on 13 October.

27 Murray and Brailsford, op. cit., page 43.

28 Quoted in the www.spartacus-educational.com entry on Rosa May Billinghurst.

29 Pankhurst, op. cit., page 225.

30 *Votes for Women*, 7 May 1909. Vera's papers are in The National Archives, impatiently awaiting the attention of a robust biographer.

31 Further research reveals the clergyman and his opponent to have been involved in a fracas during an open-air meeting in Denmark Hill,

London, in June 1914. The reverend gentleman, a supporter of Sylvia Pankhurst, was objecting to the crowd's treatment of a woman in the audience who was assaulted after heckling guest speaker Lloyd George. The incident was gleefully reported by newspapers across the UK.

32 Holton, *Suffrage Days*, page 168.

33 Elizabeth Hall of North London wrote this; quoted in Liddington, *Vanishing for the Vote*, page 255.

34 *Morpeth Herald*, 14 April 1911.

35 Ibid., 28 April 1911.

36 The hand-written police report on the incident is held in the Parliamentary Archives (HC/SA/SJ/10/12 item 26).

37 See British Film Archive on www.bfi.org.uk.

38 See Screen Archive South East (BH 001026).

6 A Beckoning Road

1 Quoted by Millicent Fawcett in *The Women's Victory*, page 78, this is from a song about Asquith in Wonderland . . .

2 Cicely Hamilton in her autobiography, *Life Errant*, page 68.

3 Pankhurst, *Suffragette Movement*, page 485.

4 Frye, *Campaigning for the Vote*, page 105.

5 *Bexhill-on-Sea Observer*, 25 July 1908.

6 Newnham College Club, *Newnham College Letter*, 1907–8, pages 22–3. Subsequent quotes are from this article.

7 *Derby Daily Telegraph*, 24 July 1908.

8 Two of the speakers on the first ever tour of the *Clarion* van were tailoress Ada Nield (1870–1945; later Mrs Chew) and mill worker Sarah Reddish (1850–1928), both of whom, with their friend Selina Cooper, went on to play a prominent part in the suffragist campaign among the textile workers of the north-west.

9 Fulford, *Votes for Women*, page 266.

10 *Scotsman*, 15 October 1912.

11 *Suffrage Annual*, page 145.

12 *Suffragette*, 25 October 1912, page 25.

13 Cutting in a 'Suffrage Scrapbook', New Family Papers, David M.

Rubenstein Rare Book and Manuscript Library, Duke University (RL.11080).

14 Suffolk Record Office (HA47/B3/367).

15 *Thame Gazette*, 29 July 1913.

16 *Bucks Free Advertiser*, March 1913; quoted in Cartwright, *Burning to Get the Vote*, page 217.

17 Unfortunately the editor of the *Common Cause* on this occasion consistently spelled Emily's surname 'Davieson'. I have corrected the error.

18 *Common Cause*, 13 June 1913.

7 Stepping Out

1 Ida Beaver and K. M. Harley, 'The Pilgrimage', in *Englishwoman*, vol. 19, issue 57 (1913), page 259.

2 *Yarmouth Independent*, 12 July 1913.

3 *Nottingham Free Post*, 10 May 1913.

4 See Liddington and Norris, *One Hand Tied Behind Us*, for more on this remarkable campaigner.

5 Robert Burns, 'Green Grow the Rushes, O', verse 5.

6 Gladys Duffield's unpublished account of the Pilgrimage, *On the March. A Personal Story of the Watling Street Route . . . Dedicated to the Women of Britain*, is in Cumbria Archive Centre, Carlisle (DX 33/1).

7 I am indebted to Anne Blunt for pointing me in the direction of Dr Mabel Ramsay's typescript reminiscences, held by the Royal College of Physicians in London (MS87).

8 Annie Ramsay's notes for a talk on the Pilgrimage are in the Women's Library, London (7 ARA).

9 *Western Times*, 7 May 1913.

10 My thanks to Deborah Scriven, who has written about the Wakefield pilgrims in 'The Pilgrims' Progress: Wakefield Welcomes the 1913 Suffragette [*sic*] Pilgrimage' for the *Wakefield Historical Society Journal*, vol. 16 (2012).

11 Reported in a letter by Ethel Kenway, July 1913, Cornwall Record Office (ST/1121).

12 This and other Watling Street songs were published by the NUWSS

for distribution among the pilgrims. Marjory Lees added a few extra verses to her copy.

8 Sufferage

1 Harriet Blessley's Pilgrimage Diary, Portsmouth History Centre (1155A/1(a)).

2 Alice Margery New's Pilgrimage Diary, New Family Papers, David M. Rubenstein Rare Book and Manuscript Library, Duke University (RL.11080).

3 See Cowman, *Mrs. Brown*, for information about Jane Colquitt.

4 Margaret Ashton (1856–1937) was a well-known local politician in Manchester and chair of the North of England Society for Women's Suffrage, 1906–15. She was one of the NUWSS's most talented public speakers.

5 Queen's College was a medical school in Paradise Street in the centre of Birmingham.

6 This was probably Jane Mason of Bolton.

7 Ethel Kenway Papers, Cornwall Record Office (ST/1121/4).

8 Margaret Nevinson in *Women's Franchise*, 24 September 1908.

9 *Exeter and Plymouth Gazette*, 27 June 1913.

10 *Cheltenham Examiner*, 17 July 1913.

11 See *Cambridge Daily News*, 21 July 1913.

12 Annie Ramsay's Pilgrimage notes, Women's Library (7 ARA).

13 Noted by independent scholar Simon Colbeck in his research into suffragist Catherine Marshall. Source not seen.

14 Quoted in Ferguson, *Victorian Bouquet*, page 26.

15 Quoted in Peacock, 'Votes for Women', page 17.

16 *Portsmouth Evening News*, 18 July 1913.

17 Harriet Blessley's Pilgrimage Diary; see note 1.

18 *Daily News*, 21 July 1913.

19 Ibid.

20 Sadly, the banner is now lost, but an image of the design survives as a postcard in the John Johnson ephemera collection, Bodleian Library, Oxford.

9 We Are People, Too

1 Keir Hardie, 'Citizenship of Women', page 14. Hardie was ahead of his time when he made this comment in 1905.

2 Mrs Mary Siddall was the brush-manufacturer's wife; she was also a school manager and a workhouse visitor. Another Oldham pilgrim, Rachel Bridge, had been a headmistress. See Berry, *Female Suffrage Movement*, page 26.

3 All quotations from Marjory Lees in this chapter are taken from various versions of her diary (see Chapter 1, note 2).

4 Similarly, all quotes from Gladys Duffield are from her unpublished memoir *On the March* (Cumbria Archive Centre, Carlisle DX 33/1).

5 Unattributed newspaper cutting in the collection of Mansfield Women's Suffrage Society Papers, Nottinghamshire Archives (DD1354/71/iv).

6 *Common Cause*, 25 July 1913.

7 Ibid.

8 *Bucks Herald*, 2 August 1913.

9 *Daily News*, 28 July 1913.

10 Harriet Blessley's Pilgrimage Diary, Portsmouth Library and Archive Service, Portsmouth City Council (1155A/1(a)).

11 Eliza Vaughan, *Humours of the Road*. Unpublished typescript in Essex Record Office (T/Z 11/27).

12 *Chelmsford Chronicle*, 25 July 1913.

13 Marjory writes that news about High Wycombe spurred Sarah Lees into sending the gardeners to rescue her. But given that the High Wycombe meeting took place only the evening before they arrived, it would make more sense if she was motivated by reports of what had happened at Thame.

14 *Common Cause*, 1 August 1913.

15 Ida Beaver and K. M. Harley, 'The Pilgrimage', in *Englishwoman*, vol. 19, issue 57 (1913), pages 254–62.

16 One such is in the collections of the Museum of London (63.104/52).

17 *Manchester Guardian*, 26 July 1913.

18 See Elizabeth Crawford's blogpost on Alan's Tea Rooms on

womanandhersphere.com/2012/09/04/suffrage-stories-suffragettes-and-tearooms-alans-tearooms.

19 Recorded in a draft of Alice New's Diary, New Family Papers, David M. Rubenstein Rare Book and Manuscript Library, Duke University (RL.11080).

20 Ibid.

21 *Common Cause*, 1 August 1913.

22 *Folkestone, Hythe, Sandgate and Cheriton Herald*, 26 July 1913.

23 *Cambridge Independent Press*, 15 August 1913; *Manchester Courier and Lancashire General Advertiser*, 24 October 1913; Fawcett, *The Women's Victory*, page 60. McKenna's comment was made in the course of setting up an inquiry into police handling of the crowds at trouble spots during the Pilgrimage, the findings of which are held in the National Archives (HO45/10701). The general consensus was that the police had tried to do the best they could for the pilgrims in the face of unmanageable rowdiness, but the NUWSS disputed that, insisting that on some occasions there should have been a larger police presence at places where trouble was anticipated.

24 Millicent Fawcett's correspondence, Women's Library (7MGF/A/1/082).

25 Transcription of the NUWSS deputation's meeting with Herbert Asquith published in *Common Cause*, 15 August 1913.

26 Ibid.

27 Transcription of the NUWSS deputation's meeting with David Lloyd George, Parliamentary Archives (LG/C/17/3/24).

10 *Patriotism Is Not Enough*

1 Ruskin, *Sesame and Lilies*, page 117.

2 Malleson, *A Woman Doctor*, page 220.

3 Frye, *Campaigning for the Vote*, page 163.

4 Ibid., page 181.

5 Ibid., page 179.

6 Ibid., page 181.

7 *Kent Argus*, 25 June 1913.

8 Unattributed newspaper cutting, Portsmouth Library and Archive Service, Portsmouth City Council (1155A/1(6)).

9 Ibid.

10 *Englishwoman*, vol. 19, issue 57 (1913), page 261.

11 Quoted in Liddington and Norris, *One Hand Tied Behind Us*, page 259.

12 Winifred told her story in an interview on BBC radio's *Woman's Hour* in 1958.

13 Rosen, *Rise Up, Women!* page 201.

14 This and subsequent quotes are from an article in *Votes for Women*, 7 August 1914, page 681. For more information on Frances Parker and her peers, see June Purvis's paper 'The Prison Experiences of the Suffragettes in Edwardian Britain', *Women's History Review*, vol. 4, no. 1, pages 103–33.

15 *Common Cause*, 7 August 1914.

16 Ibid., 17 October 1913.

17 *Daily Sketch*, 27 January 1915.

18 Pankhurst, *Unshackled*, page 290.

19 *Aberdeen Journal*, 19 July 1915.

20 This and following quotes are from Florence Lockwood's War Diaries, West Yorkshire Archive Service (KC329). Florence embroidered a beautiful banner for the Huddersfield branch of the NUWSS, which is now housed in the town's Tolson Museum.

21 *Common Cause*, 23 July 1915. Women's Patrols were organized by the National Union of Women Workers with the Headmistresses' Association and tended to be staffed by suffragist volunteers; a similar project was administered by members of the WSPU, called the Women's Police Service. Both organizations went on to influence the appointment of women constables to the national police force in 1915.

22 See Cowman, *Mrs. Brown is a Man*, for further details about Cicely Leadley Brown's war-work.

23 See Robinson, *A Force to be Reckoned With*, Chapter 2.

24 Hilda Lorimer, Classics tutor at Somerville College, Oxford, described her experiences at the camp (located at Shenberrow, outside Stanton in

Gloucestershire) in an article for the Somerville Students' Association Report, November 1915, pages 70–3.

25 *Anti-Suffrage Review*, no. 77, March 1915.

26 Ross, *Little Grey Partridge*, page 70.

11 Half a Loaf

1 Dr Elsie Inglis, 'Three Months on the Eastern Front', in *Englishwoman*, vol. 33, issue 98 (1917), page 123.

2 Ibid., pages 123-4.

3 Ibid., page 129.

4 Laurence, *Shadow of Swords*, page 275.

5 Marjory Lees Papers, Oldham Local Studies and Archives (M90/6/7/3/13).

6 *Rochdale Observer*, 17 March 1917.

7 'War Work 1914–1918', Newnham College, Cambridge.

8 Mrs Winifred Buller was something of a celebrity, training French airmen at Hendon during the war and becoming a test pilot and air-ambulance pioneer. She served in the WRAF in 1919 and 1920. Flora Sandes (1876–1956) wrote an account of her extraordinary wartime career, *The Autobiography of a Woman Soldier: A Brief Record of Adventure with the Serbian Army, 1916–1919.*

9 From a newspaper cutting dated 28 March 1917 in Florence Lockwood's War Diaries, West Yorkshire Archive Service (KC329).

10 Erminda Rentoul Esler in *Common Cause*, 27 June 1913 (the emphasis is mine).

11 This was always Millicent Fawcett's philosophy, first expressed in a letter to the *Sheffield Evening Telegraph*, 15 July 1913.

12 *Exeter and Plymouth Gazette*, 30 March 1917.

13 *Nottinghamshire Evening Post*, 30 March 1917.

14 Millicent Fawcett's correspondence, Women's Library (7MGF/A/1/131).

15 'War Notebook', Deneke Papers, Bodleian Library (uncatalogued Mss. Box 19).

16 *Scotsman*, 18 March 1918.

17 Mansfield Women's Suffrage Society Minutes, 8 February 1918, Nottinghamshire Archives (DD1354/71).

18 *Common Cause*, 15 March 1918.

19 *Gloucestershire Echo*, 4 January 1919.

20 *Englishwoman*, vol. 41, issue 122 (1919), page 52.

21 Ibid.

22 *Sunday Mirror*, 15 December 1918; *Birmingham Mail*, 16 December 1918.

23 *Aberdeen Evening Express*, 16 December 1918.

24 Ibid.

25 *Daily Mirror*, 31 December 1918.

26 *Anti-Suffrage Review*, no. 113, April 1918.

27 *Gloucestershire Chronicle*, 14 December 1918.

28 *Lancashire Evening Post*, 14 December 1918.

12 The Sequel

1 Elizabeth Dean from Manchester, interviewed on BBC radio's *Woman's Hour*, 30 June 1978.

2 *News of the World*, 8 April 1928.

3 Hackey Papers, Lancashire Archives (DDX 1057/2).

4 Mackworth, *This Was My World*, page 120.

5 Quoted by Johanna Alberti in Purvis and Holton, *Votes for Women*, page 273.

6 Quoted in Pugh, 'Politicians and the Woman's Vote', page 367.

7 *The Times*, 6 August 1929.

8 Ferguson, *Victorian Bouquet*, page 21.

9 Marjory Lees Commemorative Book, Oldham Local Studies and Archives (M90/6/7/10/2).

Select Bibliography

Adams, Pauline, *Somerville for Women: An Oxford College, 1879–1993* (Oxford: Oxford University Press, 1996)

Alberti, Johanna, 'A Symbol and a Key: The Suffrage Movement in Britain, 1918–28', in June Purvis and Sandra Stanley Holton (eds), *Votes for Women* (London: Routledge, 2000)

Anderson, Louisa Garrett, *Elizabeth Garrett Anderson* (London: Faber and Faber, 1939)

[Anon.] *The Case Against Woman Suffrage* (London: Alston Rivers, 1907)

Anti-Suffrage Review (Journal, 1908–18)

Atkinson, Diane, *The Suffragettes in Pictures* (Stroud: History Press and Museum of London, 1996)

Barnsby, George, *Votes for Women: The Struggle for the Vote in the Black Country* (Preston: Lancashire Community Press, n.d.)

Beaver, Ida, and Harley, Katherine, 'The Pilgrimage', *Englishwoman*, vol. 19 (1913), pages 254–62

Beech, Alan, *An Exploration of the Tension Between Liberalism and Women's Suffrage in One Woman's Life: A Case Study on Marjory Lees* (BA dissertation for Manchester Metropolitan University, 1994)

Berry, Terry Jane, *The Female Suffrage Movement in South Lancashire with Particular Reference to Oldham, 1890–1914* (MA thesis for Huddersfield Polytechnic, 1986)

Billington-Greig, Teresa, *The Non-violent Militant. Selected Writings*, ed. Ann FitzGerald and Carol McPhee (London: Routledge and Kegan Paul, 1987)

Bounds, Joy, *A Song of their Own: The Fight for Votes for Women in Ipswich* (Stroud: History Press, 2014)

Boyce, Lucienne, *The Bristol Suffragettes* (Bristol: Silver Wood, 2013)

Bradbrook, M. C., *'That Infidel Place': A Short History of Girton College, 1869–1969* (Cambridge: Girton College, 1969)

Broom, Christina, *see* Sparham, Anna

Cahill, Audrey Fawcett (ed.), *Between the Lines: Letters and Diaries from Elsie Inglis's Russian Unit* (Edinburgh: Pentland Press, 1999)

Calderon, George, *Women in Relation to the State* (Hampstead: Priory Press, 1908)

Cartwright, Colin, *Burning to Get the Vote: The Women's Suffrage Movement in Central Buckinghamshire, 1904–14* (Buckingham: University of Buckingham Press, 2013)

Chew, Doris Nield (ed.), *Ada Nield Chew: The Life and Writings of a Working Woman* (London: Virago, 1982)

Cholmeley, Robert, *The Women's Anti-Suffrage Movement* (London: NUWSS, 1908)

Cockroft, V. Irene, *New Dawn Women: Women in the Arts and Crafts and Suffrage Movements at the Dawn of the Twentieth Century* (Compton: Watts Gallery, 2005)

Collier, Mary, *The Woman's Labour: An Epistle to Mr Stephen Duck* (London: for the Author, 1739)

[Collum, Vera Chute] 'Skia', Articles in *Blackwood's Magazine*, vol. CXCIX (May 1916), pages 690–8; MCCXVII (March 1917), pages 339–50; and MCCXXXVII (November 1918), pages 613–40

Common Cause (Journal, 1909–20)

Corelli, Marie, *Woman, or – Suffragette? A Question of National Choice* (no imprint, 1907)

Cowman, Krista, *Mrs. Brown is a Man and a Brother: Women in Merseyside Political Organisations, 1890–1920* (Liverpool: Liverpool University Press, 2004)

Crawford, Elizabeth, *The Women's Suffrage Movement: A Reference Guide, 1866–1928* (London: UCL Press, 1999)

—*Enterprising Women: The Garretts and their Circle* (London: Francis Boutle, 2002)

—*The Women's Suffrage Movement in Britain and Ireland: A Regional*

Survey (London: Routledge, 2006)

Crofton, Eileen, *Angels of Mercy: A Women's Hospital on the Western Front, 1914–18* (Edinburgh: Birlinn, 2013)

Dicey, A. L., 'Woman Suffrage', *Quarterly Review* offprint, January 1909

Dingsdale, Ann, *Generous and Lofty Sympathies: The Kensington Society, the 1866 Women's Suffrage Petition and the Development of Mid-Victorian Feminism* (PhD thesis for Greenwich University, 1995)

Dobbie, B. M. Willmott, *A Nest of Suffragettes in Somerset* (Batheaston: Batheaston Society, 1979)

Dove, Iris, *Yours in the Cause: Suffragettes in Lewisham, Greenwich and Woolwich* (London: Lewisham Library Service and Greenwich Libraries, 1988)

Dyhouse, Carol, *Feminism and the Family in England, 1880–1939* (Oxford: Blackwell, 1989)

Englishwoman (Journal, 1909–21)

Eustance, Claire, Ryan, Joan, and Ugolini, Laura (eds), *A Suffrage Reader: Charting Directions in Britain's Suffrage History* (Leicester: Leicester University Press, 2000)

Fawcett, Millicent Garrett, *The Women's Victory – and After: Personal Reminiscences, 1911–1918* (London: Sidgwick and Jackson, 1920)
—*What I Remember* (London: T. Fisher Unwin, 1924)

Ferguson, Rachel (ed.), *Victorian Bouquet: Lady X Looks On* (London: Ernest Benn, 1931)

Forster, Margaret, *Significant Sisters: The Grassroots of Active Feminism* (London: Secker and Warburg, 1984)

Frye, Kate Parry, *Campaigning for the Vote: Kate Parry Frye's Suffrage Diary*, ed. Elizabeth Crawford (London: Francis Boutle, 2013)

Fulford, Roger, *Votes for Women: The Story of a Struggle* (London: Faber and Faber, 1957)

Garner, Les, *A Brave and Beautiful Spirit: Dora Marsden, 1882–1960* (Aldershot: Avebury, 1990)

Gottlieb, Jane, and Toye, Richard (eds), *The Aftermath of Suffrage: Women, Gender and Politics in Britain, 1918–1945* (London: Palgrave Macmillan, 2013)

Hamilton, Cicely, *Life Errant* (London: J. M. Dent, 1935)

Hannam, June, *Isabella Ford* (Oxford: Blackwell, 1989)

Hardie, Keir, 'The Citizenship of Women', *Coming Men on Coming Questions*, no. VI (1905)

Heath, Gerald and Joan, *The Women's Suffrage Movement in and around Richmond and Twickenham* (Twickenham: Twickenham Local History Society, 1968/2003)

Holton, Sandra Stanley, *Suffrage Days: Stories from the Women's Suffrage Movement* (London: Routledge, 1996)

Housman, Laurence, *Articles of Faith in the Freedom of Woman* (no imprint, 1910)

—*The Unexpected Years* (London: Jonathan Cape, 1937)

Inglis, Elsie, 'Three Months on the Eastern Front', *Englishwoman*, vol. 33, issue 98 (1917), pages 113–29

J. R., *The Sex Symphony, or Some Missing Political Instruments* (London: Arnold Fairbairns, 1908)

Jenkins, Jess, *The Burning Question: The Struggle for Women's Suffrage in Leicestershire* (Leicester: Friends of the Record Office for Leicestershire, n.d.)

John, Angela V., and Eustance, Claire (eds), *The Men's Share? Masculinities, Male Support and Women's Suffrage in Britain, 1890–1920* (London: Routledge, 1997)

Kean, Hilda, *Deeds Not Words: The Lives of Suffragette Teachers* (London: Pluto Press, 1990)

Kenney, A., *Memories of a Militant* (London: Edward Arnold, 1924)

Latham, Francis, *Is the British Empire Ripe for Government by Disorderly Women Who Smash Windows and Assault the Police?* (London: Simpkin Marshall, n.d.)

Lawson-Reay, Barbara, *Votes for Women: The North Wales Suffragists' Campaign, 1907–14* (Conwy: Gwasg Carreg Gwalch, 2015)

Laurence, Margot, *Shadow of Swords: a Biography of Elsie Inglis* (London: Joseph, 1971)

Leneman, Leah, *A Guid Cause': The Women's Movement in Scotland* (Aberdeen: Aberdeen University Press, 1991)

—*In the Service of Life: The Story of Elsie Inglis and the Scottish Women's Hospitals* (Edinburgh: Mercat Press, 1994)

Liddington, Jill, *Rebel Girls: Their Fight for the Vote* (London: Virago, 2006)

—*Vanishing for the Vote: Suffrage, Citizenship and the Battle for the Census* (Manchester: Manchester University Press, 2014)

Liddington, Jill, and Norris, Jill, *One Hand Tied Behind Us: The Rise of the Women's Suffrage Movement* (London: Virago, 1978)

Lockwood, Mrs Josiah, *An Ordinary Life, 1861–1924* (London: privately printed, 1932)

Lytton, Constance, *Prisons and Prisoners: Some Personal Experiences* (London: Heinemann, 1914)

Mackworth, Margaret, Viscountess Rhondda, *This Was My World* (London: Macmillan, 1933)

Malleson, Hope, *A Woman Doctor: Mary Murdoch of Hull* (London: Sidgwick and Jackson, 1919)

Marlow, Joyce, *Votes for Women: The Virago Book of Suffragettes* (London: Virago, 2000)

Martindale, Louisa, *Under the Surface* (Brighton, Southern Publishing, 1910)

Maudsley, Henry, 'Sex in Mind and Education', *Fortnightly Review*, vol. 15 (January–June 1874), pages 466–83

McDonald, Lynn (ed.), *Florence Nightingale on Society and Politics, Philosophy, Science, Education and Literature* (Waterloo: Wilfrid Laurier University Press, 2003)

McLaren, Lady, *The Women's Charter of Rights and Liberties* (London: Grant Richards, 1909)

[Mill, Harriet Taylor], 'Enfranchisement of Women', *Westminster Review*, vol. 55 (July 1851), pages 289–309

Mill, John Stuart, *The Subjection of Women* (London: Longmans, Green, 1869)

Mitchell, Hannah, *The Hard Way Up: The Autobiography of Hannah Mitchell*, ed. Geoffrey Mitchell (London: Faber and Faber, 1968)

Mitra, S. M., *Voice for Women – Without Votes* (no imprint, 1914)

Morrell, Caroline, *'Black Friday': Violence Against Women in the Suffrage Movement* (London: Women's Research and Resources Centre, 1981)

Morris, Rev. F. O., *The Rights and Wrongs of Women* (London: Poole, 1870)

Murray, Janet Horowitz (ed.), *Strong-minded Women: and Other Lost Voices from Nineteenth-century England* (London: Penguin, 1984)

Murray, Jessie, and Brailsford, H. N., *The Treatment of the Women's Deputations by the Metropolitan Police: Copy of Evidence Collected by Dr. Jessie Murray and Mr H. N. Brailsford, and Forwarded to the Home Office by the Conciliation Committee for Women Suffrage, in Support of its Demand for a Public Enquiry* (London: WSPU, 1911)

Nightingale, Florence, *Suggestions for Thought to Searchers After Religious Truth*, 2 vols (London: Eyre and Spottiswoode, 1860)

Norquay, Glenda, *Voices and Votes: A Literary Anthology of the Women's Suffrage Campaign* (Manchester: Manchester University Press, 1995)

Page, Arthur, 'Woman Suffrage: Its Meaning and Effect', *The National Review* (London: National League for Opposing Woman Suffrage, 1912)

Pankhurst, Christabel, *Unshackled: The Story of How We Won the Vote* (London: Hutchinson, 1959)

Pankhurst, E. Sylvia, *The Suffragette Movement: An Intimate Account of Persons and Ideals* (London: Longmans, Green, 1931)

Pankhurst, Emmeline, *My Own Story* (London: Evelyn Nash, 1914)

Peacock, S., 'Votes for Women: The Women's Fight in Portsmouth', *Portsmouth Papers*, no. 39 (December 1983)

Pethick-Lawrence, Frederick, *Fate Has Been Kind* (London: Hutchinson, 1943)

Phillips, Ann (ed.), *A Newnham Anthology* (Cambridge: Newnham College, 1979/1988)

Procter, Zoë, *Life and Yesterday*, ed. George Baker (Lansing: Favil Press, 1960)

Pugh, Martin, 'Politicians and the Woman's Vote', *History*, vol. 59, no. 197 (1974), pages 358–74

Purvis, June, and Holton, Sandra Stanley (eds), *Votes for Women* (London: Routledge, 2000)

R., A. J. (ed.), *Suffrage Annual and Women's Who's Who* (London: Stanley Paul, 1913)

Reeves, Josette, 'The Liverpool Women's War Service Bureau and its Work, 1914–1918', *Journal of the British Association for Local History*, vol. 44 (October 2014), pages 312–24

Rhondda, Viscountess, *see* Mackworth, Margaret

Richardson, Mary, *Laugh a Defiance* (London: Weidenfeld and Nicolson, 1953)

Robinson, Jane, *Parrot Pie for Breakfast: An Anthology of Women Pioneers* (Oxford: Oxford University Press, 1999)
—*A Force to be Reckoned With: A History of the Women's Institute* (London: Virago, 2011)
—*Bluestockings: The Remarkable Story of the First Women to Fight for an Education* (London: Viking, 2009)

Rosen, Andrew, *Rise Up, Women! The Mill Campaign of the WSPU, 1903–14* (London: Routledge and Kegan Paul, 1974)

Ross, Ishobel, *Little Grey Partridge: First World War Diary of Ishobel Ross who Served with the Scottish Women's Hospitals* (Aberdeen: Aberdeen University Press, 1988)

Royden, Maude, *Plain Answers to Tangled Statements (A Reply to the Anti-Suffrage Handbook)*, (London: NUWSS, 1912)

Ruskin, John, *Sesame and Lilies*, ed. and intro. by Deborah Epstein Nord, *Rethinking the Western Tradition* series (New Haven: Yale University Press, 2002)

Sadden, John, *Portsmouth Book of Days* (Stroud: History Press, 2011)

Shoebridge, Michele, *The Women's Suffrage Movement in Birmingham and District, 1903–18* (MA thesis for Wolverhampton Polytechnic, 1983)

'Skia', *see* Collum, Vera Chute

Smith, Harold L., *The British Women's Suffrage Campaign, 1866–1928* (London: Longman, 2010)

Sparham, Anna, *Soldiers and Suffragettes: The Photography of Christina Broom* (London: Museum of London, 2015)

Spender, Dale, *There's Always Been a Women's Movement This Century* (London: Pandora Press, 1983)

Stephen Leslie, *Life of Henry Fawcett* (London: Smith, Elder, 1885)

Strachey, Ray, *Millicent Garrett Fawcett* (London: John Murray, 1931)

—*The Cause: A Short History of the Women's Movement in Great Britain* (London: Virago, 1978)

Suffragette (Journal, 1912–15)

Swanwick, H., *I Have Been Young* (London: Gollancz, 1935)

Taylor, Marsali, *Women's Suffrage in Shetland* (Raleigh, Lulu Press, 2010)

Taylor, Rosemary, *In Letters of Gold: The Story of Sylvia Pankhurst and the East London Federation of the Suffragettes in Bow* (London: Stepney Books, 1993)

'The Woman Suffrage Movement and the War: Some of its Leaders and their Ideals', supplement in the *Ladies' Field* (November 1914)

Tickner, Lisa, *The Spectacle of Women: Imagery of the Suffrage Campaign, 1907–14* (London: Chatto and Windus, 1987)

Vellacott, Jo, *From Liberal to Labour: the Story of Catherine Marshall* (Montreal: McGill-Queen's University Press, 1993)

—*Conscientious Objection: Bertrand Russell and the Pacifists in the First World War* (Nottingham: Spokesman, 2015)

Vicinus, Martha, *Independent Women: Work and Community for Single Women, 1850–1920* (London: Virago, 1985)

Vote100, *Women in Parliament: A Guide to the History of Women's Participation in Parliament and their Representation in the Historical Collections* (London: Houses of Parliament, 2015)

Votes for Women (Journal, 1907–18)

Ward, Anne, *No Stone Unturned: The Story of Leonora Tyson, a Streatham Suffragette* (Streatham: Local History Publications, 2005)

Weiner, Marie-France, 'The Scottish Women's Hospital at Royaumont, France, 1914–1919', *Journal of the Royal College of Physicians, Edinburgh*, vol. 44 (2014), pages 328–36

Women's Franchise (Journal, 1907–11)

'Women's Role in the War: The Scottish Women's Hospital at the Abbaye de Royaumont in Northern France', *Sphere* (June 1915), pages 262–3

Wright, Sir Almroth, *The Unexpurgated Case Against Woman Suffrage* (London: Constable, 1913)

Picture Acknowledgements

Every effort has been made to contact copyright holders. Any we have omitted are invited to get in touch with the publishers.

Plate section

page 1: NUWSS logo: LSE Library

page 2: 'A Woman's Mind Magnified', postcard: Alamy

page 3: *(above)* 'Somehow the Tide Keeps Rising', postcard: reproduced with kind permission of Lancashire Archives, Lancashire County Council; *(left)* 'A Suffragette's Home', contemporary postcard

page 4: *(above)* Oil painting by Bertha Newcombe: LSE Library; *(below)* 'Votes for Women', envelope reproduced with kind permission of Lancashire Archives, Lancashire County Council

page 5: Map of the Watling Street route: courtesy of Oldham Local Studies and Archives

page 6: *(above and right)* NUWSS badge; medal awarded to imprisoned members of the WSPU: both LSE Library; *(left)* Cambridge alumnae banner: reproduced by permission of the Principal and Fellows of Newnham College, Cambridge

page 7: *(above and below)* Vera Chute Collum leading pilgrims from Oxford towards Thame; Eda Sharples and Marjory Lees outside the *Ark*: both courtesy of Oldham Local Studies and Archives

page 8: *(above)* Pilgrims marching through the Lake District: courtesy of Oldham Local Studies and Archives; *(below)* Suffragists from the north-west of England: New Family Papers, David M. Rubenstein Rare Book & Manuscript Library, Duke University (Box 2)

Text illustrations

page iii: Adapted by the author from a device found on WSPU stationery

page vi: NUWSS poster: LSE Library

page xvi: An anti-suffrage 'sandwich man' joins a deputation in 1910: © Museum of London

page 3: Marjory Lees with the *Ark* in Thame: courtesy of Oldham Local Studies and Archives

page 23: Emily Davies: LSE Library

page 23: Dr Elizabeth Garrett Anderson: Wellcome Images, Wellcome Library, London

page 40: Millicent Garrett Fawcett: reproduced courtesy of ThinkStock

page 45: Emmeline Pankhurst: courtesy of Oldham Local Studies and Archives

page 54: Emma Sproson: photograph reproduced with the permission of Wolverhampton Archives and Local Studies

page 61: Sylvia Pankhurst: © Mary Evans Picture Library

page 62: Christabel Pankhurst: contemporary postcard issued by the WSPU

page 62: Adela Pankhurst: contemporary postcard issued by the WSPU

page 70: Ethel Smyth: Women's Social and Political Union scrapbook, David M. Rubenstein Rare Book & Manuscript Library, Duke University

page 74: Votes for women demonstration in Hyde Park, 21 June 1908: The Record Office for Leicestershire, Leicester and Rutland

page 83: Sarah Lees: courtesy of Oldham Local Studies and Archives

page 87: Kate Frye: courtesy of Elizabeth Crawford

page 96: Selina Cooper: reproduced with kind permission of Lancashire Archives, Lancashire County Council

page 118: May Billinghurst: Women's Social and Political Union scrapbook, David M. Rubenstein Rare Book & Manuscript Library, Duke University

page 120: Cartoon from the *Suffragette*, January 1913: from the LSE Library collection, TWL @ LSE Special Collections periodicals

page 127: Christabel Pankhurst addressing the crowds in Trafalgar Square: Women's Social and Political Union scrapbook, David M. Rubenstein Rare Book & Manuscript Library, Duke University

page 154: Advertisement for Parker's bicycles: Thame Gazette/Johnston Press

page 159: Suffrage Atelier producing banners: LSE Library

page 161: Poster advertising the Women's Suffrage Pilgrimage: courtesy of Oldham Local Studies and Archives

page 164: 'The ideal coat for the Pilgrimage': The *Common Cause,* July 1913

page 166: Lady Rochdale: courtesy of Oldham Local Studies and Archives

page 169: Gladys Duffield and her daughter Lily: courtesy of Margaret Stewart

page 177: Pilgrims from Land's End: Bodleian Libraries, University of Oxford, Deneke Papers, Box 19, Land's End Caravan

page 187: Marjory Lees: courtesy of Oldham Local Studies and Archives

page 192: Marjory Lees with the *Ark*: courtesy of Oldham Local Studies and Archives

page 198: Pilgrims from Newnham and Girton Colleges, Cambridge: reproduced by permission of the Principal and Fellows of Newnham College, Cambridge

page 204: The Pilgrimage setting off from Portsmouth, 17 July 1913: Portsmouth Library and Archive Service, Portsmouth City Council, image 1155A

page 210: 'Sandwich men': *Oxford Illustrated Journal,* July 1913

page 216: The Pilgrimage at West Wycombe: courtesy of Oldham Local Studies and Archives

page 227: Millicent Fawcett in Hyde Park, 26 July 1913: LSE Library

page 257: Katherine Harley: the *Sphere,* June 1915

page 260: Royaumont Hospital, the Western Front: the *Sphere,* June 1915

page 287: Emmeline Pankhurst with her 'war babies': courtesy of Professor June Purvis

page 296: Millicent Garrett Fawcett: reproduced courtesy of ThinkStock

page 301: Marjory Lees with her suffragist friends, 1918: courtesy of Oldham Local Studies and Archives

Index